CAN MAN LIVE WITHOUT GOD

OTHER BOOKS BY RAVI ZACHARIAS

Can Man Live Without God

Cries of the Heart

Deliver Us from Evil

Jesus Among Other Gods

CAN MAN LIVE WITHOUT GOD

RAVI ZACHARIAS

THOMAS NELSON

Since 1798

NASHVILLE DALLAS MEXICO CITY RIO DE JANEIRO

Published in Nashville, Tennessee. Thomas Nelson is a trademark of Thomas Nelson, Inc.

Thomas Nelson, Inc. titles may be purchased in bulk for educational, business, fundraising, or sales promotional use. For information, please e-mail SpecialMarkets@ThomasNelson.com.

Unless otherwise indicated, Scripture quotations used in this book are from The Holy Bible, New International Version (NIV). Copyright © 1973, 1978, 1984, International Bible Society. Used by permission of Zondervan Bible Publishers.

Scripture references indicated KJV are from the King James Version of the Bible.

Scripture references indicated NKJV are from the New King James Version of the Bible, copyright © 1979, 1980, 1982, 1990, Thomas Nelson, Inc., Publisher. Used by permission.

Library of Congress Cataloging-in-Publication Data

Zacharias, Ravi K.
    Can man live without God / Ravi Zacharias.
        p.   cm.
    ISBN 13: 978-0-8499-1771-4 (HC)
    ISBN 13: 978-0-8499-4528-1 (SC)

    1. Christianity and atheism.   2. Apologetics—20th century. 3. Atheism—Controversial literature.   4. Jesus Christ—Appreciation. I. Title.
BR128.A8Z33   1994
239—dc20   94-34205

Printed in the United States of America

12 QG 25 24 23 22 21

To my wife, Margie,
a treasured gift from God,
a beautiful life lived for Him.

CONTENTS

CONTENTS

FOREWORD

I AM an inveterate tape listener. I have a tape on whenever I'm driving, sometimes when I'm working around the yard, or even occasionally while organizing papers on my desk. Over the years, I may have listened to thousands of Christian tapes.

But seldom have I heard any that impressed me as much as Ravi Zacharias's presentation at Harvard entitled "The Veritas Series." Ravi put the case for Christianity appealingly, understandably, and convincingly before some of the best and brightest American students. He fielded questions deftly.

I listened to the series twice, then called his office and suggested that it ought to be turned into a book. Hence, I may hope that my suggestion had something to do with the appearance of this volume. I believe it is one of the most critical that could be written in our time.

Most of us fail to realize that the battle of ideas being waged in modern America—euphemistically known as the culture war—is merely a symptom. We Christians invest enormous amounts of energy running to fight this battle here or that battle there. But we can never win the culture war that way.

What we have to do is attack the deeper cause of the cultural conflict. We have to dig down to the philosophical roots of the battles we are fighting. The truth of the matter is that over the past thirty years, the American mind has been transformed dramatically.

One of the most telling examples is our view of truth. In the 1960s, 65 percent of Americans said they believed the Bible is true; today that figure has dropped to 32 percent. Even more dramatically, today 67 percent of all Americans deny that there's any such thing as truth. Seventy percent say there are no moral absolutes.

This confusion over truth is the fundamental crisis of our age.

What good does it do for us to say, "The Bible says . . . ," if two-thirds of our listeners don't believe the Bible is true? What good does it do for us to say Jesus is the truth if two-thirds of the American people believe there is no such thing as truth? This is not to deny that the Word of God has the power to convict even the hardest heart. But if Christians are to be heard by the modern mind and make effective inroads into our culture, we must first develop what Francis Schaeffer called a cultural apologetic: We must defend the very concept of truth.

That is precisely what Ravi Zacharias does in this book—and he does it brilliantly. He presents an apologetic defense of the Christian faith that is powerful and compelling.

It has always frustrated me that many Christians shy away from intellectual arguments. Many deem an intellectual defense unspiritual—as though all that matters is our religious experience, as though arguing on intellectual grounds weakens our faith.

But anti-intellectualism is *not* more spiritual. The Bible explicitly commands us to take every thought captive to the obedience of Christ. If we fail, we will find it increasingly difficult to present the gospel, and we will lose our influence in the culture.

What is needed is for lay Christians to be equipped with the kind of logic and analysis you will find in these pages. Then we need to sit down with our secular neighbors to defend truth and the historicity of the Christian faith.

I hope you will not read this book lightly and lay it aside. Study it. Become conversant with its arguments, and use what you learn here to advance the cause of truth with your neighbors.

The culture in which we live is nearly lost. But often at the darkest moments, God raises up people—indeed prophets—to speak to our age. Ravi Zacharias is just such a man for these times. I hope and pray he will equip you for the good fight that we wage.

CHARLES COLSON

ACKNOWLEDGMENTS

A RECENT acknowledgment I read began with the words "This book comes to publication trailing clouds of the kindness of others." Those gracious sentiments well represent what follows in these pages as well. There are many whose kindness has resulted in the publication of this volume. Naturally I cannot single out each one by name but do want to at least make special mention of those who have played a key role in bringing this about. First I would like to thank the students of Harvard University and Ohio State University who attended the lectures I delivered there. The extraordinary planning and organizing of the meetings merits my sincere appreciation to the groups that invited me and hosted the forums.

My gratitude is also due to Charles Colson for planting the idea in my mind to carry this material into print. His suggestion got this effort under way.

The process of transcribing the spoken material demanded hours of painstaking and meticulous work, which Karen Mayhem carried out with the utmost of competence. Her efforts provided a vital link in the chain. My sincere thanks to her are well in order.

I would also like to express my appreciation to all my colleagues whose own sacrifice in my absence was made without complaint. Of special mention in this list is Dan Glaze, my "perpetual encourager," who led them in their support. Also in that group is my research assistant, Danielle DuRant, who kept a close eye for me on all related subject matter and served a vitally important role. She has diligently labored, particularly in the final stages of this manuscript. I am also deeply indebted to Joan Houghton for her skilled and kind help in meeting the demands of the language. She has been an outstanding teacher.

Throughout this effort the entire W Publishing Group staff I worked with have been exemplary in their courtesy and encouragement. Kip Jordon and Joey Paul have been kind friends and wise counselors. Their experience and accessibility have become a wonderful resource for me.

Most importantly, my wife, Margie, has, in every sense of the term, worked longer and harder than I did in editing this manuscript from the beginning to its final form. If computers took on the personalities of the ones using them, ours would reflect her image. This book would not have been possible without her patient, affectionate, and needed corrections. I cannot gainsay her monumental role.

Naturally, the freeing of her time and mine was made possible by three young lives whom we both so dearly cherish, to whom we say thank you from the depths of our hearts. I speak of our children, Sarah, Naomi, and Nathan. Even vacations got interrupted to meet deadlines, but they were generous in their understanding and throughout this project have cheered us on. Indeed, this book comes trailing clouds of kindness, and I am spiritually enriched by these lives.

INTRODUCTION

"WE HAVE educated ourselves into imbecility," quipped the noted English journalist Malcolm Muggeridge as he bemoaned the many nefarious ideas that are shaping modern beliefs. Venting an identical disillusionment in his commentary on the American culture, George Will averred that there is nothing so vulgar left in our experience for which we cannot transport some professor from somewhere to justify it.

Why this association of aberrant behavior with the halls of learning? The answer is well worth pursuing if we are to deal with our present cultural malaise by understanding its progenitors and to thwart what looms as a future with terrifying possibilities. It is not unprecedented that as a young nation begins to reach its adolescent years, it craves freedom from any restraint and, in psychological terms, seeks to repudiate its father. But the grasping after this sort of unbridled liberty and absolute individual autonomy could be fraught with opposition, and the best hope for securing such release is to undermine the convictions and philosophies that have hitherto held sway and to counter with claims of greater knowledge, newer truths, and superior insight into the issues that divide the past from the present.

Emulating a legal proceeding in which an attorney tries valiantly to discredit witnesses who injure his or her case, secular thinkers unleashed a concerted effort to prejudice the minds of this generation. If even a slight doubt could be raised upon any minutiae of theistic belief, it was exultantly implied that the whole worldview should be deemed false. The goal was to forge a breed of iconoclastic young scholars and opinion makers who would be perceived as saviors, delivering society from the tyranny of a God-infested past and remaking culture in their own image.

Such machinations, which combine linguistic trickery and the distortion of truth, are familiar fare in law courts, bringing about the desired end of an utterly confused juror. And this, may I suggest, has been the precise approach taken in the battle of ideas that has occupied center stage for centuries. The road from the Renaissance through the Enlightenment, right down to our postmodern deconstructionist worldview was predict-able. All through those centuries warnings were sounded that if, indeed, man was the measure of all things, someone had to determine "which man." Was it going to be Hitler or Hugh Hefner, Stalin or Mother Teresa? But that question was too discomforting and the answer too foreboding. Since questions that bring such unease or expose contradiction are often buried under a welter of verbiage or vitriolic counterattacks, the strategic course taken was to establish a new reigning worldview by merely casting aspersions upon ideas that stood in the way and to "win" the battle by sheer default.

The principal means to accomplish this was to take control of the in-tellectual strongholds, our universities, and under a steady barrage of "scholarly" attack change the plausibility structure for belief in God so that God was no longer a plausible entity in scholastic settings. This assault on religious belief was carried out in the name of political or academic free-dom while the actual intent was to vanquish philosophically anything that smacked of moral restraint. Unblushingly, the full brunt of the attack has been leveled against Christianity as Eastern religions enjoy a patronizing nod and the protection of mystical license. As for Islam, no university dares offend. Hand in hand with this unmasked intellectual cowardice and concealed duplicity came mockery and ridicule of the Christian, which has now become commonplace, a "civilized" form of torture.

In such fashion came the onslaught on all that had gone before; the pen became the sword and the professorial lectern, the pulpit. If young, fertile minds could be programmed into believing that truth as a category does not exist and that skepticism is sophisticated, then it would be only a matter of time before every social institution could be wrested to advantage in the fight against the absolute.

However, over time the sword has cut the hand that wielded it, and learning itself has lost its authority. Today as we look upon our social land-scape, the answers to the most basic questions of life—from birth to sexuality to death—remain completely confounded. The very scholars who taught their students to question authority are themselves disparaged by the same measure. No one knows what to believe as true anymore; and if anything is believed, the burden of justification has been removed. Interestingly, the word *university* means "to bring unity in diversity," and the idea of the academy was to impart knowledge and virtue. Neither of these goals is recognizable today. Jean-Paul Sartre's longing to unify knowledge was left unfulfilled. It is now a tacit assumption that the hallmark of modern education is skepticism, harking back more to the seventeenth-century model of René Descartes, whose quest for certainty began with the certainty of doubt. However, tragically, unlike Descartes, there is no god postulated to guard us against deception, and where Descartes began the modern skeptic has ended.

Many years ago author Paul Scherer alerted us to this downward slide. Referring to the volatile exchanges between the church and its detractors he said:

> One by one the generation that refused to be bound by the Pope, and refused to be bound by the Church, decided in an ecstasy of freedom that they would not be bound by anything—not by the Bible, not by conscience, not by God Himself. *From believing too much that never did have to be believed, they took to believing so little that for countless thousands human existence and the world itself no longer seemed to make any sense.* Poets began talking about the "wasteland," with "ghostly lives," as Stephen Spender put it, "moving among fragmentary ruins which have lost their significance." Nothingness became a subject of conversation, nihilism a motive, frustration and despair a theme for novelists and dramatists, and the "edge of the abyss" as much of a nautical term among the intelligentsia as it was for explorers in the days of Columbus! (emphasis mine)[1]

Yet, all is not lost. In spite of the varied and willful attempts made by antitheistic thinkers to undermine the spiritual and to thrust it into the arena of the irrational, or at best deem it a private matter, the hunger for the transcendent remains unabated. After nearly three decades of crisscrossing the globe and lecturing at numerous campuses around the world, it is evident to me that the yearning for the spiritual just will not die. In fact, at virtually every engagement I have found the auditorium filled to capacity and the appreciative response quite overwhelming, even in antagonistic settings. There is no clearer demonstration of this unrelenting hunger than the experiences of Russia and China as each has, in its own way, tried to exterminate the idea of God, only to realize that He rises up to outlive His pallbearers.

Our universities tell a similar story. Though proud skepticism is rife in academic bastions, the human spirit still longs for something more. This tension must be addressed, especially at this time of cultural upheaval, and it is imperative that the answers we espouse meet not only the intimations of the heart but the demands of the mind. Here the greatest question of our time must be considered: Can man live without God? It must be answered not only by those who are avowedly antitheistic, but also by the many who functionally live as if there were no God and that His existence does not matter.

But in all fairness, there is another side to this story, justifiably provoking the contempt of the skeptic. Much of what has passed for the Christian message has been nothing more than frothy God-talk—mindless, thoughtless, and in its exploitation of people, heartless. This, too, will not do. Just as so much of antitheistic thinking when scrutinized is sensically impoverished, so also much religious verbiage, seeped in emotional drivel and bereft of reason, can be tossed at unsuspecting audiences in the name of orthodoxy. The ruinous end of the latter, in its destruction of lives plundered materially and spiritually, may be greater than the ideas perpetrated by the openly cynical. Is there an answer to all this? I sincerely trust there is. And it is to find that common ground of interaction that this material is presented.

In this book I have included the material from two lectures that were delivered at Harvard University at the invitation of several groups, and along with them, one lecture delivered at Ohio State University. As the theme was addressed extemporaneously, it was not always possible to present the full context of the argument. I have therefore expanded the original content so as to pull together the loose ends. However, in a subject as wide ranging as this, one cannot muster every argument in a few brief lectures. Hopefully I have given sufficient reason to defend strongly the theistic worldview in general and the Christian worldview in particular. By contrast, I hope I have shown the many logical and social breaking points of antitheistic thinking, which is just too incoherent to be true and as a system of thought is incapable of dealing with the intellectual and existential rigor that life places before us.

I should add further that the responses of the audiences were extremely gratifying and greatly encouraging. Even at points of disagreement the students nevertheless respected the arguments and the presentation. For their heartfelt applause and expressions of thanks I will ever be grateful.

I have positioned the material in three major sections, each one logically flowing from the preceding one. The first section analyzes the antitheistic worldview, demonstrating both its built-in logical contradictions and its existential inadequacies that ultimately make it philosophically unlivable. The antitheist often makes an issue of what he calls the "imposition" that theists enjoin upon society by their explicit assumption that there is such a thing as a transcultural ethic. In making this charge, the antitheist draws more theistic blood by the reminder of the untold havoc, as he sees it, that religion has wrought upon civilization. All this is done, supposedly, to contend for the tolerance and solace granted by a worldview that denies the transcendent and is neutral to absolutes. Conveniently forgotten by those antagonistic to spiritual issues are the far more devastating consequences that have entailed when antitheism is wedded to political theory and social engineering. There is nothing in history to match the dire ends to which humanity can be led by following a political and social philosophy that consciously and absolutely excludes God. The ramifications are pervasive for society as a whole and life-altering for each individual. Santayana's aphorism still haunts—he who refuses to learn from history is forced to repeat its mistakes.

The end of the first section leads to the logical conclusion that a philosophy of meaninglessness is an unavoidable consequence of the antitheistic starting point. This is readily admitted by antitheists, but it is cavalierly espoused by them as liberating. Can this really be so? Within the human experience, the hunger for meaning in each succeeding generation is neither diminished nor dispelled, scientific advances and new psychological or social theories notwithstanding. What best explains this hunger for meaning, and how can it be satisfied? French mystic Simone Weil warned of the incalculable error made when one assumes this hunger to be merely a belief and not a certainty. Thus, the second discussion defends the certainty of the longing for meaning and provides some cogent answers in that search.

Intrinsic to those answers, and to all others offered by Christian theism, is the centrality of the person of Jesus Christ and of who He claimed to be. His answers to life's deepest questions are presented, not only as relevant for our time, but as compellingly unique, both in detail and in extent. To the implications of His life and message the most obvious question surfaces—how do we know Jesus Christ to be the truth as He defined life's essence and destiny? Humanist Ted Turner, for example, openly debunks Christianity as outdated and irrelevant. Is his assessment correct? What about all the other options available in a volitionally pluralistic society? Can truth really be so exclusive? Television talk-show host Larry King made a very perceptive comment when he was asked who he would most like to have interviewed from across history. One of those he named was Jesus Christ. "What would you have asked Him?" came the rejoinder to Mr. King. "I would like to ask Him if He was indeed virgin born, because the answer to that question would define history." As trite as it may sound on the surface, Larry King was absolutely right in identifying the hinge upon which all history turns. If, indeed, Jesus Christ is who He claimed to be, any castigation of His message is the ultimate expression of futility. On the other hand, if His claims were false, all of Christendom and much of history has been built upon a lie. It is to the gnawing question of the tenability of the Christian message that the third section of this book addresses itself. This is, without a doubt, the most important portion of the book and must be studied in its entirety, and with care.

Following these three essential themes that respond to the question "Can man live without God?", Appendix A includes the questions that were raised at Harvard following this presentation. These challenges well represent those most frequently posed in this context.

The final section, Appendix B, is a brief thumbnail sketch of the "personal side" of some of the leading thinkers who have shaped the modern mind-set, both popular and academic—thinkers such as Bertrand Russell, Jean-Paul Sartre, and others. I have also endeavored to engage the heart of their antitheistic arguments and have presented what are clearly self-stultifying fallacies implicit in their philosophies. I trust the reader will find this material thought provoking.

There may be points where, for some, the argumentation will get heavy. I urge you to stay with the material with the assurance that either an illustration or an explanation will follow that will clarify the issue being discussed. The relevance of these ideas for all of us cannot be gainsaid. And if, indeed, some ideas do remain somewhat elusive, by the end of the book the principal arguments will stand, unobstructed and distinct. The lines will be clearly drawn. I, for one, believe that this generation longs to think again and that we do it a disservice by not providing that opportunity.

The familiar adage rings true that the mind is too great an asset to waste, for it is the command control of each individual life. It is my desire that through the unfolding of these ideas each of us may recognize the greatest mind of all, even God Himself, whose existence or nonexistence is essential to defining everything else.

RAVI ZACHARIAS

PART I

ANTITHEISM IS ALIVE—AND DEADLY

1

Anguish in Affluence

"GIVE ME THE MAKING of the songs of a nation," said eighteenth-century Scottish political thinker Andrew Fletcher, "and I care not who writes its laws."[1] His confident words not only divulge a major cultural access point to our contemporary mind-set, but also acknowledge the extraordinary control of song lyrics upon the moods and convictions of the young, who are embattled by the tug of so many allurements.

I readily grant Mr. Fletcher his assertion. My own experience testifies to the impressions carved upon my consciousness by popular music. Beyond that, such music accorded me the privilege of identifying with the expression of shared sentiments. I recall an occasion in that pliable stage as a teenager when I sat in my living room in New Delhi, India, suspended between the dreary world of my physics textbook on my lap and the low sound of music from the radio in my ear. In this "between-two-worlds" state of mind, I was suddenly captivated by the sentiments of a song that seemed to echo the struggles in my own heart. The strange blend of Eastern chant in the background and the crisp baritone voice of the singer, a Westerner, conveyed a sense of universality to the obvious anguish that imbued each line and articulated the crowded questions I had painfully suppressed:

> From the canyons of the mind
> > we wander on and stumble blind,
> Wade through the often tangled maze
> > of starless nights and sunless days,
> Hoping for some kind of clue—
> > a road to lead us to the truth.
> But who will answer? . . .

3

Is our hope in walnut shells
    worn 'round the neck with temple bells?
Or deep within some cloistered walls
    where hooded figures pray in shawls?
Or high upon some dusty shelves,
    or in the stars,
    or in ourselves?
Who will answer?[2]

The songwriter persuasively touched the emotions as he grappled with the pain that life's passages engender—the overwhelming despair of a family when love is lost; the agony for one in the death of a child; the torment of another struggling with suicide; the noise and din in a night club for some as they seek to escape the haunts of loneliness; the apprehension of all, living under the threat of a nuclear conflagration. Each scenario ended with the question, "Who will answer?" Finally the chorus thundered forth the intensity of the conflict deep within the human consciousness.

If the soul is darkened
    by a fear it cannot name,
If the mind is baffled
    when the rules don't fit the game,
Who will answer?
Who will answer?
Who will answer?

It was remarkable to me, even at that stage of my life, that the candid admission of such emptiness emerged from the world that symbolized the new Eden—America. And even more to the point, it came from that segment of society that epitomized the success for which millions of young people clamor—Hollywood, that bastion of perpetual enchantment. How could this be? Had the breadth of such anguished questioning been articulated from my native soil, it would have been understandable, for Indian culture has never been reticent to voice the tragedy that life portends. V. S. Naipaul, one of the world's finest writers, has appropriately captured India's angst in referring to her as a wounded civilization.

Coincidentally, at that very time in my life, one of India's finest artistic accomplishments had won international acclaim with a film called *Mother*

India. The film portrayed a family's life-and-death struggle to bring some measure of dignity and decency to their mortal existence. Between warding off disease and death, battling the vicissitudes of national disasters, and coping with family clashes, life had become synonymous with pain. The chorus of the film's theme song summed it up well.

> Since I have come into this world,
> I must live.
> If living means drinking poison,
> I have to drink it.

The fatalism, the nihilism, the "take-life-by-the-throat" philosophy with all of its existential trauma, were endemic to a nation so victimized by centuries of conflict and struggle. But how was it that the same questions that were predictable from within a "wounded" context were also raised by those who apparently did not experience the same impoverishments and lived in a country where life's physical deprivations had been in large measure conquered?

Although I wrestled with these issues then as much as it was possible for a young mind to do, years later my deep sense of puzzlement remains. But the struggle has taken on a new twist. Now, as I live in the West and witness the dying moments of this century of progress, the songs of the nations have not changed, and my bewilderment lies in the conspicuous absence of any answers; even more so, in the complete failure of our cultural elites to grasp the reason behind the life-defining questions the music asks. Listen, for example, to the words of two very thought-provoking songs performed by King Crimson as they scream forth their own confusion.

> Cat's foot iron claw
> Neurosurgeons scream for more
> From paranoia's poison door
> Twenty first century schizoid man.[3]

Once again the mind is taken captive as the imagination wanders through the senseless violence, the needless hate, and the heartless cruelty human beings foist upon each other. The unshakable barrenness of soul and the uncertainty of the future are tellingly anchored to the extermination of the spirit.

5

The wall on which the prophets wrote
Is cracking at the seams.
Upon the instruments of death
The sunlight brightly gleams.
When every man is torn apart
With nightmares and with dreams,
Will no one lay the laurel wreath
As silence drowns the screams.

Between the iron gates of fate,
The seeds of time were sown,
And watered by the deeds of those
Who know and who are known;
Knowledge is a deadly friend
When no one sets the rules.
The fate of all mankind I see
Is in the hands of fools.[4]

The end of life is summed up in one word—*confusion,* a suitable epitaph for the "morning after" of life itself, which promised not laughter, but tears. Despite all its melodrama and pardonable overkill, the underlying message of the futility of life is irresistible.

I recognize the risk in beginning this hard look at hard questions with the popular philosophers of our time, musicians. But I do so because I credit them with a greater degree of honesty and unmasked vulnerability in recognizing the anguish within the human heart than the academician, who often conceals such a struggle behind a facade of self-assurance. It is easier to hide behind philosophical arguments, heavily footnoted for effect, than it is to admit our hurts, our confusions, our loves, and our passions in the marketplace of life's heartfelt transactions. With all the education to which we now lay claim that has pushed back the horizons of knowledge undreamed of a generation ago, the messages of popular songs have not changed because the conflicts still remain; if anything, they have only intensified. That intensification in search of a spiritual answer still continues in spite of the fact that every now and then there arises on the educational landscape some new antitheistic voice, arrogantly sounding forth with an air of omniscience, mocking religion and debunking the sacred. "We have outgrown this myth," is the boast. But the masses just ignore such gloating, intellectual posturing because they are well aware that these "experts" are woefully unable to force-fit life's mental furniture by restructuring reality.

Albert Camus confessed decades ago, as did psychologist Viktor Frankl more recently, that the search for meaning is life's fundamental pursuit; all other questions they deemed secondary. And so it is that every generation—ours being no exception—raises the issue of life's essence, the latest theory or invention of science and technology notwithstanding. Cognizant of this search that cuts across time, generations, and cultures, I venture to present some answers. But we will first need to define the dilemma clearly and set some boundaries so that we can begin these considerations for our time from some points of agreement.

Intense Heat, Diminishing Light

There is a story told, whether factual or not I do not know, of the one-time heavyweight boxing champion of the world, Muhammad Ali, flying to one of his engagements. Ali's name has never been synonymous with humility, and thus whether this story is fact or fiction, the notoriously yet affectionately branded "Louisville Lip" at least made possible such an anecdote. During the flight the aircraft ran into foul weather, and mild to moderate turbulence began to toss it about. All nervous fliers well know that when a pilot signals "moderate turbulence," he is implying, "if you have any religious beliefs, it is time to start expressing them." The passengers were accordingly instructed to fasten their seatbelts immediately. Everyone complied but Ali. Noticing this, the flight attendant approached him and requested that he observe the captain's order, only to hear Ali audaciously respond, "Superman don't need no seatbelt." The flight attendant did not miss a beat and replied, "Superman don't need no airplane either."

I draw attention to that story because of the immediate and larger context in which many of us find ourselves. Unquestionably, we live in a nation of immense wealth with an array of possibilities for material and educational success. Some among us will have access, as a result, to the finest education available anywhere and thereby position ourselves for extraordinary success in a fast-changing world. By the same token, such a sophisticated environment can easily induce within us an air of invincibility, leaving us thoroughly deceived that the prosperity procured or the educational gains we have made have elevated us above the "ignorant

7

masses," and that we are better equipped for life itself, no matter what jolts and bumps lie ahead. Academic or material advancement unfortunately does not necessarily confer wisdom. It would be foolhardy of us to take what generations preceding us have revered in coping with the turbulence of life and censoriously cast it all aside just because we are modern. Should we fall victim to such a posture, the appropriate word to describe that self-exaltation is *hubris*, translated into English from the Greek as "pride." But the connotation of the original word is much deeper, implying a wanton self-aggrandizement that looks down its sympathetic nose at the hoi polloi, seeing them as bereft of any intellectual strength and as plagued by confusion from which the educated, successful self is exempted. I ask, therefore, that as we deal with some of these lofty ideas, we do so with an attitude of humility. Falsely posing as supermen makes a crash landing certain, for history is punctuated with reminders of the peril of such grandiose delusions. It is quite ironic that the self-deifying concept of man as Superman surfaced again in one of the darkest moments of the twentieth century— when the Third Reich harnessed and enfleshed Nietzschean philosophy. Hopefully that reminder alone should spell caution to any enterprising boast of human exaltation to the exclusion of God.

We must approach what Will Durant, popular historian and philosopher, has appropriately categorized the greatest question of our time—Can man live without God?—with arguments and attitudes that demonstrate not only intellect and candor but also a tenacious honesty. It has been my privilege to address such philosophical issues in many parts of our world, and I hold the view that all philosophizing on life's purpose is ultimately founded upon two fundamental assumptions, or conclusions.

The first is, Does God exist? and the second, If God exists, what is His character or nature? The questions are impossible to ignore, and even if they are not dealt with formally, their implications filter down into everyday life. It is out of one's belief or disbelief in God that all other convictions are formed.

One further reminder is pertinent when engaging in a discussion as important and controversial as the question of God's existence. Having been transplanted from the East to the West, I have personally witnessed what religious anger or ideological despotism can do, and I know that emotions in matters such as these can easily run amok. It seems quite self-defeating, though, to argue on issues of ultimate good while forsaking all goodness in the process. Is it not possible, I ask, to wrestle with these ideas and work through any disagreements without being disagreeable? Obviously feelings run deep on such matters, but why is it so often the case that discussions on these issues end up generating more heat than light? When cordiality is lost, truth is obscured. And it is truth, especially when trying to answer a question such as the one before us, that provides for us the very rationale and foundation for a civil existence.

No one can deny that great minds have held forth on opposite sides of the issue. Antitheistic scholars often boast that it was Immanuel Kant who provided the rational grounds for societal ethics apart from the existence of God. (Ironically, I have heard that vociferously boasted both in North America and in Russia. I shall leave you to work through the ramifications of the ensuing contradictory political and economic theories.) But interestingly enough, I have heard none of them represent what Kant concluded as he drew his *Critique of Pure Reason* to a close:

> In other words, belief in a God and in another world is so interwoven with my moral sentiment that as there is little danger of my losing the latter, there is equally little cause for fear that the former can ever be taken from me.[5]

During my brief time as a visiting scholar at Cambridge University in England, I well remember the lectures of Professor Don Cupitt, dean of Emmanuel College, renowned for his British Broadcasting Corporation series "The Sea of Faith," which one critic has appropriately referred to as "faith at sea." (Brian Hebblethwaite, a philosopher colleague of his at Cambridge, has powerfully refuted Cupitt's position in his book *The Ocean of Truth.*) Cupitt is at once an atheist and an ordained Anglican priest. The only consolation in reconciling these twin credentials is that if you do not like what Cupitt believes, come back next semester when the sea may well have borne away this mystic and his ideas and deposited his conclusions in a new and different mix. On that campus, as on many others, the tide never settles with intellectual heavyweights on opposite ends.

One of the most extensive forums ever held on the subject of God's existence in the North American context is featured in the book *Does God Exist?* in which two very fine scholars debated this question from opposing views while several others critiqued their presentations.[6] Philosopher J. P. Moreland did a masterful job of defending the theistic position although most of his arguments were completely ignored by his antagonist, Kai Nielson of the University of Calgary. Nielson, in effect, insisted that no argument contrary to his own had any validity because theism could not deliver any denotative proof. In his analysis, Professor Dallas Willard of the University of Southern California delivered a scathing rebuttal to Nielson's reasoning. (For any serious student, this book, which includes contributions from some noted thinkers of our time such as Anthony Flew and Peter Kreeft, treats the subject very cogently and comprehensively.) The debate once again proved beyond any doubt that only ignorance or prejudice calls the theistic position uninformed or intellectually wanting. I sincerely hope that we can rise above those dispositions to the heart of this issue and that we can establish clearly on which side is the so-called "leap of faith."

Leveling with Philosophy

One of the challenges in presenting this content is to be fair to the tough critic and, at the same time, not to allow the argumentation to become so abstruse that it becomes inconsiderate of the many serious thinkers who are nevertheless uncomfortable with intense philosophical banter. I am keenly aware of this necessary balancing act and have therefore developed a system that realistically reflects the way philosophical thinking penetrates our lives. I believe this takes place at three different tiers, or levels, at which we as individuals formulate our conclusions or establish our convictions. This system has been helpful to me in dialoguing both with those for whom philosophy is a serious academic discipline and with those for whom it is not. I believe it was C. S. Lewis who once remarked that unless a complicated argument could be simplified to appeal to the average person, the chances were that the one doing the explaining did not understand it either. That demand is a difficult one to meet but is a needed reminder.

Let me describe the three levels to you. Level one, which is foundational, is the level of theory. It is here that we engage one another in the great ideas of philosophy and in the categories that have been provided for reasonable discourse. When two individuals dialogue or dispute at this level, there has to be a clear epistemological base, that is, the establishment of the process by which one arrives at the truth. Such dialogue involves the rigorous application of the laws of logic and the advancement of the argument through sound reasoning. Here neither feeling, culture, sentimentality, nor tradition have any prior claim. The introduction of a knee-jerk emotional response, however passionately felt, must be set aside, for it has no validity in defending the truthfulness of propositions or systems. Shouting louder does not help if truth has been lost. Understanding the role this first level plays in the pursuit of truth is paramount. There is no way to ignore or circumvent these laws of argument, for in effect one is forced to apply them in order to refute them. We shall return to this later, but it is important to note here and now that this level is often disregarded by those who do not enjoy the hard-nosed rigor of logic while, at the same time, employed by them when they are denouncing an opposing view.

Critical thinking is a basic skill. Auguste Comte was right in his observation that "ideas govern the world or throw it into chaos."[7] The German philosopher Arthur Schopenhauer once suggested, "It would be a very good thing if every trick could receive some short and obviously appropriate name, so that when a man used this or that particular trick, he could at once be reproved for it."[8] To that I would add that this kind of chicanery—playing word games when dealing with the most monumental issues of life—can be one of the most insidious and destructive forces in the life of a nation. History has shown that crimes of logic can be more catastrophic for humanity than crimes of passion. The latter can be readily recognized and countered, but if the very judgment to which an act is subjected is impaired or malevolent, the jeopardy is doubled.

I have deliberately taken time to stress the importance of sound reasoning and to warn against its abuse. One of the more subtle, yet drastic upheavals of our time is the way some special-interest groups have illogically fought for certain positions by cleverly redefining words and prostituting ideas. As a sloganeering culture, we have unblushingly trivialized the serious and exalted the trivial because we have bypassed the rudimentary and necessary steps of logical argument. Reality can be lost when reason and language have been violated.

As foundational as this level is, few people ever crack open a text in logic, and matching their disinterest in this discipline, they develop a contempt for any use of logic by anyone who challenges their illogic. It is understandable why textbooks in logic do not hit the bestseller list, but the laws of logic must apply to reality else we may as well be living in a madhouse.

Recognizing this aversion to reason, we must then ask ourselves how most among us come to our belief systems. What about those with whom we work or travel each day? If the reasoning process is not properly pursued as other disciplines are, what compelling influences determine our decisions and shape our values?

May I suggest that in this sense we are possibly a unique generation. A massive global assault has been launched upon us, and it is the arts more than any other single force that predominate as an influential agent, molding our character, our values, and our beliefs. This invasion bypasses our reason and captures our imagination. Never before in history has so much been at stake as is now in the hands of the imagemakers of our time. There is something very ironic here. Western man has long prided himself as being the offspring of the Enlightenment, nurtured at the feet of sophisticated thinkers. Yet he has, in turn, brought about the humiliation of reason by the instruments that were born from the strength of the mind.

This second level of philosophizing, through the arts, has shaped the national mind-set in everything from determining war strategy to electing presidents, to finding one's identity in cars and deodorants. Existentialist philosophers such as Jean-Paul Sartre and Albert Camus did not waste their time establishing syllogisms. They harnessed the passion of an empty world within the human psyche and fused it with their own ethos, affecting the mood and feeling of an educated herd. A homogenization of our cultural tastes quickly ensued, and a fastening upon our sensitivities or rather, a desensitization of conscience, was securely in place. Through technology the whole world has now become the media's parish, talk-show hosts the prophets, actors and musicians the priests, and any script will do for the Scriptures as long as moral constraints are removed. Sitting before a well-lit box is all the cultic performance needs, and each person can enthrone his or her own self as divine. Truth has been relegated to subjectivity; beauty has been subjugated to the beholder; and as millions are idiotized night after night, a global commune has been constructed with the arts enjoying a totalitarian rule.

To be sure, the arts have always had, and should have, a role in the imagination and entertainment of a society. What is so unique in our society, though, is the all-pervasive influence of the arts, even upon matters of transcending importance—in effect, desacralizing everything and programming our very beings.

The third level inevitably follows—kitchen-table conversation—where some very profound questions can be asked in nonthreatening situations. This level is often reduced to sheer shrug-of-the-shoulder or wave-of-the-hand prescriptivism. After all, if the formally trained teacher is handcuffed by the questions of right and wrong, how can Grandpa and Grandma or Mom and Dad so nonchalantly answer them in this brave new world of many voices?

As an aside, may I mention that every calling has its hazards? At neighborhood parties, doctors are an abused group, enduring the questions posed by friends as each presents his or her own litany of maladies in the hope of a cure. Lawyers at such gatherings are induced by newly introduced acquaintances to provide free counsel on any personal matter. I once heard of a doctor who was exasperated at this constant professional exploitation and was, on a particular occasion, commiserating with a friend who was a lawyer, asking him what she should do when her professional expertise was taken advantage of in such settings. The lawyer suggested that an easy solution would be to send a bill to the abuser of such a privilege. The doctor's gratitude for the good advice was nevertheless short-lived when the next day she received a bill for legal counsel from the lawyer.

Over the years I have been invited to enjoy a meal in hundreds of homes, only to realize once there that, yet again, the true reason for the request has been to solve some great mystery of ethics, philosophy, or science—that is the hazard of my trade. In a very tangible way, I have learned that there is no free lunch. Sitting around a table, though, I have heard questions that are deep and complex sometimes coming even from young teenagers, but the solutions I have heard most often offered to them are, quite frankly, superficial and simple. Many frustrated young people have expressed, "All I hear my parents or preachers saying is that the Bible says this is so and therefore it is so, and that is the only answer necessary to give. What they do not realize," the young person passionately pleads, "is that when I begin my answer at school (or in the university) with 'the Bible says,' my answer is immediately dismissed as irrelevant, and in some instances I am torn to bits." I often remind them that the same type of "authority referencing" is given by irreligious persons who also provide no defense for why their source has served as canonical for them, be it this philosopher or that movie star. Both starting points undefended are open to question.

Can one prescribe just anything for any reason? From Woody Allen to Howard Stern, the list of pontiffs making pronouncements *ex cathedra* and shaping the opinions of this generation is unending. Sheer prescriptivism is clearly at the mercy of contrary prescriptions if all that is necessary for something to be believed is just to believe it. How can one possibly prescribe a moral principle, or the lack of one, without justifying the authority of the source? And yet, this is the level at which so many issues are argued. Whether by talk-show hosts or politicians, the opposing positions are constantly and contemptuously castigated as an imposition on their own position, forgetting that at the same time an imposition takes place in reverse when they offer their solution as superior.

Level three is where most of us live. From coffee shops to neighborhood parties to the kitchen table—life-defining and life-transforming conversations take place by a seemingly casual exchange of ideas.

This leads to my summation on the three-level theory of philosophy—logic, the arts, and table talk. If one is to come to a correct conclusion when debating any issue I propose we must abide by a rule, and that is this: Argue at level one, illustrate at level two, and apply at level three. The reasoning process provides the foundation, the arts the infrastructure and illustration, and the kitchen table the superstructure and application. If this process is rearranged, meaningful debate is precluded, and there is no point of reference for truth.

What I hope to do as we deal with the question of God's existence is to initiate the discussion from the common ground of the second level—where we all feel, and live, and act—to arrive at a place of agreement on the intellectual and existential struggle we all confront. Before we end, however, we will return to the first level to establish why the message of Jesus Christ operates on sound reasoning and why His message provides a solution to the questions and agonies of our time. Then we can bring authority to our table discussions when dealing with life's ultimate dimensions.

2

Straying through an Infinite Nothing

A FEW YEARS AGO I was at a very unusual family gathering of some Middle Eastern friends. It did not take long, amid all the back-slapping hilarity and laughter, for me to realize that although they were all related to one another, they came from different countries where the animosities of one for the other ran very deep, and have for centuries. I wondered whether politics ever entered into their light-hearted conversations, or was there a tacit understanding that guarded such discussions as sacrosanct?

I soon had my answer when one of them volunteered that he never feared getting too deeply mired in political issues because even the starting points, he was sure, would be debated to death. To illustrate his cultural traits, he told this interesting satire, which revealed not only how idiosyncratic they each were as individuals, but also how each culture in its own way is locked into a peculiar tunnel vision.

The story was of a roving reporter conducting a survey from country to country. In America, the first stop, he asked a person on the street, "What is your opinion on the shortage of meat in the world?" The bemused American replied, "What is shortage?"

Continuing in his single-minded survey, his next stop was in a deprived nation weighed down by the pain of famine. The reporter inquired, "What is your opinion on the shortage of meat in the world?" and the famished individual predictably responded, "What is meat?"

His third location was a country strangled by a dictatorial regime, and there the reporter asked a person standing in a long line for food, "What is your opinion on the shortage of meat in the world?" Having been stripped of all individuality, the puzzled person intoned, "What is opinion?"

Finally, the frustrated reporter ended up in the Middle East and quizzed a harried individual on his way to work, "What is your opinion on the shortage of meat in the world?" Wildly gesturing, the Middle Easterner countered, "What is, what is?"

As laughter erupted all around me, my host welcomed me to his family where, he said, "in true Middle Eastern fashion we cannot even agree on the question, so we really do not fear disagreement on the answer." I must confess that it took a burden off me to know that they could break the tension in issues so great by seeing the lighter side of their dispositions. Nevertheless, it was a solemn reminder of how tedious even starting points can be in some deliberations.

But here we find ourselves in search of answers, albeit on a volatile subject, so let us at least agree on some common ground on which to start.

Defining the Terms

Etienne Borne provides a clear definition of atheism and its ramifications for life:

> Atheism is the deliberate, definite, dogmatic denial of the existence of God. It is not satisfied with appropriate truth or relative truth, but claims to see the ins and outs of the game quite clearly being the absolute denial of the absolute.[1]

The second is taken from the *Encyclopedia of Philosophy.*

> An atheist is a person who maintains that there is no God; that is, that the sentence "God exists" expresses a false proposition. . . . a person who rejects belief in God.[2]

In her book *What on Earth Is an Atheist?* popular atheistic protagonist Madalyn Murray O'Hair asserts:

> We need a decent, modern, sophisticated and workable set of standards by which we can get along with ourselves and with others.

> We atheists . . . try to find some basis of rational thinking on
> which we can base our actions and our beliefs, and we have it. . . .
> We accept the technical philosophy of materialism. It is valid phi-
> losophy which cannot be discredited. Essentially, materialism's
> philosophy holds that nothing exists but natural phenomena. . . .
> Materialism is a philosophy of life and living according to rational
> processes with intellectual and other capabilities of the individual
> to be developed to the highest degree in a social system where this may
> be possible. . . . There are no supernatural forces, no supernatural
> entities such as gods, or heavens, or hells, or life after death. There
> are no supernatural forces, nor can there be.
>
> We atheists believe that nature simply exists. Matter is. Mate-
> rial is.[3]

May I underscore a very important point here, as do many other books
that deal with the subject of atheism?[4] *Atheism is not merely a passive unbelief in God but an assertive denial of the major claims of all varieties of
theism; atheism contradicts belief in God with a positive affirmation of matter
as ultimate reality.* Some atheists avoid this frontal attack upon theism and
try to soften that absolute denial of God. Their argument asserts that
God's existence is rationally unprovable and is therefore at best a meaningless proposition. In effect, their atheism is arrived at by default. This
approach is often taken so as to be conveniently relieved of the burden of
defending one's own alternative view. In actual terms both the soft and the
hard form of atheism accomplish the same goal and end up denying God's
existence either implicitly or explicitly. Any attempt to escape the ramifications of its absoluteness is unsuccessful.

Once this denial is made, choices necessarily follow in virtually every
facet of life, and the undergirding philosophy that determines what choices
are made is the negation of God's existence. The atheist, often better described as an antitheist, attempts to build his or her own life in the belief
that there is no God and that there are no supernatural entities. All forms
of religion they consider irrational, but in kicking against the unavoidable
goads along life's path they bloody themselves both intellectually and socially. I am thoroughly convinced that when the last chapter of humanity
is written we will find that the implications of atheism, i.e., living without
God, if consistently carried through, will have made life plainly unlivable
within the limits of reason or even of common sense.

The Autopsy of an Idea

Possibly no philosopher articulated a more forceful refutation of the theistic worldview than Frederick Nietzsche. He posited in its place a bold espousal of the antitheistic mind-set, keenly aware of the revolutionary, world-altering ramifications of that paradigm shift. Few philosophers had such a radical impact as Nietzsche upon the history makers of the twentieth century. His powerful influence upon Hitler—and through Hitler, Mussolini—is now well documented. Although I have referred to this connection elsewhere in my writings, I will take the risk of repetition because, in my estimation, no one has so poignantly voiced the linkage between atheism and life in such trenchant terms as he. Nietzsche dramatically portrayed this in his popular parable *The Madman.*

Have you not heard of that madman who lit a lantern in the bright morning hours, ran to the marketplace and cried incessantly, "I'm looking for God, I'm looking for God!" As many of those who did not believe in God were standing together there, he excited considerable laughter. "Why, did he get lost?" said one. "Did he lose his way like a child?" said another. "Or is he hiding? Is he afraid of us? Has he gone on a voyage? Or emigrated?" Thus they yelled and laughed. The madman sprang into their midst and pierced them with his glances.

"Whither is God?" he cried. "I shall tell you. We have killed him—you and I. All of us are his murderers. But how have we done this? How were we able to drink up the sea? Who gave us the sponge to wipe away the entire horizon? What did we do when we unchained this earth from its sun? Whither is it moving now? Whither are we moving now? Away from all suns? Are we not plunging continually backward, sideward, forward, in all directions? Is there any up or down left? Are we not straying as through an infinite nothing? Do we not feel the breath of empty space? Has it not become colder? Is not night and more night coming on all the time? Must not lanterns be lit in the morning? Do we not hear anything yet of the noise of the grave-diggers who are burying God? Do we not smell anything yet of God's decomposition? Gods, too, decompose. God is dead, and we have killed him.

"How shall we, the murderers of all murderers, comfort ourselves? What was holiest and most powerful of all that the world has yet owned has bled to death under our knives. Who will wipe this blood off us? What water is there for us to clean ourselves? What festivals of atonement, what sacred games shall we have to invent? Is not the greatness of this deed too great for us? Must not we ourselves become gods simply to seem worthy of it? There has never been a greater deed; and whoever will be born after us—for the sake of this deed, he will be part of a higher history than all history hitherto."

Here the madman fell silent and looked again at his listeners; and they too were silent and stared at him in astonishment. At last he threw his lantern on the ground, and it broke and went out. . . .

It has been related further that on the same day the madman entered divers churches and there sang his *requiem aeternam deo.* Led out and called to account, he is said to have replied each time, "What are these churches now if they are not the tombs and sepulchers of God?"[5]

Nietzsche's mood, without apology, is funereal. He boldly borrows jargon from a coroner's lexicon as he philosophically performs an autopsy upon an idea whose time had gone—the idea of God's existence. Once this idea had throbbed and pulsated, sending its life-giving sustenance to the extremities of civilization. But having convinced himself of what he termed the repressiveness of Christian teaching, and signaling man's coming of age, he said it was no longer possible to certify God as a viable entity. Philosophy and freedom joined hands in the arena, and the "noblest superstition was killed." And so it was that as the madman came to publish this news, he realized that mankind was not yet ready to receive this newborn idea because old myths die hard. But the day would come, he said, when a godless world would be welcomed into the waiting arms of the philosophical deliverer.

Early in Nietzsche's career, contemporary scholarship did him an injustice by treating his highly emotive words as bereft of academic sophistication. His style was at once his strength and his own worst enemy. It is still easy to dismiss the strong images that saturate his work as exaggerations of the nihilism he enjoined. But this is precisely where Nietzsche must be commended for feeling the pathos of the artist rather than hiding behind the lectern of the placid educator. He, in effect, drew attention to the three levels of philosophy by clearly demonstrating that there is a connection between the madman in the street and the sane man in the library. He uncompromisingly prognosticated the upheaval that was in store for mankind because the foundation had crumbled. He was truly one of the "antitheistic prophets" of the twentieth century, foretelling doom and gloom as he called forth a transvaluation of our values. Life had to be redefined and rebuilt with a new "Godless" foundation. It is that foundation that now merits our scrutiny.

Smuggled Foundations

One of Nietzsche's contentions was that Christianity had paralyzed the potential of human beings. (This perspective could well have been influenced by the composer Wagner, his close friend and an avowed anti-Semite who considered Christianity to be the cursed legacy of the Jews.) In fact, Nietzsche classified the Christian message as the nadir, or lowest point, of human progress because it elevated such concepts as morality, repentance, and humility. You cannot build a civilization of power upon these self-debasing ideas, he charged, and therefore they must be destroyed. His analysis considered Christian notions to be weakening to the mind and debilitating to the greatness that lay within. He felt that the infrastructure of the European ethos was stunted because of Christian teaching. If only this scaffolding of Christendom could be dismantled and thrown away forever, humanity could break free, soar to greater heights, and scale higher mountains of individual accomplishment. He provided the alternative of a new antitheistic foundation on which to build, but he warned that the immediate entailments could be catastrophic.

Nietzsche's estimate that the negative impact of his philosophy would be temporary as it awaited the emergence of the Superman could not have been more misguided and flawed. His wrongheadedness was one of history's costliest miscalculations and lay in his belief that an atheistic foundation was indispensable to building for the future. He envisioned that atheism would provide—indeed, had to provide—a superior undergirding for man to rise above the shadows of the past. The reality is, under close examination, that this new foundation is philosophically incoherent, morally bankrupt, and unable to logically or existentially support civilization.

In the new reconstruction, we do not see the promised greatness or harmony. Instead we are trapped in a world of violence, discord, emptiness, alienation, and racial hatred. The reason for this ought to be evident to us—our musicians sing about it. But having become masters of deceit and able manipulators of reality, we have also become deaf to the truth. It is proverbial that a nut does not fall very far from the tree, and if we are not careful we will more and more resemble the offspring of the madman. The infrastructure of our society has become mindless and senseless because the foundation upon which we have built cannot support any other kind of structure.

Ah, but it is at this point that we have played a game with words and lied to ourselves a thousandfold. Let me say forthrightly that what we have actually done is smuggle in foundational strengths of Christian thought, buried far below the surface to maintain some stability, while above the ground we see humanism's bizarre experiments growing unchecked. If we truly put into place the same principles below the ground that we flaunt above the ground, we would completely self-destruct. And though in the classroom we have tried to dignify what we have done, the songwriters and artists have called our bluff.

An utterly fascinating illustration of this duping of ourselves is the Wexner Center for the Performing Arts at Ohio State University. This building, another one of our chimerical exploits in the name of intellectual advance, was branded by *Newsweek* as "America's first deconstructionist building."[6] Its white scaffolding, red brick turrets, and Colorado grass pods evoke a double take. But puzzlement only intensifies when you enter the building, for inside you encounter stairways that go nowhere, pillars that hang from the ceiling without purpose, and angled surfaces configured to create a sense of vertigo. The architect, we are duly informed, designed this building to reflect life itself—senseless and incoherent—and the "capriciousness of the rules that organize the built world."[7] When the rationale was explained to me, I had just one question: Did he do the same with the foundation?

The laughter in response to my question unmasked the double standard our deconstructionists espouse. And that is precisely the double standard of antitheism! It is possible to dress up and romanticize our bizarre experiments in social restructuring while disavowing truth or absolutes. But one dares not play such deadly games with the foundations of good thinking. And if, indeed, one does toy at the foundational level, he or she will not only witness the collapse of all reason but at the same time will forfeit the right to criticize the starting point of any other worldview. Antitheism insists that an infinite, personal, omniscient, omnipotent God as postulated by any of the major religions does not exist. "No higher answer exists," says Harvard paleontologist Stephen Jay Gould. "We must construct this ourselves."[8]

If that be so, the tidal wave of questions that emerge from such imperiousness is unstoppable, somewhat like wrenching an unreuseable cork from a container filled with toxic fumes. This is precisely the condition presented by Nietzsche and more recently confirmed by Jean-Paul Sartre. And that is why it was so important for the Superman of Nietzschean dogma to emerge and take charge. However, who Nietzsche envisioned as a savior has instead became a destroyer, because his philosophical foundation lent itself to tyranny and ultimately, to genocide.

Our Eyes Have Seen the "Gory"

One of the great blind spots of a philosophy that attempts to disavow God is its unwillingness to look into the face of the monster it has begotten and own up to being its creator. It is here that living without God meets its first insurmountable obstacle, the inability to escape the infinite reach of a moral law. Across scores of campuses in our world I have seen outraged students or faculty members waiting with predatorial glee to pounce upon religion, eager to make the oft-repeated but ill-understood charge: What about the thousands who have been killed in the name of religion?

This emotion-laden question is not nearly as troublesome to answer if the questioner first explains all the killing that has resulted from those who have lived without God, such as Hitler, Stalin, Mussolini, Mao, et al. The antitheist is quick to excoriate all religious belief by generically laying the blame at the door of all who claim to be religious, without distinction. By the same measure, why is there not an equal enthusiasm to distribute blame for violence engendered by some of the irreligious?

But the rub goes even deeper than that. The attackers of religion have forgotten that these large-scale slaughters at the hands of antitheists were the logical outworking of their God-denying philosophy. Contrastingly, the violence spawned by those who killed in the name of Christ would never have been sanctioned by the Christ of the Scriptures. Those who killed in the name of God were clearly self-serving politicizers of religion, an amalgam Christ ever resisted in His life and teaching. Their means and their message were in contradiction to the gospel. Atheism, on the other hand, provides the logical basis for an autonomous, domineering will, expelling morality. Darwin himself predicted this slippery slope of violence if evolutionary theory were translated into a philosophy of life. Nietzsche talked of the enshrouding darkness that had fallen over mankind—he saw its ramifications. The Russian novelist Fyodor Dostoevski repeatedly wrote of the hell that is let loose when man comes adrift from his Creator's moorings and himself becomes god—he understood the consequences. Now, as proof positive, we witness our culture as a whole in a mindless drift toward lawlessness—we live with the inexorable result of autonomies in collision.

In case you fear that I am carrying this too far, I present the following for your consideration. It is not always easy in life to pinpoint moments that dramatically change you for the future. Sometimes, however, in retrospect we are able to look back upon such a moment and say, "For me, that was it." Let me introduce you to one such experience for me.

A few years ago when I was speaking in Poland I was taken to the Nazi death camps of Auschwitz and Birkenau. I shall never be the same. Many, many times in silence I have reflected upon my first visit there, where the words of Hitler envisioning a generation of young people without a conscience are aptly hung on a wall, grimly reminding the visitor of the hell unleashed when his goal was realized.

> I freed Germany from the stupid and degrading fallacies of conscience and morality. . . . We will train young people before whom the world will tremble. I want young people capable of violence—imperious, relentless and cruel.

On display for all to behold are thousands of pounds of women's hair, retrieved and marketed as a commodity by the Nazi exterminators, architects of the final solution that sent multitudes to the gas ovens. The incredible reminders—from rooms filled with pictures of abused and castrated children to the toiletries and clothing that are stacked to the ceiling—cast an overwhelming pall of somberness upon the visitor.

That this was conceived and nurtured in the mind of the most educated nation at that time in history and brought forth on the soil that had also given birth to the Enlightenment almost defies belief. But it was atheism's legitimate offspring. Man was beginning to live without God.

3

The Madman Arrives

I S THERE AN EXPLANATION for Auschwitz, this mind-boggling historical scar on the face of humanity? I believe there is, and it comes from one who survived Auschwitz, Viktor Frankl.

> If we present man with a concept of man which is not true, we may well corrupt him. When we present him as an automaton of reflexes, as a mind machine, as a bundle of instincts, as a pawn of drive and reactions, as a mere product of heredity and environment, we feed the nihilism to which modern man is, in any case, prone. I became acquainted with the last stage of corruption in my second concentration camp, Auschwitz. The gas chambers of Auschwitz were the ultimate consequence of the theory that man is nothing but the product of heredity and environment—or, as the Nazis liked to say, "of blood and soil." I am absolutely convinced that the gas chambers of Auschwitz, Treblinka, and Maidanek were ultimately prepared not in some ministry or other in Berlin, but rather at the desks and in lecture halls of nihilistic scientists and philosophers.[1]

If we in the West, living under the illusion of neutrality, insist on removing the Ten Commandments from our moral code, perhaps we might consider displaying these remarks of Frankl's to remind us that the impetus for the Holocaust did not come from a military strategy as much as it did from the educated elite, unblushing in their antitheistic philosophies and materialistic assumptions.

The Pathology of a Belief

A story I heard personally from Malcolm Muggeridge (that stirred me then and still does even yet) was his account of a conversation he had with Svetlana Stalin, the daughter of Josef Stalin. She spent some time with Muggeridge in his home in England while they were work-ing together on their BBC production on the life of her father. Accord-ing to Svetlana, as Stalin lay dying, plagued with terrifying hallucinations, he suddenly sat halfway up in bed, clenched his fist toward the heavens once more, fell back upon his pillow, and was dead. The incredible irony of his whole life is that at one time Josef Stalin had been a seminary student, preparing for the ministry. Coming of Nietzschean age, he made a decisive break from his belief in God. This dramatic and com-plete reversal of conviction that resulted in his hatred for all religion is why Lenin had earlier chosen Stalin and positioned him in authority— a choice Lenin too late regretted. (The name Stalin, which means "steel," was not his real name, but was given to him by his contemporaries who fell under the steel-like determination of his will.) And as Stalin lay dy-ing, his one last gesture was a clenched fist toward God, his heart as cold and hard as steel.

Is there a connection between Stalin's antitheism and his mastermind-ing the large-scale murder of his own people, some fifteen million of them? During those final days of the collapsing Marxist experiment in the Soviet Union, Soviet novelist Chingiz Aitmatov retold the following story, which has been paraphrased here.

On one occasion, so it was narrated, Stalin called for a live chicken and proceeded to use it to make an unforgettable point before some of his henchmen. Forcefully clutching the chicken in one hand, with the other he began to systematically pluck out its feathers. As the chicken struggled in vain to escape, he continued with the painful denuding until the bird was completely stripped. "Now you watch," Stalin said as he placed the chicken on the floor and walked away with some bread crumbs in his hand. Incred-ibly, the fear-crazed chicken hobbled toward him and clung to the legs of his trousers. Stalin threw a handful of grain to the bird, and as it began to follow him around the room, he turned to his dumbfounded colleagues and said quietly, "This is the way to rule the people. Did you see how that chicken followed me for food, even though I had caused it such torture?

People are like that chicken. If you inflict inordinate pain on them they will follow you for food the rest of their lives."[2]

With that promised debasement, Stalin reduced humanity to the level of animals, and intoxicated with power, he ruthlessly exterminated millions of his countrymen, prompting the suicides of several members of his immediate family. Stalin's starting point of building a world without God led him down the road to one of the goriest experiments in all of genocidal history.

Let me make clear what I am implying. I am not hereby suggesting that this is the way all antitheists are or that this is the kind of thinking all antitheists endorse. Nor am I suggesting that this is the only outworking of antitheistic thought. Obviously, there have been others in history who, though denying God, may have chosen for themselves the path of philanthropy. But here is the point. A Stalinistic-type choice is one that the philanthropic atheist is hard-pressed to rail against once he or she has, by virtue of atheism, automatically forfeited the right to a moral law. And that is the inescapable quandary. The ground of autonomous, individual morality can give rise to any choking weed that saps the life from all else.

Is this, indeed, the utopian humanistic dream? Is this the colorful personality walking across the tightrope of time, shoving out the wobbling "religious" man as he struggles to keep his balance? Do you remember that imagery from Nietzsche? I refer to his parable "Thus Spake Zarathustra," which is a melodramatic epic poem, rich in colorful detail that reveals his linguistic genius. The message intended by Nietzsche in that parable is both pathetic and pointed. Zarathustra, so the story goes, is the master ethicist who, at one stage in his life, sought a world of his own making and cloistered himself in the seclusion of a mountain. After years of trying to frame a morally ideal world on his own, he abandoned his quest for virtue as unreasonable and false. Reluctantly conceding to himself that he had been in serious error, Zarathustra discarded his once-treasured belief and left his hermetically sealed world. His mission as he traveled down his mountain was to proclaim to the world below this newfound knowledge that liberated him from the shackles of moral constraint.

On his way he met with a hermit who also had sacrificed the love of everything else "for the love of God." In the ensuing conversation, the hermit inquired of Zarathustra where he was going. Zarathustra stated that he was leaving the mountain and returning to the "depths" to shatter the myths that man believed—the myths of virtue, morality, and God. As he turned his back on the hermit who continued to plead with him to abort this mission—for it was wrong to disavow morality—Zarathustra whispered to himself in pity for the hermit, "Has no one told him that God is dead?"

Immediately upon his arrival in town, Zarathustra began to preach his new message to the people in the marketplace who had gathered to watch a tightrope walker cross between two towers. Zarathustra wrested the opportunity to advantage and used the acrobat to illustrate his point.

> Man is a rope, stretched between the animal and the Superman—
> a rope over an abyss. A dangerous crossing, a dangerous wayfaring,
> a dangerous looking back, a dangerous trembling and halting.

Elaborating on his theme that man is at present a halfway stop between the beast and the overman, Zarathustra added:

> Ye have made your way from the worm to man, and much within
> you is still worm. Once were ye apes, and even yet man is more of
> an ape than any of the apes. . . . Believe not those who speak unto
> you of superearthly hopes! Poisoners are they, whether they know it
> or not. Despisers of life are they, decaying ones and poisoned ones
> themselves, of whom the earth is weary: So away with them! Once
> blasphemy against God was the greatest blasphemy; but God died,
> and therewith also those blasphemers.[3]

Just as this one-time moralist was finishing his prologue, insisting that man needed to progress and abandon his idea of morality and God, the tightrope walker began to make his way across the chasm. Halfway across, he stopped and staggered. All of a sudden, a colorfully clad clown appeared behind him, stridently crying out:

> Go on, haltfoot! Go on, lazybones, interloper, sallow-face!—lest I
> tickle thee with my heel! What dost thou here between the towers!
> In the tower is the place for thee, thou shouldst be locked up; to one
> better than thyself thou blockest the way!

With each word, the buffoon came closer to the acrobat, and then, with a devilishly bloodcurdling cry, he leaped over him. Shaken by the sight and feel of the clown having overtaken him, the acrobat lost his courage, his pole, and his balance and plummeted to the ground, a whirlpool of arms and legs. Zarathustra stood calmly over the bloodied man, who was twitching and gasping on the brink of death and moaning in fear of hell.

> "On mine honor, my friend," answered Zarathustra, "there is nothing of all that whereof thou speakest: there is no devil and no hell. Thy soul will be dead even sooner than thy body: fear, therefore, nothing anymore." The man looked up distrustfully. "If thou speakest the truth," said he, "I lose nothing when I lose my life. I am not much more than an animal which has been taught to dance by blows and scanty fare." "Not at all," said Zarathustra, "thou hast made danger thy calling; therein there is nothing contemptible. Now thou perishest by thy calling: therefore will I bury thee with mine own hands."
>
> When Zarathustra had said this the dying one did not reply further; but he moved his hand as if he sought the hand of Zarathustra in gratitude.[4]

This parable dramatically captures Nietzsche's message to the world. It was the message of antitheism. According to Nietzsche, Zarathustra, the master ethicist and moralizer, had conclusively come to realize that all talk of ethics was nonsensical for the concept did not have any truth in ultimate reality. Convinced of his new deduction, he began his mission to enlighten the masses to his great discovery: The quest after morality was an ill-fated pursuit imposed by Christianity, dwarfing man and imprisoning him with fear. In atheistic terms, man is only halfway through his journey from being the beast to becoming the Superman. All that stands in his way should be obliterated. The main obstruction is the Christian, the religious man, "the worm theologian," for religion is a farce, engendered by fear of the world beyond. Push the Christian aside! Bury him! Tell him of his illusion and ignorance! Tell him he does not belong in this new world. And when you see his arms and legs twitching as he falls and dies, give him the greatest news of all. Proclaim to him that there is no heaven to be gained and no hell to be feared, and as he breathes his last he will reach out his hand to clasp yours with gratitude. Go and bury him so that you see his face no more, once and for all removing this burden of God that misguided "saints" have placed upon us.

New Promises and Old Betrayals

In Nietzschean antitheistic terms, Zarathustra performed the greatest of all deeds by transvaluing reality. The good news was no longer salvation; that was a poisonous concoction blended by religious powermongers. The good news is that the desire for salvation was unjustified, and one did not need to bear the weight of glory anymore. One could now drink deeply of the cup of antitheism—pure, unadulterated matter.

How does one deal with such a fierce tirade? The only way is to examine the ideas propounded and to remember their consequences. Upon close scrutiny, it soon becomes obvious that, while this emotionally charged outburst against the existence of God comes garbed in intellectual terminology, what one really finds is an agenda and "reason" that lurks behind the outwardly academic assault. The agenda is unblushingly admitted by a few. Aldous Huxley was one of them:

> For myself, as, no doubt, for most of my contemporaries, the philosophy of meaninglessness was essentially an instrument of liberation. The liberation we desired was simultaneously liberation from a certain political and economic system and liberation from a certain system of morality. We objected to the morality because it interfered with our sexual freedom; we objected to the political and economic system because it was unjust. The supporters of these systems claimed that in some way they embodied the meaning (a Christian meaning, they insisted) of the world. There was one admirably simple method of confuting these people and at the same time justifying ourselves in our political and erotic revolt: We could deny that the world had any meaning whatsoever.[5]

In the same context, he had prefaced his remarks with these words:

> I had motives for not wanting the world to have a meaning; consequently I assumed that it had none, and was able without any difficulty to find satisfying reasons for this assumption. Most ignorance is vincible ignorance. We don't know because we don't want to know. It is our will that decides how and upon what subjects we shall use our intelligence. Those who detect no meaning in the world generally do so because, for one reason or another, it suits their books that the world should be meaningless.[6]

Most of our God-killers today are not as forthright in admitting their motivation for such conclusions. There are some exceptions, but even they attempt to smuggle in the justification for their deductions on the shoulders of academic strength. Honesty demands that we ask of such thinkers what preceded what. Was it the desire to be free from all moral entailments that drove the intellect to manufacture a rational basis for that desire, or was it the genuine path of reason that led to the banishment of God? Stephen Jay Gould stated the following:

> We are here because one odd group of fishes had a peculiar fin anatomy that could transform into legs for terrestrial creatures; be- cause comets struck the earth and wiped out dinosaurs, thereby giving mammals a chance not otherwise available (so thank your lucky stars in a literal sense); because the earth never froze entirely during an ice age; because a small and tenuous species, arising in Africa a quarter of a million years ago, has managed, so far, to sur- vive by hook and by crook. We may yearn for a "higher" answer— but none exists. This explanation, though superficially troubling, if not terrifying, is ultimately liberating and exhilarating.[7]

There is a terrible irony in all of this, isn't there? What is the exhila- ration and liberation he is talking about? Am I missing something? Is this liberation synonymous with the fact that we have become one of the most violent and drugged nations on earth? Is this the exhilaration that makes sedatives and antacids the most highly sold drugs across pharmaceutical counters, to slow us down from our mad rush for ever-increasing wealth? Is this the exhilaration that is sending our songwriters and musicians into a frenzy on the stage and into a stupor in their homes? Is this the exhilaration venting forth on our talk shows that pride themselves in profane argument as entertainment? Is this the exhilaration that has fragmented our families and often victimized the weakest in our midst? Is this the exhilaration of living in the bloodiest century in history? Is this the exhilaration of a generation of young people often fatherless, many times hopeless? Is all this reason for exhilaration? Or are we playing deadly word games once again?

I say again that one may angrily argue that I am misrepresenting antitheism and that not all antitheists are immoral or despondent. The anger I can understand, but the argument is illogical. It is *true* that not all antitheists are immoral, but the larger point has been completely missed. Antitheism provides every reason to be immoral and is *bereft of any objective point of reference* with which to condemn any choice. Any antitheist who lives a moral life merely lives *better* than his or her philosophy warrants. All denunciation implies a moral doctrine of some kind, and the antitheist is forever engaged in undermining his own mines. This is precisely what makes Nietzsche's admission so terrifying.

Now let me return to the parable of Zarathustra and highlight how Nietzsche's philosophy fueled his own life. It is quite heartrending to read a description of his morbid mind and lifestyle as he ambled to his desk each day to pen his celebratory tirade against God. His life bore all the marks of physical and mental deterioration. Stooped, five-foot-eight, and almost blind, he would return to his routine in his small, freezing, and unkempt room. On a table innumerable scraps of paper recording his erratic thoughts were stacked. In a corner his only possessions, a threadbare suit and two shirts, lay in an old wooden trunk. Other than that, with no color or decoration, there were only books and manuscripts and a tray holding numerous jars and bottles containing drugs and potions to alleviate the debilitating pain of migraines and stomach ailments that often sent him into fits of vomiting. The sedatives and painkillers rendered him almost senseless for hours, but it was only this frightful arsenal of poisons and drugs that brought him any relief in his fast-disintegrating world. He would write for hours, wrapped in his overcoat and scarf, hunched beside a stove that belched forth fumes and no heat, his eyes wearing double glasses, getting ever closer to the pages before him. Endlessly he poured his thoughts onto paper, his body shivering and his eyes burning, while his life, driven by turbulent thought, sputtered toward an inglorious end.

The line that most poignantly and painfully sums up Nietzsche's beleaguered state is that "Zarathustra is the work of an utterly lonely man."[8] Ironically this is the same man who branded believers in God "poison-mixers" when his own life was the blend of a fatal mix.

Voltaire once scathingly attacked Christianity's bold pitch for meaning, saying that it was not in keeping with reality. That biting rebuke is here reversed by the blatant contradiction of Nietzsche's "good news," which was patently incongruous with the reality to which his philosophy gave birth. His pathetic physical debilitation and emotional turmoil, clearly exacerbated by his syphilitic condition, showed itself more blatantly in his writings as the years progressed. All his talk of the colorful buffoon playing to the stands ever remains the humanistic utopian dream, still unrealized.

The insanity that Nietzsche predicted for the world overtook him personally. In his autobiography, *Ecce Homo,* he had chapters titled "Why I Am So Intelligent," "Why I Write Such Good Books," and "Why I Am Fate." He identified himself as the "successor to the dead God." The end for Nietzsche came while he was in Turin, the city of Cesare Lombroso, psychiatrist and author of the widely known *Genius and Insanity.* Nietzsche collapsed in the street and was taken to Basel and later to an asylum. In a strange and sinister way, he microcosmically portrayed the fulfillment of a philosophy that wantonly denied God and chose to live without even a hint of divine command. He may turn out to be the most important philosopher of the last two centuries because he tried in practical terms to answer the greatest question of our time in his own being.

There is one episode in young Nietzsche's life that is at once tragic and definitive, pinpointed by several biographers as the turning point in his moral and spiritual outlook. Upon his arrival in Cologne as a student, he asked a guide to direct him to a hotel. Evidently, this malevolent individual took him instead into a brothel. When Nietzsche found himself surrounded by "women of the night" and their unwashed, unkempt customers, he was rudely shaken. He did not hide his contempt for those engaged in such a lurid practice. After playing a few chords on the piano, he stormed out, stating that the only object with any soul in that place was the piano. Many who knew him intimated that the allurement may have trapped Nietzsche and that he returned thereafter. Three years later he did admit to having contracted syphilis during that time. In a tragic way, his life had been transformed, for that which he had once despised he later embraced, and that which he embraced killed him. It is to that transformation I allude when I speak of a parallel for our nation. For Nietzsche's own utopia and the utopia he envisioned for Germany were not to be.

In his dreadful condition of madness, he possibly embodied and foreshadowed the lunacy unto death that seems to possess Western civilization today as it denies the very idea of God any access into the lives of this generation. Certainly, God has been barred from the institutions that determine society's thinking and behavior. I, for one, see Nietzsche's life and death as a blueprint for where we are headed inexorably as a nation, having committed ourselves to an antitheistic form of government and education.

4

The Homeless Mind

THE REASON FOR THE COLLAPSE of antitheism's literal and figurative utopia is that at the center of the thesis lies a devastating inability to build an ethical theory that is reasonable, coherent, and consistent without reducing it to sheer pragmatism. And this inability to arrive at goodness apart from God is not because of a failure to try. In fact, some of the most impressive thinking ever done on the subject of ethics was done by the watershed thinker of the Enlightenment, Immanuel Kant, who sought to establish a moral impetus within man and to postulate a system of right and wrong from reason alone. Historians of moral theory point out that the two centuries spanning 1630 to 1850 became the foundation on which our present Western edifice is built. Morality became defined as rules of conduct that were neither theological in their basis nor legal nor aesthetic, but were freed from those disciplines and given cultural space of their own.[1] Writing in the late eighteenth and early nineteenth centuries, Kant ironically planted the intellectual seed that lovers of reason watered on the fertile soil of Western culture as it burgeoned toward a secular worldview. Ironically, I say, because, as I previously stated, both democracies and totalitarian regimes lay claim to Kant's philosophy as the groundwork for their own social theories. This is an all-too-important fact, conveniently forgotten by the extremists and radicals of our time who seem to think that it is the plaintive cry of democratic freedom that echoes a rationalistic ethic. The terrifying truth is that the atheistic demagogues of the former Soviet Union also lovingly quoted Kant as the basis for their moral theory.

Reasoning That Failed the Test of Reason

Since Kant is cited as the godfather of goodness procurable apart from God, let us give our attention to him for a moment. Kant began with two very simple theses. First, he asserted that the rules of morality were rational and hence compelling for all rational beings. These rules, he argued, were as indisputable as the syllogisms of logic or the certainty of mathematics. His foundational premise was clearly and without equivocation that human beings—Eastern or Western, urban or suburban, religious or irreligious—could arrive by unaided reason at a normative dictum for right and wrong.

Second, Kant believed that this dictum was not merely a theoretical "ought" that was unreachable. Rather, he believed that mankind had within itself the capacity to perform that "ought" in its most noble demands upon the will. Therefore, by our reason we can know what is right, and by our will we can do what is right.

But at this point in his argument Kant presents two very important qualifiers to his rational justification for morality. The first is that God is not necessary as a revealer of right and wrong since we can come to pure reason apart from God. (Kant does not deny that God has given us some commands. He just denies the need for that revelation since reason alone, he contends, impels us to what is right.) While the first is constantly thrown at the theist by the antitheist, the second he conveniently ignores.

What is that second qualifier that the skeptic loves to forget? Kant stated without equivocation that an individual's moral choices were not to be determined by the happiness test, meaning that one ought not to choose a certain path for life just because it makes one happy. Again, Kant does not deny the need for happiness in all of us, just as he does not deny the existence of God. But he demolishes those contingencies as a basis for choosing between right and wrong. Strangely enough, while the Marxist world latched on to this reasoning by expelling God from its society and imposing humiliation and pain on the masses (because the greatest good was for the state rather than for individual happiness), the new world of democratic utopia inscribed the pursuit of individual happiness as a fundamental right for all individuals at the cost of the collective good. In both arenas, Kantian ethics were deviously mangled.

Our culture is so quick (as are we in these academic settings) to insist that God is unnecessary for understanding morality, quoting Kant ad nauseum. But have we brushed aside his other equally emphatic qualifier, that one must choose an ethic apart from one's own happiness? Kant argues that moral demands have an unconditional character to them as surely as mathematics does. They simply and categorically stand, independent of our preferences. Morality, then, is not fabricated by our desires or our longings or our rights, however we may term them.

I will not debate the Kantian system at this juncture. Any student of ethics ought to know that Kant's principal assertions have numerous assumptions that even the modern antitheist will not accept. His belief that a normative ethic can be arrived at apart from any divine revelation is fraught with philosophical, social, and historical contradictions.

I want to point out, further, that this bold presupposition in some forms of Western thought—claiming that morality can be deduced from reason alone—is precisely the reason for a total breakdown of understanding between East and West. The categories of right and wrong emerging from a secular viewpoint find no common ground with cultures whose ethics and political theories are born out of their religious commitment. The unbridled anger often vented in so-called Third World countries against certain positions in the West, from sexuality to politics, at least ought to alert us that "reason" alone has not served as a point of commonality. What may be reasonable in India may not be reasonable in France, and what may be reasonable in America may be "satanic" in Iran.

Even more troubling is that secularized Western man has actually extrapolated Kantian principles and assumed that, having arrived on the scene by chance with no transcendental accountability, he can still boldly talk of reason as objective. His reasoning processes are given authority by pointing to himself or to his culture. His culture, in turn, is justified by his reason— the argument gets pathetically circular.

For the Middle Eastern world of Islam, truth has been "revealed"; for the Far Eastern world of Hinduism and Buddhism, truth is "intuitive"; for the Western world, truth is "reasoned"; and for secularized Western man, his own happiness is paramount. How does one reason against intuition, revelation, and personal happiness when each comes with proportionate passion and conviction?

An assumption Kant invoked that often goes unnoticed illustrates this point. He reasoned that there were normative virtues that were universal, categorical, and internally consistent, and this led him to formulate his maxim that we should each will and act in keeping with the way everyone should always will and act. Kant himself said that some "oughts" were always binding, such as "Always tell the truth," "Always keep promises," "Be benevolent to those in need," "Do not commit suicide." The trouble with all these noble maxims is that they need Mishnaic or Talmudic types of interpretations, and each can easily die the death of a thousand qualifications and still be universalized. For example, it is easy to universalize a principle that states "Always tell the truth—unless it will lead to the death of another person." There are myriad others. Kant's argument is unprovable within his own stated parameters and involves some glaring oversights.

Ethicist Alisdair MacIntyre has also pointed out the influence of Kant's Christian background on his thinking, whether or not Kant himself admitted to it. All ethical theorists are influenced by their religious presuppositions that help forge their own ethical theories, a factor clearly present in the theories of Kierkegaard, Hume, and Diderot. Their respective religious upbringings of Lutheranism, Presbyterianism, and Jansenist-influenced Catholicism were implicit in their nonnegotiable maxims. Here again the antitheist fails to see the "higher answer" that cannot be suppressed, or he is hard pressed to adjudicate between conflicting ethical norms that cannot be sustained or countered apart from first defending a transcendent basis of ethics.

On a side note, it is important to mention that most of the ethicists that antitheists like to quote held a high and sacred view of marriage and would have had extraordinary difficulty with the way marriage is trivialized today by modern philosophers. I think particularly of a man like Bertrand Russell and his complete disregard for his own marital commitments. While riding his bicycle one day, Russell suddenly decided that he did not love his wife anymore; hence, it was time, he concluded, to walk out on her. This behavior he was to repeat several times in his life. Love and marriage have, indeed, fallen upon hard times, and men like Kant would not feel complimented at being told that they had provided the ethical groundwork for this collapse of commitment.

The Choice Against Reason

In conclusion, Kant's effort to provide a rational basis for ethics apart from God or personal happiness was unsuccessful, but he paved the way for others, not the least of whom were the existentialists. The one best known in *that* struggle to find an ethic is Sören Kierkegaard, the Danish philosopher. The step from Kant to Kierkegaard was long but predictable. The former approached ethics from the perspective of reason; the latter from that of the will and of the individual's power to choose. The key word in Kierkegaardian thinking is *choice,* which he presents in his book *Either-Or.* This choice between the ethical and aesthetic was not so much the choice between good and evil, he said, as it was the decision whether or not to choose *in terms of* good and evil. The doctrine that emerged in his writings was that when the ethical way of life is adopted, it should be adopted for *no specific reason* but as a choice that lies *beyond reason.* Once he had made his choice, said Kierkegaard, the ethical person had no problems of interpretation. Once again a deep incoherence surfaces as reason is jettisoned. The trend was the same for Hume and Diderot.

It is not at all difficult to see why this so-called Enlightenment experiment in ethics failed. It failed because one by one the basic presupposition of its propagators was uncovered. And that presupposition was this: In every instance, the purpose for life was presupposed before there was a postulation of ethics, and a purpose for life apart from God makes the ethical battleground a free-for-all. Time and again it was proven that it is not possible to establish a reasonable and coherent ethical theory *without first establishing the telos, i.e. the purpose and destiny of human life.* Even Kant concluded that without a *telos* it all got wrongheaded. If life itself is purposeless, ethics falls into disarray. As Dostoevski said, if God is dead, everything is justifiable.

This, may I suggest, is North America's predicament. This is the albatross around our educators' necks. This is the goad that keeps stabbing away at us as we bleed one another. We continue to talk of values and ethics; we persist in establishing moral boundaries for others while erasing the lines that are drawn for life itself. If my happiness is a right and the ultimate goal of life, why worry about anyone else's claims to happiness? And if I *must* worry about someone else's happiness, whose?—and why his or hers, and not another's? If life is pointless, why should ethics serve any purpose except my own? If I am merely the product of matter and at the mercy of material determinism, why should I subject myself to anyone else's moral convictions?

If, on the other hand, I am fashioned by God for *His* purpose, then I need to know Him and know that purpose for which I have been made, for out of that purpose is born my sense of right and wrong. There are two worlds represented in these options.

Creed or Chaos

Having abandoned God and finding both reason and choice to be insufficient guides in life's deepest issues, a solution is even more elusive when other worldviews enter the picture. The Muslim is thoroughly at peace with himself, universalizing his ethical beliefs. The Marxist is even more content, universalizing his or her own utopian dream at the cost of the individual. Their graves bespeak their hearts' convictions. To all of this the existentialist affirms his own choice as sufficient reason. And so we stare at a nation with condoms flung at worshipers, scuffles and derisive cries outside abortion clinics, and consenting adults victimizing unconsenting children. And in our search for morality and happiness outside of God, we have effectively lost all three—God, morality, and happiness.

Malcolm Muggeridge, that peripatetic journalist who traveled the globe for more than six decades of his life, said that if God is dead somebody else is going to have to take His place. It will either be megalomania or erotomania, the drive for power or the drive for pleasure, the clenched fist or the phallus, Hitler or Hugh Hefner. To that I might add—either economic or sexual exploitation. Muggeridge went on to add that we have lost our moral point of reference because we have forgotten that most empirically verifiable (though most denied) part of human experience—the depravity of man. And Muggeridge was right.

But it is not just Muggeridge who postulated this conviction. In crisp and evocative words, Iris Murdoch, professor at Oxford University, England, responded to Kant's *Groundwork on Ethics* and his argument for ethics from reason alone, apart from God.

How recognizable, how familiar to us, is the man so beautifully portrayed in the *Groundwork*, who confronted even with Christ turns away to consider the judgment of his own conscience and to hear the voice of his own reason. . . . This man is with us still, free, independent, lovely, powerful, rational, responsible, brave, the hero of so many novels and books of moral philosophy. The *raison d'être* of this attractive but misleading creature is not far to seek. He is the offspring of the age of science, confidently rational, and yet increasingly aware of his alienation from the material universe which his discoveries reveal . . . his alienation is without cure. . . . It is not such a long step from Kant to Nietzsche to existentialism, and the Anglo-Saxon ethical doctrines which in some ways closely resemble it. . . . In fact, Kant's man had already received a glorious incarnation nearly a century earlier in the work of Milton: his proper name is Lucifer.[2]

Is this philosophical indictment any different from the warning cry of the King Crimson rock group: "Knowledge is a deadly friend when no one sets the rules; the fate of all mankind I see is in the hand of fools"?[3] It brings to my mind the touching reminder of a recent town-hall meeting after the city of Atlanta had experienced one of the bloodiest months of murder in its modern history. One after another, several of these hurt and victimized young people stood up and pleaded with their elders and politicians to "please bring God and prayer back into our schools" while the city and civic leaders looked on helplessly, hoping that other, more socially acceptable solutions would be forthcoming. The heaviest price exacted from a society living without God is paid by its young people.

Yes, there is a connection—a logical connection—between telos and ethics, between the purpose of life and the "oughts" that entail, between God and morality.

The well-known social critic Dennis Prager, debating the Oxford atheistic philosopher Jonathan Glover, raised this thorny question: "If you, Professor Glover, were stranded at the midnight hour in a desolate Los Angeles street and if, as you stepped out of your car with fear and trembling, you were suddenly to hear the weight of pounding footsteps behind you, and you saw ten burly young men who had just stepped out of a dwelling coming toward you, would it or would it not make a difference to you to know that they were coming from a Bible study?"

Amid hilarious laughter in the auditorium, Glover conceded that it would make a difference.[4] Of course it makes a difference, because there is a logical connection.

Dorothy Sayers, the British theologian and novelist, echoes the same sentiments in the title of her essay *Creed or Chaos*. The modernist's creed betrays his bankruptcy. No one says this better than Steve Turner, the English journalist, in "Creed," his satirical poem on the modern mind:

> We believe in Marxfreudanddarwin.
> We believe everything is OK
> as long as you don't hurt anyone,
> to the best of your definition of hurt,
> and to the best of your knowledge.
>
> We believe in sex before, during, and
> after marriage.
> We believe in the therapy of sin.
> We believe that adultery is fun.
> We believe that sodomy's OK.
> We believe that taboos are taboo.
>
> We believe that everything's getting better
> despite evidence to the contrary.
> The evidence must be investigated
> And you can prove anything with evidence.
>
> We believe there's something in horoscopes,
> UFO's and bent spoons;
> Jesus was a good man just like Buddha,
> Mohammed, and ourselves.
> He was a good moral teacher although we think
> His good morals were bad.
>
> We believe that all religions are basically the same—
> at least the one that we read was.
> They all believe in love and goodness.
> They only differ on matters of creation,
> sin, heaven, hell, God, and salvation.

We believe that after death comes the Nothing
Because when you ask the dead what happens
they say nothing.
If death is not the end, if the dead have lied, then it's
    compulsory heaven for all
excepting perhaps
Hitler, Stalin, and Genghis Khan.

We believe in Masters and Johnson.
What's selected is average.
What's average is normal.
What's normal is good.

We believe in total disarmament.
We believe there are direct links between warfare and
    bloodshed.
Americans should beat their guns into tractors
and the Russians would be sure to follow.

We believe that man is essentially good.
It's only his behavior that lets him down.
This is the fault of society.
Society is the fault of conditions.
Conditions are the fault of society.

We believe that each man must find the truth that
is right for him.
Reality will adapt accordingly.
The universe will readjust.
History will alter.
We believe that there is no absolute truth
excepting the truth
that there is no absolute truth.

We believe in the rejection of creeds,
and the flowering of individual thought.[5]

He then adds this postscript called Chance:

CAN MAN LIVE WITHOUT GOD

If chance be
the Father of all flesh,
disaster is his rainbow in the sky,
and when you hear

State of Emergency!
Sniper Kills Ten!
Troops on Rampage!
Whites go Looting!
Bomb Blasts School!

It is but the sound of man
worshipping his maker.[6]

Indeed, the hope of atheism moves it inexorably to a creedless chaos. On the heels of the Enlightenment, existentialism was waiting to be born. Passion became the fashion, and decency had "gone with the wind." When existentialism spent itself the deconstructionists dismantled all that was left. Colin Gunton's book, which follows existentialism to its ultimate end, is suitably titled *Enlightenment and Alienation*. There remains no moral point of reference that is both coherent and logically prescriptive.

This is the first point of breakdown when attempting to live without God. The ramifications are terrifying. Let us go on to the second.

5

Where Is Antitheism When It Hurts?

T HE RENOWNED PREACHER Joseph Parker once said, "If you preach to the hurts of people, you will never lack for an audience." It is a point well taken, for the shared experience of pain and suffering transcends cultural and linguistic barriers. The fact and abundance of human suffering not only draws empathy out of us, one for the other, but also prompts within the human spirit the deeply felt question: Where is God when it hurts? While I do not intend to answer this question from the Christian perspective until later, I do want to frame the question now within its legitimate parameters.

Someone has said, "Virtue in distress and vice in triumph make atheists of mankind." This is undeniably the single greatest barrier to belief in God. Alfred, Lord Tennyson worded it simply yet cogently, "Never morning wore to evening but some heart did break."[1] The poet has the luxury of focusing on the emotions without apology.

When we look at human suffering, we look at a dilemma of cosmic proportions. It is a question that spawns scores of others. The same question, when related to the scientific worldview, surfaces as a counterpoint to the argument from design. In other words, just as the scientist may grant that the eye is well designed but not perfect, so the philosopher admits that this is, to a certain extent, an ordered world but sees capriciousness in it because of the inordinate amount of human suffering. From the antitheist's point of view, religious faith does not really answer the question; its prescriptions are merely swallowed with a whole dose of other superstition. And that, he contends, only serves to temporarily tranquilize the individual without really answering the question of why there is pain and suffering in this world if, indeed, an all-loving or all-powerful

45

God is at the helm. The whole struggle is further accentuated by the human experience of death—the ultimate form of pain and suffering—which, according to Camus, is philosophy's only problem.

At first glance one does not realize how intricate and extensive this question can be. But the more one seeks a satisfying answer the more one understands how complex an issue this is for *every* worldview. For example, philosophers deal with the metaphysical problem of evil (the authorship of evil), the moral problem of evil (God's role in it), and the physical problem of evil (where there is no human agency involved). A necessary part of the discussion entails what is commonly known as "the best of all possible worlds."

The skeptic generally presents four options that God could have exercised in creation (if, in fact, He does exist): first, to create no world at all; second, to create a world in which there are no such categories as good and evil—an amoral world; third, to create a world in which one could only choose good—a kind of robotic world; fourth, to create the world as we know it, with the possibility of both good and evil. Why, the skeptic asks, would God choose *this* model, knowing that evil would ensue?

These are the philosophical battle lines. Obviously, it is not possible to deal with all the issues here, but I do hope in my defense of Christianity in Part III of this book to answer the thorniest of them as well as I can.

Before the antitheist, however, are two unshakable dilemmas. The first is the philosophical challenge he or she faces in defending the question of existent evil. The second is the problem of death. Here again, the irrationality of life when one tries to live without God is exposed. It is extremely important that, as I unfold this argument dealing with evil, it be treated as a whole. Each portion of it links up with another, and if it is taken piecemeal, injustice is done to the answer. Just as Christianity cannot deal with the difficulties of this question in isolation, neither can atheism. The assumptions and deductions are part of a larger system.

One of the most provocative responses to the experience of death and the search for hope was presented by Professor Wilfred McClay of Tulane University after he had attended a funeral. I quote now his comments quite extensively because these words expose the twin edges of the question, both for the antitheist and for the theist.

> Where the rest of us had been stunned into reflective silence, awed and
> chastened by this reminder of the slender thread by which our lives

hang, the minister had other things in mind. . . . He did not try to comfort her family and friends. Nor did he challenge us to remember the hard words of the Lord's Prayer, "Thy will be done." Instead, he smoothly launched into a well-oiled tirade against the misplaced priorities of our society, in which millions of dollars were being poured into "Star Wars" research while young women such as this one were being allowed to die on the operating table. That was all this minister had to say. His eulogy was, in effect, a pitch for less federal spending on defense and more spending on the development of medical technology. . . . The only thing omitted was an injunction that we write our Congressman, or Ralph Nader, about this outrage.

I could hardly believe my ears. . . . Leave aside the eulogy's unspeakable vulgarity and its unintentional cruelty to the woman's family. Leave aside the flabby and cliché quality of language and speech. Leave aside the self-satisfied tone of easy moral outrage. . . . Leave aside the fashionable opinions. . . . I am willing to concede, for the sake of argument, that the minister may have been right in everything he said. All of these considerations are beside the point. Nothing can alter the fact that he failed us, failed her, and failed his calling by squandering a precious moment for the sake of a second-rate stump speech, and by forcing us to hold our sorrow back in the privacy of our hearts, at the very moment it needed common expression. That moment can never be recovered.

Nothing that religion does is more important than equipping us to endure life's passages by helping us find meaning in pain and loss. With meaning, many things are bearable; but our eulogist did not know how to give it to us. All he had to offer were his political desiderata. For my own part, I left the funeral more shaken and unsteady than before. Part of my distress arose from frustration that my deepest thoughts (and those of many around me, as I later discovered) were so completely unechoed in this ceremony and in these words. But another part of my distress must have stemmed from a dark foreboding that I was witnessing another kind of malpractice, and another kind of death.[2]

I find it intriguing that in spite of all the vilifying attacks religion has to face, it is still deemed the only bastion of hope in the face of death, both for the deceased and for the grieving survivors. The points Professor McClay raise here, implicitly and explicitly, are pertinent to our discussion. The events that provoked these impassioned words from him were tragic. The woman by whose grave he stood had been a friend from the university; she had died rather suddenly while giving birth to her baby. All the euphemisms and abstruse philosophizing could not conceal the pain or bypass the questions. Here atheism meets a stiff challenge.

C. S. Lewis insightfully suggested that only we human beings spell pain the way we do. His contention was that we do not merely posit the reality of pain; rather, we position the question in a decidedly moral context, specifically the morality of justice. Why? Why? Why? Elsewhere, Lewis strongly argued that pain may well be God's megaphone to a morally deaf world.[3]

These twin issues of the *context* and *purpose* of pain underscored by Lewis are constantly ignored by the antitheist because they stab antitheistic thinking in the heart of its most potent criticism against God's existence. By raising the question of pain and death in a moral context, an antitheist betrays a glaring contradiction in his understanding of reality if at the same time he denies God's existence. If this is not a moral universe, why position the question morally? Why *spell* pain the way he does?

Alternatively, if it *is* a moral universe, could not the whole experience of pain and suffering indeed be God's megaphone to draw mankind's attention to a moral reality? But if this is a moral world, the question actually becomes self-indicting. The antitheist is on the painful horns of a moral and logical dilemma. If the question is meaningful for him to raise, then it is also self-indicting—the implication is that this is a moral universe and therefore the critic must also deal with his or her own immorality. Conversely, if the question is meaningless, because evil is not an appropriate category in a purely materialistic and Godless world, then the critic lives in contradiction by positioning his criticism of God in moral terms. One way or the other, either the question or the questioner self-destructs.

One of the most remarkable conversions to Christianity was that of the poet W. H. Auden. It was remarkable because of the route he took in his own mind as he searched for answers to the very deep question of evil. In an interview with social analyst Ken Myers, Professor Alan Jacobs of Wheaton College poignantly describes this path taken by Auden. Jacobs narrates an event in 1940 when Auden entered a predominantly German section of a movie theater in Manhattan where the Third Reich's filmed version of its conquest of Poland was being shown. To the sheer shock and dismay of Auden, every time a Pole would appear on the scene, the angry screams of the crowd would resound in the theater. "Kill him . . . Kill them!" they would shout, somewhat reminiscent of the bloodthirsty cries of the Roman masses as they thronged the arena to witness the gladiatorial orgies of savagery and sadism.

Auden left the theater tremendously shaken and confounded by this experience of unmitigated hatred he had witnessed. His dismay lay not merely in his inability within his humanistic framework to find a solution to such a moral plague, but in his obvious inability to even explain the existence of such inhuman passions holding the mind in its grasp. He was having difficulty "spelling" evil, given his presuppositions. That struggle led to his Christian conversion, which coherently provided an explanation both to the depravity of man and an answer for its cure.

Auden well understood the question. Apart from God the question of pain and death not only remains unanswered; it even defies justification.

Let me try, as briefly as I can, to pull the problem together and find some daylight. Return to Professor McClay's frustration and notice that he also reveals another disappointment. His legitimate expectation and implication were that it is within the role of religion to bring hope to an otherwise irremediable situation. Trapped in the barren desert of hopelessness, the mourners needed something more than the terribly inappropriate political sermonizing on something as tragic as death. But is this not also part of the bankruptcy of our time? Blaming anybody and everybody, we start looking to education, political theory, and social progress as a way out of our moral quicksand, imagining that they can somehow build shelters along the way from the scorching heat of reality and perhaps even rescue us from death and hopelessness. Is this not a dislocation of the problem brought about by trying to live without God? Certainly Professor McClay saw this displacement.

True, religion is not justified purely because it provides relief from hopelessness. It matters for nothing if it is only a psychologically induced solution. If religious truth is approached by an uncritical intellect and sought as an escape from a painful reality, then to use the scriptural analogy, the exorcism of the demon of hopelessness only opens wide the psyche to the stranglehold of a sevenfold possession, deceiving the one possessed by the more pathetic illusion of a future. If, on the other hand, religious belief is based on truth and is submitted to the greatest scrutiny, then the peace and hope that are sought after and realized for life and death are legitimate.

That scrutiny in search of truth is demanded before one submits to the claims of any religion. But here is the point: Why is that *same* scrutiny not given to the thinking that directs a life lived without God? In short, where is antitheism when it hurts?

Here again, as in the struggle against a moral law, antitheistic thinkers argue in a circle and give an answer that flies in the face of reason. How can thinking men and women ever be given ultimate hope when life itself is death-bound? Any hope imparted is only realized by robbing reality in order to pay appearances. The Nietzschean assurance that the dying person will reach out and shake your hand when you assure him that extinction is imminent is, at best, a good-news/bad-news joke. The bad news is that he is dying; the good news is that when he dies he will not want anything anymore. So the bad news is not really bad, after all; in fact, it is the consummate liberation.

In a strange way, this has Buddhistic overtones without the moral or spiritual impetus of Buddhism. Gautama Buddha, as you may recall, began his whole quest for the answers to life because he witnessed old age, disease, and death. This quest led to the abandonment of his wife, home, and all material comforts. The answer lay in his belief that at the heart of all human suffering was desire, and if only desire could be extinguished, Nirvana lay around the corner. Classical Buddhism was, of course, atheistic with gnostic overtones, and it taught that the answer to suffering lay in the eradication of desire. For the Buddhist, meditation, self-renunciation, and the transmigration of the soul would bring that enlightened state.

For the antitheist, the death of desire occurs only in death itself, so death in fact becomes the deliverer from desire. It was in recognition of this conundrum that Jean-Paul Sartre raised the question of why he did not commit suicide, for that would indeed remove all his suffering. If life is defined apart from God, this is a very legitimate question. Sartre's answer was absurd—that he did not commit suicide because to do so would be to use his freedom to take away his freedom. Like many antitheistic answers, this, too, is hollow, and the rejoinder is obvious. Why would one hesitate to take away that freedom if freedom itself is the problem, bringing with it aimlessness, pain, and despair? The loss of something that is never thought of, felt, or sought for when lost is not a loss at all. Death, in effect, becomes a cure-all because it delivers one from such a state. If it is a cure-all, then it is not an evil except for the survivors. But that only pushes the solution one step further. In a strange way, death is transvalued from being an evil to being the ultimate good. With this kind of reasoning, man can create the best of all possible worlds by mere extinction. Enter once again the world of antitheistic word games.

With all the attempts to impart hope, trying to live without God ends up in a vicious circularity, raising questions the answers to which raise even greater questions. In short, atheism has no answer for why we spell pain the way we do. And the grim, barbaric options between stoicism and epicure-anism, now called optimistic humanism, do not even spell relief. If one were to borrow Edward Murrow's definition of an optimist—"someone who tells you to cheer up when things are going his way"—it is evident why optimistic humanism is called such, though it effectually redefines both terms for its optimism is artificially induced, and its humanism devalues humanity. Optimism here is an obscured reason's substitute for hope.

The trouble with much philosophizing is that it can easily become a process of establishing one construct after another in an attempt to alter reality. With all of atheism's talk of hope or utopia, never before in history has such hopelessness enshrouded so many people, as the heart's deepest longings remain unmet.

The fundamental problem in Russia today is hopelessness, and the same pertains for millions of young people in our own country. Not long ago, following an address I had delivered to leaders of the Peace Accord in South Africa, a young Asian stood up in an open session and asked, "Mr. Zacharias, what answers can you give us to keep us from becoming another Bosnia?" When a young teenager can voice a question such as that, laden with such emotion and fear, it is evident that life without God is not work-ing. The question really should be, What is going to keep the whole world from becoming another Bosnia?

Noted optimistic humanist Ted Turner made the comment once that if Cable News Network (CNN) had existed in the 1940s, the holocaust would never have happened. I infer from his boast that he means that the dissemination of information would arrest evil in its march, and human energy for the good would prevail. With all respect for his en-trepreneurial brilliance, I wonder what he would say to the innocents awaiting slaughter in Bosnia and Rwanda? Hope can never be imparted merely by technological advance when death stares you in the face—only a grim stoicism prevails. We may run from reality, but like many attempts to cosmetically cover scars, we cannot evade its deep and private pain.

The very sharp edge of pain and death is felt universally, and every religion or philosophy of life has to deal with it. A philosophy that espouses no belief in God cannot even justify the question, let alone provide an answer except for the hope for extinction. If this gap in human knowledge could only be filled, just think of how it would redefine everything. Honesty of mind drives every generation to seek an answer that does not smack of ignorance or arrogance, and life's passages demand something better for each life before the curtain falls. For the Christian there is an answer.

Diminishing Darkness, Increasing Light

A short while ago I happened to be speaking in a church that drew quite a few members of the local leadership in government and business. A member of the pastoral staff asked me if I would be willing to visit someone whom I did not know but who had been at some meetings that I had addressed a year before. She had evidently cherished those meetings and enjoyed listening to tapes of the messages. Now she was dying of AIDS. I, along with my wife and a colleague, immediately took the opportunity to visit her.

I wish I could fully express to you my emotions on that occasion. There, coalesced in that room, were both the pitiful reality of an undignified death and the greatness of courage and faith within the human heart. The apartment building was situated in a prime location where the city's renowned historic landmarks could be viewed. But our dying friend could no longer enjoy that view—her life was quickly ebbing away. As we entered her apartment, we started down the stairs that led to the living room. On a sofa sat her parents, and by her side stood a friend. She herself lay pathetically emaciated and utterly without strength. Nevertheless, she turned her head feebly at the sound of someone coming, not knowing who it was, and when she caught sight of us she gasped. As I bent down and hugged her, she kept repeating, "I don't believe it. I don't believe it." I shall spare you the details of our conversation, but I would like to share two simple thoughts.

As I looked around the room, I saw on a table within her reach a tape recorder and some tapes, and a book opened, facedown. The title of the book said it all—*The Hunger for Significance.* Before I left, I asked if we could pray together, and with much delight she agreed. I looked at her dreadful physical condition, completely bereft of any form, just skin and bones. We bowed our heads and prayed, and when I opened my eyes I caught the twinkle in hers. She reached out for me, and I hugged her again before we left. She well knew that life for her was at its end, but from within her glowed a hope that transcended the present. Although some of life's choices had taken their toll, she had in the previous two years made the greatest choice she could, the choice to trust God to take her through this, and then beyond the grave. Five days later she died, and according to the promise of Scripture, I know she realized that hope. Christ lived, died, and rose again to proclaim the promise of heaven.

Let me transport you from the aroma of death in a foreboding setting to a palace in London. The occasion was a Christmas Eve address to the British Commonwealth delivered by King George VI. His closing quotation, during those difficult days for Britain and the world following World War II, have been etched in the memories of those who were in positions of leadership at that time in history.

> I said to the man at the Gate of the Year, "Give me a light that
> I may walk safely into the unknown."
> He said to me, "Go out into the darkness, and put your hand in
> the hand of God, and it shall be to you better than the light, and
> safer than the known."[4]

As he spoke, his listeners were unaware that the king was dying of cancer. These words were to become an anchor in his own time of need.

From individual need to international struggles, the only hope that makes sense and is legitimate is the hope that comes from God, the hope for life and beyond death. Where there is no answer for death, hopelessness inevitably invades life. Pascal knew whereof he spoke when he said that he had learned to define life backwards and live it forwards. By that he meant that he first defined death and then his life accordingly. That makes complete sense. All journeys are planned with the destination in view. The apostle Paul said, referring to Jesus, "I want to know Christ and the power of his resurrection and the fellowship of sharing in his sufferings" (Phil. 3:10). The resurrection of Christ informs suffering, and that is why the existence of God and the confidence of hope go together. Life is no longer seen through the foggy glass of finitude but through the clearer vision of God Himself, who brings victory over death.

It is the privilege and prerogative of those who deal in matters of the spirit to respond to these struggles. But with equal force I state that antitheism leaves the questioner doubly indicted, for it negates the very justifiability of the question and dispels the problem of pain as strictly a moral aberration in an otherwise progressing species. Bertrand Russell affirmed that his life was built on the foundation of unyielding despair; perhaps that is why he issued a joint statement with Albert Einstein, just two days before Einstein's death, confessing that "those of us who know the most are the gloomiest about the future."

With a commitment to matter as ultimate reality, "gloominess" is a very logical outcome. Denying God leaves man free to abolish the past and decree the future, but those who know the most do not find hope in man's decrees. The lack of certainty and of a future hope was the canker in the heart of paganism. Evidently our neopaganism fares no better—the canker has become cancerous, and man's behavior and character certainly do not alleviate the fear of the future.

Writing a quarter of a century ago, Archibald McLeish sounded this warning cry of humanity's pyrrhic victory over God.

> There is, in truth, a terror in the world, and the arts have heard it as they always do. Under the hum of the miraculous machines and the ceaseless publications of the brilliant physicists a silence waits and listens and is heard.
>
> It is the silence of apprehension. We do not trust our time, and the reason we do not trust our time is because it is we who have made the time, and we do not trust ourselves. We have played the hero's part, mastered the monsters, accomplished the labors, become gods— and we do not trust ourselves as gods. We know what we are.
>
> In the old days when the gods were someone else, the knowledge of what we are did not frighten us. There were Furies to pursue the Hitlers, and Athenas to restore the truth. But now that we are gods ourselves we bear the knowledge for ourselves. Like that old Greek hero who learned when all the labors had been accomplished that it was he himself who had killed his son.[5]

Those words describe the consequences of trying to live without God. One has no right to a future hope, either personal or cosmic.

6

In Search of Lower Meaning

WE HAVE NOW COME to the third dilemma of antitheism. Severed from a rationally defensible moral law and from the existential fulfillment of hope, the individual is set upon a collision course that has wiped the slate of human existence clean of any meaning. The *tabula rasa* (the blank slate of the human mind) is an invitation to any graffiti, for how do contradictory meanings compete in an arena of unreason and hopelessness? Stephen Jay Gould has, without apology, drawn the lines clearly. He says:

> The human species has inhabited this planet for only 250,000 years or so—roughly .0015 percent of the history of life, the last inch of the cosmic mile. The world fared perfectly well without us for all but the last moment of earthly time—and this fact makes our appearance look more like an accidental afterthought than the culmination of a prefigured plan.
>
> Moreover, and more important, the pathways that have led to our evolution are quirky, improbable, unrepeatable and utterly unpredictable. Human evolution is not random; it makes sense and can be explained after the fact. But wind back life's tape to the dawn of time and let it play again—and you will never get humans a second time. . . . We cannot read the meaning of life passively in the facts of nature. We must construct these answers ourselves—from our own wisdom and ethical sense. There is no other way.[1]

These are very strong statements, and there can be no doubt of where Professor Gould stands on this matter: He says, in effect, "We are here by accident . . . we have no intrinsic meaning . . . we must construct these answers ourselves. . . . There is no other way." Obviously, not all critical thinkers of his caliber are in agreement with him. For that matter, not even all who submit to the evolutionary theory are in agreement with him. For Gould and his ilk, clearly life must be lived without God; his philosophical extrapolations are not just mild-mannered reflections, but an aggressive philosophy to be propagated. His tirades against Philip Johnson, professor of law at Berkeley, have revealed the anger with which he reacts should anyone challenge his cultic commitment to atheistic evolutionary belief.[2]

But there is at least one thing that both theists and antitheists agree on, and that is that no matter what the starting point, we must all attempt to answer the question of life's meaning. For a philosophy that defines life apart from God, there is a plethora of options, each necessarily forfeiting the right to judge anyone else's choice. For a philosophy that espouses God, life is directed by the concepts and precepts that are revealed by His character and purpose.

One of the most common refrains we hear from those who have reached the pinnacle of success is that of the emptiness that still stalks their lives, all their successes notwithstanding. That sort of confession is at least one reason the question of meaning is so central in life's pursuit. Although none like to admit it, what brings purpose in life for many, particularly in countries rich in enterprising opportunities, is a higher standard of living, even if it means being willing to die for it. Yet, judging by the remarks of some who have attained those higher standards, there is frequently an admission of disappointment. After his second Wimbledon victory, Boris Becker surprised the world by admitting his great struggle with suicide.[3] Jack Higgins, the renowned author of *The Eagle Has Landed,* has said that the one thing he knows now at this high point of his career that he wished he had known as a small boy is this: "When you get to the top, there's nothing there."[4]

This, I dare suggest, is one of the more difficult of life's realities to accept. Those who have not yet experienced the success they covet find it impossible to believe that those who have attained it find it wanting in terms of giving meaning to life. The driving force behind our thriving marketing industry and the sovereignty of technopoly (to use Neil Postman's phrase) is to create new hungers to help us forget old ones. If the wheel of fortune does not deliver, we turn our attention toward the deception and enamorment we have with becoming the object of artistic adulation. This high-speed pursuit between the Scylla of wealth and the Charybdis of fame is exacerbated by the breadth of its allurement for all ages, and even the young are forced into discovering that reaching the pinnacle of fame exacts a price. Perhaps a mature adult can cope with the deceptiveness of the plastic image—of being surreal and idolized. But it is another thing entirely to thrust this upon a child or a young person who has not yet learned to distinguish fact from fantasy. The slippery slope to self-destruction has trapped many a child actor. How many lives will Madison Avenue toy with before the heartless deceit is admitted? The search for fulfillment never ends because the cure for boredom requires something loftier.

Ernest Van den Haag underscores this seemingly timeless insatiability across all demographic lines:

> Though the bored person hungers for things to happen to him, the disheartening fact is that when they do he empties them of the very meaning he unconsciously yearns for by using them as distractions. In popular culture even the second coming would become just another barren "thrill" to be watched on television till Milton Berle comes on. No distraction can cure boredom, just as the company so unceasingly pursued cannot stave off loneliness. The bored person is lonely for himself, not, as he thinks, for others. He misses the individuality, the capacity for experience from which he is debarred. No distraction can restore it. Hence he goes unrelieved and insatiable.[5]

It is evident that the problem is far too acute for some novel invention to solve or for a simplistic solution to be offered. (We have even come to artificially induced realities—gradually erasing the line between the true and the false, the actual and the fantasized—ultimately making life itself a contradiction.) Great thinkers of every stripe have addressed this problem. Voltaire posited the inexorable circularity of life as he saw it—from man to worm, each in its own way either a predator or prey completing the cycle and the miseries of each making the good of all. But, in all this, man ever remains a stranger to his own research.

What has been the result of our constant search for something that will make sense of life apart from God? Either pragmatism—doing whatever works (a philosophy in which we in America specialize)—or some form of mysticism with a smuggled-in spirituality during a few private moments to prepare us for the fast lane once again. Is it possible that just as pain spelled with moral connotations raises the moral dilemma, so our miseries in search of meaning really reflect our grandeur? Are we held hostage to a physical determinism thrust forward by the prebiotic soup, or are we here by the fashioning will of a Grand Designer?

Living without God and espousing the first option presents another insurmountable obstacle. Lee Iacocca stated this human malady well in his book *Straight Talk:* "Here I am in the twilight years of my life, still wondering what it's all about. . . . I can tell you this, fame and fortune is for the birds."

Dissonant Voices

Let me end by quoting a few perspectives forthrightly stated and representative of different approaches in search of a solution to the problem of meaning.

I have previously referred to *Life* magazine's publication on mankind's search for meaning. It is a fascinating cross section of words and pictures—from philosophers to drug addicts, from painters to plumbers. The arguments—or should I say, the contradictions—provide hours of reading that are not dissimilar to being on an emotional roller coaster. I present a sampling, beginning with José Martinez, a taxi driver, who provides the nihilistic sound bite:

> We're here to die, just live and die. I live driving a cab. I do some fishing, take my girl out, pay taxes, do a little reading, then get ready to drop dead. You've got to be strong about it. Life is a big fake. Nobody gives a damn. You're rich or you're poor. You're here, you're gone. You're like the wind. After you're gone, other people will come. It's too late to make it better. Everyone's fed up, can't believe in nothing no more. People have no pride. People have no fear. People aren't scared. People only care about one thing and that's money. We're gonna destroy ourselves, nothing we can do about it. The only cure for the world's illness is nuclear war—wipe everything out and start over. We've become like a cornered animal, fighting for survival. Life is nothing.[6]

Raymond Smullyan, a mathematical logician, speaks quite defiantly:

> I have always been extremely puzzled by those who have claimed that
> if there is no God, then life is meaningless. Is there the slightest
> shred of evidence that secular humanists find life less meaningful
> than do religious believers? I am not claiming that there is no God,
> nor am I claiming that there is one. All I am claiming is that life is
> extremely meaningful to most of those who live it—God or no God!
>
> I cannot help but think of the marvelous haiku: "Quite apart from
> our religion, there are plum blossoms; there are cherry blossoms."[7]

Ironically, Smullyan creates puzzles for a living. I assume they are intended with a solution in mind unless, of course, it is all right to recut the
pieces to suit each individual. What does it matter so long as it is enjoyed?
And don't ask Smullyan whether there should be a moral solution to Bosnia
or racism; just keep planting cherry trees and apple trees so that all the
combatants may enjoy them on their shellshocked paths to the grave.
It seems quite bizarre to read such cynical castigations of the ideas of
meaning, implying, I suppose, that the very denial of meaning has been
"meaningfully" offered.

I shall resist an immediate analysis of Smullyan's type of thinking except
to say that it is indefensible in the real world of moral, political, social, and
religious struggle. It is an ivory-tower brazenness devoid of sense, to which
the blood of humanity cries out, "Have mercy on me."

In contrast, albeit generating equally intense questions, are the words
of Andrei Bitov, Soviet novelist and short-story writer. He first portrays
his agnosticism and then dramatically leaps into this sentiment:

> In my twenty-seventh year, while riding the metro in Leningrad, I was
> overcome with a despair so great that life seemed to stop at once, pre-
> empting the future entirely, let alone any meaning. Suddenly, all by
> itself, a phrase appeared: Without God life makes no sense. Repeat-
> ing it in astonishment, I rode the phrase up like a moving staircase,
> got out of the metro and into God's light and carried on living.
>
> Faith is the only truth and the rarest of gifts. Exaggeration with-
> out faith is dangerous whether man recognizes the existence of God
> or denies it. If man does recognize it, his misinterpreting leads him
> down the path of idolatry so that he ends up idolizing both the

CAN MAN LIVE WITHOUT GOD

random and the particular. If man denies God, he is certain to take the particular for the whole and the random for the regular, becoming imprisoned by the logic of denial.[8]

Bitov's warning is appropriate. On the one hand, if man denies God, there is an ensuing exaggeration and confusion of the random and of the particular as well as a great cost in missing the purposeful and normative. This, I believe, is another blind spot of antitheism. On the other hand, Bitov uses two words that stand out. What does he mean by *faith* and *God?* If these ideas are properly defined and defended, then he speaks not of credulity, but he presents the answer of ultimate value. That will be our challenge as we look to the next part of this book, which leads me back to where I began:

> Is our hope in walnut shells
>   worn 'round the neck with temple bells?
> Or deep within some cloistered walls
>   where hooded figures pray in shawls?
> Or high upon some dusty shelves,
>   or in the stars,
>   or in ourselves—
> Who will answer?[9]

When one attempts to live without God, the answers to morality, hope, and meaning send one back into his or her own world to fashion an individualized answer. Living without God means lifting oneself up by his or her own metaphysical bootstraps, whichever way is chosen. In a world where cultures now freely intermix, one would imagine that progress is being made in finding common ground on the issues of the "supernatural." Yet, the closer we come to each other, the further apart our inner worlds seem to be.

May I add just one brief idea to this? It is not merely that living without God creates an enormous tension for morality, hope, and meaning; living without God is also making an absolute commitment to a philosophy of life's essence and destiny which, if wrong, affords absolutely no recourse should it be proven false. That is the degree of faith required of one who espouses an antitheistic lifestyle. Bertrand Russell and others, in their own maverick ways, bragged about what they would say to God should they happen to be surprised and meet Him after death. But those grandstanding words impress *us* more than I believe they will God, and they sound better before the final crossover than they will after.

Can man live without God? Of course he can, in a physical sense. Can he live without God in a reasonable way? The answer to that is No! because such a person is compelled to deny a moral law, to abandon hope, to forfeit meaning, and to risk no recovery if he is wrong. Life just offers too much evidence to the contrary.

Outside of Christ there is no law, no hope, and no meaning. You, and you alone, are the determiner and definer of these essentials of life; you, and you alone, are the architect of your own moral law; you, and you alone, craft meaning for your own life; you, and you alone, risk everything you have on the basis of a hope you envisage. As a cynic once put it, "We are all in this together, alone." You have made life's greatest decision, taken the greatest gamble, and answered the greatest question of our time—if you choose to live without God.

The lines are clearly drawn; the answers are worlds apart. You bring the tests of truth to evaluate the reasons that have led to your conclusions. Can life make sense anymore? That now merits our attention.

PART II

WHAT GIVES LIFE MEANING?

7

The Science of Knowing
and the Art of Living

Who am I? They often tell me
I would step from my cell's confinement
calmly, cheerfully, firmly,
like a squire from his country-house.

Who am I? They often tell me
I would talk to my warders
freely and friendly and clearly,
as though it were mine to command.

Who am I? They also tell me
I would bear the days of misfortune
equably, smilingly, proudly,
like one accustomed to win.

Am I then really all that which other men tell of?
Or am I only what I know of myself,
restless and longing and sick, like a bird in a cage,
struggling for breath, as though hands
were compressing my throat,
yearning for colors, for flowers, for the voices of birds,
thirsting for words of kindness, for neighborliness,
trembling with anger at despotisms and petty humiliation,
tossing in expectation of great events,
powerlessly trembling for friends at an infinite distance,
weary and empty at praying, at thinking, at making,
faint, and ready to say farewell to it all?

Who am I? This or the other?
Am I one person today, and tomorrow another?
Am I both at once? A hypocrite before others,
and before myself a contemptibly woebegone weakling?
Or is something within me still like a beaten army,
fleeing in disorder from the victory already achieved?[1]

During his imprisonment by the Nazis, Dietrich Bonhoeffer penned these words. No reader can reasonably ignore the pathos and poignancy that so eloquently expresses the search for an answer that could bring some sense to life and to its vicissitudes. Under similar circumstances, someone else once said that he could endure many a "what" about life if he could only answer the "why." Stephen Hawking ends his bestselling book *A Brief History of Time* having explained the "what" and even the "how" of this universe with the words, "Now if we only knew why, we would have the mind of God."[2] His inescapable implication is that the answer to that final question would have to come from a mind that transcends our material universe. The "what" gives us the stuff of existence; it is the "why" that provides the glue to all that we live for and the larger interpretation of why we are here in the first place.

As with many of life's hard questions, it is easy to force a false dichotomy by totally separating two equally necessary components within the answer. The "what" and the "why" of life are inextricably bound together in everyone's assumptions. That is how it ought to be. It is only as an individual has concluded on the "why" of life that the "what" of life becomes defined. If I am a creation of God, then life must be deemed sacred. But if I am the product of pure chance, the body may be profaned, for life itself is disposable. These two facets, therefore—the "what" and "why"—have intermeshed from the time of the ancient gnostics to our modern-day hedonists. The two components are inseparable when dealing with the subject before us: what gives life meaning.

But I must state at the outset that before we can find the solution to this quest for life's meaning we must first engage in a serious scrutiny of the question itself. How futile it would be to address the meaning of life if the parameters of the question itself are unclear or absurd.

The subject of what gives life meaning surfaces in every generation and possibly in every life, often addressed in both informal conversation and in

66

formal philosophical presentations. Every now and then I am tempted to ask the speaker in an academic setting what he or she means by the statement "I have found meaning in life." Is there an agreed-upon unit of measurement by which we can all exclaim "There it is!"? Or are we condemned to wallow in culturally relative quotients, ever changing the point of reference and relegating meaning to a sense of happiness or to how one feels at a given moment? More often than not I fear, this is, indeed, the level to which any treatment on meaning is reduced; why else would a nation consider the pursuit of happiness as fundamental to its existence?

I once had a professor who creatively articulated the various philosophical postures on this subject by contrasting the thinking of two existentialists, Jean-Paul Sartre and Martin Heidegger. For Heidegger, he said, the meaning of life would be expressed by "I know we are all on this ship and that the ship is going down. But I am going to stand on the deck and salute because it looks better." Sartre, on the other hand, would exclaim "No! No! No! I know the ship is going down, but let's descend to the lower bunk and play a last game of poker. At least we can enjoy life while the ship is going down!" Philosophers are keenly aware of how Heidegger's philosophy led him to even endorse the Nazi regime, and as for Sartre, he shocked everyone when, on his deathbed, he disavowed the choice by which he had lived.[3]

In like manner we, too, swing from the grimness of Stoicism to the indulgence of Epicureanism—either maintaining a sullen resoluteness in the face of despair or rushing unchecked in a pleasure-crazed lifestyle, knowing it will all come to nought. Such is a common posture in our times, reminding me of Ethelbert Stauffer's book *Christ and the Caesars,* in which he compared the addiction to merriment in Rome to the effect of the sardonian root, a poisonous plant that forced a convulsive smile across the face of the dying.

Knowing the Script

Any student of science or philosophy will be familiar with the name of Michael Polanyi. A fellow of the Royal Society of England, Polanyi was professor of physical chemistry and social studies at the University of Manchester and a fellow of Merton College at Oxford. He possessed an extraordinary intellect and authored some of the finest works in his field

CAN MAN LIVE WITHOUT GOD

of expertise, in particular, epistemology, that branch of philosophy that deals with the nature and the grounds of knowledge. In his book *Meaning*, Polanyi argued powerfully that science is a normative form of knowledge and that society gives meaning to science, rather than the reverse that science gives meaning (and/or "truth") to society. He cautioned that if science mis-applies its role it is in danger of destroying life, not contributing to it. Religion, poetry, and art are the disciplines, Polanyi stated, that infuse meaning into existence—not science. And most interestingly, this philosopher of science asserts that it is the imagination that synthesizes and provides the glue for the otherwise chaotic and disparate elements of life.

I introduce Polanyi and the strictures he places upon science at this stage because undoubtedly it is the scientist who will become uneasy with the extent to which we will involve the imagination during the early part of the discussion. Naturally, the epistemological or truth base will have to be established on a surer footing—as I have done in the preceding section and will be doing briefly in the latter part of this discussion. But here I need to reverse the procedure. I highly recommend to you Polanyi's book and his cogent argument that there are many intimations of reality beyond the laboratory.

One word of admonition from him demands our immediate attention before moving into the heart of the subject.

> Intellectual assent to the reduction of the world to its atomic elements acting blindly in terms of equilibrations of forces, an assent that has gradually come to prevail since the birth of modern science, has made any sort of teleological view of the cosmos seem unscientific and woolgathering to us. And it is this assent, more than any other one intellectual factor, that has set science and religion (in all but its most frothy forms) in opposition to each other in the contemporary mind.[4]

Polanyi is saying that by reducing all of life to atomic elements and blind forces, science has, in effect, made the pursuit of the meaning of life meaningless. But he warns that it is not for science to make this determination or to assign purpose to life. Polanyi's concern cannot be gainsaid as we approach this subject. Our hard-core, materialistically driven society, living with the myopia of scientific single vision, seems determined to live under the illusion that science alone is our consummate deity, delivering us from all ills—our new champion in the arena that has felled God with its random punch. Any legitimate understanding of the disciplines cannot reasonably arrive at such an indefensible conclusion. When the sharp edges of reality are exposed—from infancy to maturity—the "whys" of life proliferate, silencing the scientific voice and stumping the philosophical mind.

The challenge before us is to respond to the larger question of life's purpose itself, which in turn addresses the "whys" and "whats" of living a meaningful life. Consider for a moment two very profound and provocative statements that admit to a pervasive, omnipresent emptiness in life—a loneliness—notwithstanding all our advances in knowledge. The first is from D. H. Lawrence.

> We want to delude ourselves that of the problem of our emptiness, love is at the root. I want to say to you, it isn't. Love is only the branches. The root goes beyond love. A naked kind of isolation. An isolated me that does not meet and mingle and never can. It is true what I say. There is a beyond in you and a beyond in me which goes further than love, beyond the scope of stars. Just as some stars are beyond the scope of our vision, so our own search goes beyond the scope of love. At least, I think that it is at the root, going beyond love itself.[5]

Echoing the same sentiments Thomas Wolfe says:

> The whole conviction of my life now rests upon the belief that the sense of loneliness, far from being a rare and curious phenomenon peculiar to myself and to a few other solitary people, is the central and inevitable fact of human existence. All this hideous doubt, despair, and dark confusion of the soul a lonely person must know, for he is united to no image save that which he creates himself. He is bolstered by no other knowledge save that which he can gather for himself with the vision of his own eyes and brain. He is sustained and cheered and aided by no party. He is given comfort by no creed. He has no faith in him except his own and often that faith deserts him leaving him shaken and filled with impotence. Then it seems to him that his life has come to nothing. That he is

ruined, lost, and broken past redemption and that morning, that bright and shining morning with its promise of new beginnings, will never come upon the earth again as it did once.[6]

Thomas Wolfe, in his short, thirty-eight-year life, microcosmically reflected in these words the mood that predominates a large body of literature. I cannot resist interjecting here the same sentiments expressed by Bertrand Russell, putting his own imprint on this reality. Russell's summation was that the only sensible posture of life was one of unyielding despair and that any attitude other than despair was merely a seduction of the mind. The message is clear: Simplistic answers that seek escape from this malady by predicating "love" as the answer just do not understand the question. The struggle to find meaning is far too complex for such a vacuous solution. If this struggle to find meaning is treated with such scant intelligence, the mind becomes captive in the inescapable clutches of despair and purposelessness.

Few people know the epidemic proportions of this syndrome of despair and meaninglessness as well as professional counselors or ministers. For many years I thought this ache from the surrender of meaning was only felt and talked about by certain cultures, but I have found that the difference lies not so much in the felt need as in the willingness or reticence to talk about it. From the Middle East to the Far East, from Europe to the Americas—when the door is shut the accents may differ, but the sentiments remain virtually identical. May I relate one such story that will reveal the depth and breadth of humanity's struggle in search for meaning?

Several years ago when I was speaking at a series of meetings, a particular woman sat in the front row each night, thoroughly engrossed in the subject matter and taking frequent notes as the talk unfolded. Toward the end of the week, she and her family invited me to have lunch with them in their home. I had been informed that a deep tragedy had overtaken their lives, a tragedy that gave her heart no rest until she could find some answers. Although it was not very long before I was able to guess where her story was headed, the details nevertheless came as a shock.

She spoke at great length of her husband and his many professional accomplishments. He had earned a reputation and a following as a pioneer in his field, and financially he was riding the crest of success. In short, he was admired, envied, and well loved by all who knew him. His whole life—from home to office—breathed contentment, success, and influence. How then, could she explain the events of one fateful night?

She told me of a sudden and awful sound that jolted her awake from her sleep. Taking a moment to get oriented, she looked across the bed and saw that her husband was not there by her side. She nervously made her way in the direction of the sound until she saw her husband doubled over at the kitchen table, the stare of death upon his face and a scrawled note lying by his extended hand. With a hurried glimpse at the piece of paper her world fell apart, and since that night myriad questions had plagued her mind. The letter was a suicide note, beginning with the words, "Some people die natural deaths. Others, unable to face life anymore, choose to cut it short." Then followed a protracted, heartfelt apology with a plea for forgiveness for this betrayal and the assurance to the family that all their financial needs were well provided for.

I could feel the terrible burden of this heartrending experience even though this woman was a complete stranger to me. Her story was continually punctuated by the words "I cannot understand it. Why did he do it?" So ran the pitiful cry of a forsaken wife who now felt the greatest rejection of all.

Obviously, I could not answer why, but let me tell you what I did tell her. For many in our high-paced world, despair is not a moment; it is a way of life. Momentary lapses into disconsolation or even purposelessness are not uncommon, and we all at some time experience these moments. But the resigned posture that deems life to be completely devoid of ultimate purpose and bereft of meaning can hardly be touted as a rationally comforting dogma. Yet it is this conclusion that doggedly haunts the modern mind, little different from Heidegger's solution to "stand on the deck and salute" as the ship is going down.

You may find the approach I am taking to address this ubiquitous, lifelong struggle for meaning to be surprising. Nevertheless, I have chosen to take this route so I can touch upon some themes one is not accustomed to in an academic setting. Put it down to an Eastern methodology, if you will. I only ask for your patience and that you not jump to conclusions until I have finished the totality of the argument. If you falsely leap to a deduction even at the halfway point, you will miss the picture I am trying to portray.

I have no doubt that the subject necessitates intricate philosophical argumentation. For now, let us resist the tantalizing allurement to equate sophistication with wisdom. I cannot guarantee this approach will uncover all the answers you are seeking, but I will do my best to position the malady as clearly as I can so that there are some incontrovertible points of reference by which the answers can be tested.

During a brief time of study at Cambridge University in England, I pursued research into the works of some of the Romantic poets—Coleridge, Blake, Shelley, et al. The reasons for my interest were twofold. First, I wanted to better understand the historic slide that took the Romantic mind-set from the euphoria of a utopian dream envisaged by the best of them following the French Revolution to the dark despondency and despair of the Napoleonic Wars. I think, for example, of Robert Southey's exhilaration following the storming of the Bastille and his declaration that "Man has been born again." That optimism was rudely cast aside only a few years later.

Why, I wondered, is history so replete with graphic and dramatic drifts from one extreme to another? Was Martin Luther right that history is like a drunken man reeling from one wall to another, knocking himself senseless with every hit? Is the Dickensian description of the best of times and the worst of times perennially axiomatic?

The second reason I wanted to study the Romantic poets was because of their understanding of the imagination and their cognizance of its role in conveying to the mind intimations of reality. Thus, I turn now to the artist, the poet, and the romanticist for the preliminary ideas in this study before turning to the rigors of the philosopher.

Drawing the Curtain

Let us begin by looking at that familiar passage in William Shakespeare's play *As You Like It.*

> All the world's a stage,
> And all the men and women merely players:
> They have their exits and their entrances;
> And one man in his time plays many parts,
> His acts being seven ages. At first, the infant,
> Mewling and puking in the nurse's arms.
> Then, the whining schoolboy, with his satchel,
> And shining morning face, creeping like a snail

Unwillingly to school. And then, the lover,
Sighing like a furnace, with a woeful ballad
Made to his mistress' eyebrow. Then, a soldier,
Full of strange oaths, and bearded like the pard,
Jealous in honour, sudden and quick in quarrel,
Seeking the bubble reputation
Even in the cannon's mouth. And then, the justice,
In fair round belly, with good capon lin'd,
With eyes severe, and beard of formal cut,
Full of wise saws and modern instances;
And so he plays his part. The sixth age shifts
Into the lean and slipper'd pantaloon,
With spectacles on nose, and pouch on side;
His youthful hose well sav'd, a world too wide
For his shrunk shank; and his big manly voice,
Turning again toward childish treble, pipes
And whistles in his sound. Last scene of all,
That ends this strange eventful history,
Is second childishness, and mere oblivion;
Sans teeth, sans eyes, sans taste, sans everything.[7]

In these seven stages Shakespeare presents the script to be acted out in life—infancy, schoolboy, lover, soldier, middle age, decline, and old age. And the last scene of all, which ends this strange, eventful history, presents life as toothless, sightless, tasteless—and meaningless.

Long before our electronic means of entertainment, expounding on the relationship between life and art, Fyodor Dostoevsky predicted that at first art would imitate life, then life would imitate art, and finally, that life would draw the very reason for its existence from art. I believe he was quite prophetic, and if Shakespeare's analogy is taken to be true, we have indeed erased the difference between the two theaters of life and drama; if anything, the theater has upstaged our real world. One can almost detect here a hint of Eastern mythology, which holds that the "gods" are playing out the conflict of good and evil in the lives of us mortals.

For our purposes, let us divide life into four stages—childhood, adolescence, young adulthood, and maturity—and in that context demonstrate and explore how, at each stage, meaning is pursued, attained, and sometimes lost.

8

The Romance of Enchantment

THE FIRST STAGE we will consider is the world of a child. I am deeply indebted here to the writings of G. K. Chesterton, who unabashedly proclaimed that he learned more about life by observing children in a nursery than he ever did by reflecting upon the writings of any of the philosophers. We shall pardon his overstatement, but we dare not miss the point of it.

What is it about a child that fascinates us? More to the issue, what is it that fascinates a child? The answer to both questions is the same. Is it not that sense of wonder that pervades much of what the child sees and experiences? Listen to young fathers or mothers who have just welcomed a little one into their arms and their home—they themselves are starry-eyed, enveloped in the wonder of this lovely bundle of life that has im-measurably enriched their own lives.

Let me narrate for you an experience my wife and I had several years ago when I was speaking in the Middle East. At that time the political situation in that subcontinent had reached an ignition point. In fact, for-eign delegations were in the vicinity trying to stem the tide of hate and hoping to bring some semblance of peace to that troubled spot of the world. Our journey took us by taxi from Jordan to Israel by way of the West Bank, crossing over at the Allenby Bridge.

When we arrived at the bridge, we got out of the taxi on the Jordanian side and walked with the help of the Jordanian porter to the midpoint of the bridge, which was as far as he was allowed to go. At that juncture an Israeli porter picked up our baggage and escorted us to the Israeli side of the bridge. The lines were very clearly drawn. Once on Israeli soil, we were taken into a highly secured immigration building for routine but rigorous questioning, which was to precede our procurement of a visitor's visa. My wife, our small daughter Sarah, and I stood in one of the lines, having been warned to expect an emotionally taxing, drawn-out morning, possibly taking up the entire day.

I really did not know how best to prepare my daughter for the experience as she was barely two years old. We were surrounded on every side by machine-gun-clutching soldiers whose glares led us to believe that we were all guilty of something. There were sandbags piled against every wall, and a real sense of unease pervaded the room.

Finally it was our turn to be interrogated. Unknown to me, as she surveyed the room filled with armed guards, Sarah had locked eyes with a young Israeli soldier who was staring back at her in eye-to-eye "combat." Suddenly and strangely there was a moment of silence in the room, broken by the squeaky little voice of my daughter asking the soldier, "Excuse me, do you have any bubblegum?"

Words alone cannot fully express to you what that little voice and plea did for everyone in the room, where hitherto the weapons of warfare and the world of "adult ideas" had held everyone at bay. All who understood English could not repress a smile, and all who did not understand English knew a soldier's heart had been irresistibly touched. All eyes were now on him.

He paused for a moment, then carefully handed his machine gun to a colleague. He came over to where we were standing, looked endearingly at Sarah, and picked her up in his arms. He took her into a back room and returned a few minutes later with her in one arm, and in the other hand, he carried three glasses of lemonade on a tray—one for my wife, one for Sarah, and one for me. We were in and out of the immigration office in twenty-five minutes. In fact, the young soldier brought his jeep to the door and drove us to the taxi stand, sending us on our way to Jericho. If you will pardon the pun, another wall had fallen! I have often remarked that Sarah earned her year's keep with one little question voiced at the right time.

The incredible power of a child! For one fleeting moment in that room, she brought war to a standstill. Indeed, such is the strength of innocence, is it not? One soldier at least saw something in her—maybe the face of his own little girl back home—and the sentiments he felt transcended his immediate world of guns, hatred, and distrust. The wonder-filled face of a two-year-old girl made it possible for him to rise above the all-pervading air of suspicion, and for the sake of life's infancy and essential beauty, to momentarily trade away all other fears. The very strength of that child's influence was only buttressed by the fact that she was not even aware of the power she wielded or of what she had accomplished.

Is it enough, though, to merely recognize the power of a young life? I am fully aware of the flip side to this wondrous world of a child, that flip side which speaks of a gullibility. But if we rush ahead too quickly to grapple with that downside of childhood, we cheat ourselves of some of the grandest lessons life beckons us to heed from the splendor-filled strengths that infant lives offer—their capacity for enjoying and engendering wonder. It is out of that enthrallment and sense of wonder that a world of meaning ensues for a child. From gazing into the eyes of its mother as the child is nursed in her arms to the ecstasy that is experienced when riveted to the twinkling lights of a Christmas tree—a child gasps a dozen times a day, overwhelmed by life's sublime offerings. Watch the face of that child at her first taste of ice cream as her whole body gyrates, pleading for more. Listen to him chuckling as his father chases him at play in the front lawn. The laughter and merriment from simple yet exquisite delights keep the youngster's heart full. Each experience is entered into fully, resisting only sleep lest the little one miss a moment of fun.

Nothing is a greater indicator of this sense of wonder and of the world of fantasy than the child's love for the fairy tale. Walt Disney built a world empire on this propensity. And I believe that it is in the world of the fairy tale that we gain our first clue to life's meaning. No one, in my estimation, better captures this enchantment than the genius mind of G. K. Chesterton in what I consider to be his masterpiece and possibly one of literature's greatest essays, brilliantly titled *The Ethics of Elfland*. Chesterton at once retains and unravels the mystery of a child and his or her love for fairy tales. He brings to light three ever-present components in every tale of fantasy. These three elements weave themselves into the conscience and imagination of a little one to such a degree that when they unfold in the story, there is never a hint of disappointment and always the posture of ready acceptance.

The first element is that of a moral principle that emerges as the chief lesson of every story. (In fact, the very word *moral* first obtained its usage from the world of such literature.) These principles are intended to impart some of life's most inviolable virtues. In *Beauty and the Beast,* the moral is that you have to love something before it is lovable; in *Cinderella,* it is the exaltation of the humble and the rescue of the oppressed; in *Sleeping Beauty,* it is that one can be blessed with all that life offers yet still be cursed with the reality of death, and that death itself can be softened to the effect of a sleep, ultimately vanquished by truth. All this enchant-ment—all this wonder—occasions a moral lesson.

But that is not all these stories convey. The second component to the fairy tale is that of a very specific and unalterable condition. This condi-tion is not up for negotiation. It is not always explained; it is not even defended. The condition is merely stated: "If you do not come back by such-and-such you will become a such-and-such."

The third element is even more axiomatic—the one to whom the condition is given never says, "How come?" The condition is accepted without contest. Chesterton suggests that if the one so warned were to question the injunction of the fairy godmother, she might well reply, "If that is the way you want it, tell me how come there is a fairyland!"

That, may I say, is an incredibly important reminder. Mystery and awe are legitimate responses in a world of such stupendous dimensions, requir-ing some parameters of behavior without which no promise for a brighter tomorrow pertains. At some point the questioner must surrender to the grander mind that lays the stipulation.

And yet, I say to you, that few dispositions of the modern mind are as patently audacious as our assumption that we are owed a grasp of re-ality of limitless proportions. We pursue that quest for knowledge to a degree that demands the removal of all mystery, even from life's most sublime intimations. We want no part of a God who denies us the slight-est bit of information on any matter to which we feel we are entitled. I think of all the grand mysteries of life with which we are privileged to live and of the many whose essence we have destroyed by rendering them commonplace.

I think of the great mystery and blessing of human sexuality—the wonder that God has endowed in the consummation of love shared within the sanctity of marriage. Yet we have remorselessly profaned it. I think of the marvel of childbirth—how within the body of a woman a young life can be formed to perfection. But now the child is conceived in a world surrounded by self-centered wills of humanity that have reduced it to an abstraction as a "product of conception." I think of the wonder of a little life, nurtured at the breast of its mother. But alas! We live in a day in which we have lost the splendor of motherhood, and if we had our way we would even eradicate physiological differences between genders. I think of the glory of a sunrise or a sunset, all now part of a mindless universe cyclically doing its thing to no end. Oscar Wilde once said that we do not appreciate sunsets because we do not have to pay for them. Oscar Wilde was wrong. We can "pay" for sunsets by living in accordance with the purpose of our Creator and of His grand design. In leaving the bounteous world of our childhood, we have not merely walked out of fairyland; we have brazenly wandered into a barren desert bereft of wonder and meaning, supposedly having torn away the horizon of our finitude and seen nothing there. The quest was understandable, the departure legitimate; but the journey was wrongheaded.

From Misery to Mystery

The Bible is not unaware of humanity's hunger for knowledge, and the God of the Bible understands this longing well. The book of Job, for example, is one of the better-known books in the Bible because it seeks an answer to the myriad questions of the mind and particularly to the problem of God in relation to humanity and suffering. I suspect there are more questions raised in that book than in any other book in the Scriptures.

But I want to underscore the process of argumentation that God employs in bringing Job through his quest for an explanation to a glad submission to the divine will. We are all aware that Job was experiencing the dark night of the soul—his theology was falling apart, for he had been "good" but he was not being "blessed." He had lost everything, and he yearned not only for respite but also for an answer from an all-knowing God. It is soon obvious that the flurry of questions Job tossed at his would-be sympathizers was actually a conduit for venting his frustration with God. "Why am I suffering when I have lived a righteous life? . . . Unless I have the answer here and now to dispel all doubt and fear, I cannot go on."

In a dramatic and unexpected manner, God broke into the tedious and repetitive tirades and said, "All right, Job, I will answer you." That got

79

Job's attention. At last the heavens no longer seemed as brass, and the human mind could touch the eternal in its desire to understand one of life's thorniest enigmas. Yet the first part of God's answer was a series of sixty-four questions beginning with, "Brace yourself like a man; I will question you; and you shall answer me. Where were you when I laid the earth's foundation?" (Job 38:3–4). If that scenario of God questioning Job were put into the format of a game show, Job would have won the "I-don't-know" award of the year.

What was God really doing in that very personal interchange with a devoted and intelligent man? May I propose that God's purpose was two-fold. First it was to enable Job to recognize the legitimacy and sensibility of human limitation. We delude ourselves into believing that these finite minds of ours not only can know, but should know everything about everything. God's answer is "You don't—and you can't; and what is more, there is legitimate mystery that breeds a needed sense of wonder."

But there is a second part to God's purpose for Job, and we must notice it because this is where modern man in distinction to his predecessors, more than at any other time in history, has impoverished himself. God appeals to Job by compelling him to open up his modest stock of certainties within which was his uncompromising belief that the world itself was the handiwork of God, who was sovereign and good. "If you grant that I am the author of this universe and you recognize both its wonder and its mystery, why can you not trust me to take you through this struggle, too, without pushing back the curtain completely?" In that common ground of Job's belief in God as creator, Job could trust Him to be the preserver also.

This is where God's question becomes totally irrelevant to our sophisticated modern who actually thinks he has solved the riddle of the origin of the universe with his laboratory instruments. An audacious theory of time plus matter plus chance is confidently espoused. With that abandonment of the marvel of this universe as the expression of an omniscient God, the expulsion of all moral principles follows, culminating in a pompous demand of the Creator—"How come?" The "ethics of elfland" has given way to the tyranny of darker instincts.

Let me illustrate how this attitude is demonstrated in the most sophisticated quarters of academia. I once recall reading an extensive article by Professor Kenneth Miller of Brown University entitled "Life's Grand

Design." The subtitle reads "Though some insist that life as we know it sprang from a grand designer's original blueprints, biology offers new evidence that organisms were cobbled together layer upon layer by a tireless tinkerer called evolution." The author launches another of those all-too-familiar attacks on the classical argument for the existence of God from design. More specifically, he has addressed himself to the illustration of the human eye, giving special attention to the positioning of the neural wiring. As you may know, photoreceptor cells located in the retina of the eye pass impulses to a series of interconnecting cells and eventually process information to the cells of the optic nerve, which leads to the brain. This is how Miller describes our "imperfection":

> An intelligent designer working with the components of this wiring would choose the orientation that produces the highest degree of visual quality. No one, for example, would suggest that the neural connectors should be placed in front of the photoreceptor cells— thus blocking the light from reaching them—rather than behind the retina. Incredibly, this is how the human retina is constructed. Visual quality is degraded because light scatters as it passes through several layers of cellular wiring before reaching the retina. Granted, this scattering has been minimized because the nerve cells are nearly transparent, but it cannot be eliminated because of the design flaw.
>
> Moreover, the effects are compounded because a network of vessels, which is needed to supply the nerve cell with a rich supply of blood, also sits directly in front of the light-sensitive layer, another feature that no engineer would propose.[1]

I shall resist addressing some glaring philosophical weaknesses in Miller's article. Even at a foundational level his argumentation makes three fundamental mistakes. First and foremost, he makes the same blunder that most antitheistic evolutionary thinkers make—he forms a caricature of biblical thinking and then tears it into shreds. Nowhere does the biblical teaching of Creation say that man in his present condition is perfectly designed. Ask any woman who has gone through a painful labor during childbirth whether she has doubts about the perfection of the design of the human body! Miller does not need to look only to the eye to portray what he calls a "flaw."

Second, if his deduction is indeed valid and the design of the organ of sight is terribly flawed because of its physiological and structural inadequacies, what makes Professor Miller think that his brain has made a perfect deduction, for the brain itself could be impeded by shoddy design? In his materialistic assumption, Professor Miller knows that the eye engenders sight and that the liver secretes bile; therefore, he must also hold that the brain secretes thought. Why is the latter secretion assumed to be perfect, rising above its deterministic shackles and being transcendingly aware of the imperfections and shortcomings of the organic subagents?

Finally, Professor Miller must be aware of other fine scholars who have demonstrated the limitations that would have applied to the eye had the design been reversed, as he has envisioned.

A few years ago when my oldest daughter was thirteen years old, we were all at a golf course for an afternoon of fun. At one point she stood behind the shoulder of my nephew as he prepared to drive the ball some distance. He was unaware of how close she was to him, and as he took a powerful swing the club caught my daughter in the eye with full force. She immediately fell to her knees while blood poured from her eye through her hands with terrifying profusion.

One look at her and we were sure she had lost that eye. To this day thoughts of the experience are numbing. Within minutes she was in an ambulance and within hours was in the hands of one of America's finest pediatric eye surgeons. Following emergency surgery, assessed by the surgeon as totally successful, she was released from the hospital several days later and has fully recovered her vision. When we thanked the doctor for his care and skill he explained to us that his task had been simplified by the marvelous structure of the eye's design and by the protection afforded its most sensitive parts by virtue of its design.

I do not want to push this too far, but I have to wonder about criticisms offered by the Professor Millers of this world and their ilk. Here is the point. In audaciously tearing away the curtain of the eye with a dissaffection similar to that of opening the hood of a car, this distinguished educator has lost the wonder of a marvelous facility.

I will grant you that the theist sometimes unfortunately overstates his or her argument from design, especially in the case of the eye. But certainly the argument *to* design, when positioned alongside other evidences, is not bereft of reason.[2] In fact, in a strange and puzzling way, Professor Miller ends his own article with these words:

William Paley once hoped that the study of life could tell us something about the personality of the creator. Although Paley was wrong about the argument from design, he may have been right about the notion of personality. To the deeply religious, evolution may be seen not as a challenge but rather as proof of the power and subtlety of the creator's ways. The scope and scale of evolution can only magnify our admiration for a creator who could set such a process in motion. The great architect of the universe might not have written down each DNA base of the human genome, but that architect would still have been very clever indeed.[3]

In patronizingly doffing his hat to the theist, Miller has tried to cover his own tracks, which, in his scheme of origins, have arisen from nowhere. Driven by arrogance, the loss of wonder leaves the critic doubly impoverished, both by his rejection of truth and by his inability to experience legitimate enjoyment. Polanyi's warning has gone unheeded by Miller, and in an attempt to defend his discipline his unscientific postscript betrays some shoddy philosophizing.

Intellect and Sublimity

It would be very easy for the skeptic to say, "Ah! But you are not going to take a child's view of the universe against a man of such letters, are you?" To raise that question is to miss the point. I am arguing that for a child meaning is procured by his recognition of the awe-inspiring reality that surrounds his life. That reality is fused with wonder and design, engendering purpose. The world is not seen as mindless or capricious. But, with the jettisoning of these factors, life itself loses meaning, so why consider any criticism to be meaningful? Further, and more importantly, the same data that the Millers of this world use are drawn upon by equally—if not better—qualified individuals who with great academic prowess establish the impossibility of an explanation for this universe—apart from God. Those scholars see not only an intelligible and tightly knit universe; they equally gain from it the wonder that brings meaning because they recognize behind it all the mind and hand of a designer. To them, the moral principles accordingly pertain, and they know when to stop asking, "How come?" Their worldview is far more coherent, unlike that of Miller, who has to sneak in a passing caveat at the end of his critique.

As an example, let me transport you to a sophisticated lecture hall in Cambridge University where I sat listening to a lecture by quantum physicist Dr. John Polkinghorne, president of Queens College, Cambridge. His book *The Quantum World* has been hailed by *Physics Bulletin* as one of the finest in its genre. In his book *One World,* Polkinghorne eloquently argued that the existence of God is intimated by our finely tuned and intelligible universe, with exactitude demanded in every detail that antitheistic thinkers are hard pressed to explain.

> In the early expansion of the universe there has to be a close balance between the expansive energy (driving things apart) and the force of gravity (pulling things together). If expansion dominated then matter would fly apart too rapidly for condensation into galaxies and stars to take place. Nothing interesting could happen in so thinly spread a world. On the other hand, if gravity dominated, the world would collapse in on itself again before there was time for the processes of life to get going. For us to be possible requires a balance between the effects of expansion and contraction which at a very early epoch in the universe's history (the Planck time) has to differ from equality by not more than 1 in 10^{60}. The numerate will marvel at such a degree of accuracy. For the non-numerate I will borrow an illustration from Paul Davies of what that accuracy means. He points out that it is the same as aiming at a target an inch wide on the other side of the observable universe, twenty thousand million light years away, and hitting the mark![4]

I recall another occasion when I sat in the auditorium of the University of Witwatersrand in Johannesburg, South Africa, awaiting my turn to speak. Before my talk, I was privileged to hear a noted astronomer, Professor David Block (who was inducted into the British Astronomical Society at the age of nineteen) make his presentation on why he believed in a designed universe. One of his slides showed a picture of one hundred billion stars, drawing attention to the mind-boggling magnificence of the universe whose quantities are interdependent. Dr. Block reminded the audience that if they were to count one star per second they would be there for two thousand, five hundred years.

The likes of Drs. Block and Polkinghorne are not, if you will pardon the pun, starry-eyed infants. I am aware of David Hume's rejoinder to this kind of argumentation and of his castigation of the causal principle in philosophy extrapolated from science. But is empiricist John Locke's claim—"Man knows by an intuitive certainty that bare nothing can no more produce any real being than it can be equal to two right angles"— a farcical assertion? Maybe the child in its intuition has something to teach us here, further sustained by the adult intellect. From the toddler in the nursery to Queen's College in Cambridge—there is enjoyment, enthrallment, and wonder when God is seen behind the marvels of this universe. But when the curtain is pushed back to gain knowledge for the sake of knowledge, the hunger is insatiable and the wonder is lost.

Let me sum this up with the words of Christopher Morley:

> I went to the theater with the author of a successful play. He insisted on explaining everything. He told me what to watch, the details of direction, the errors of the property man, the foibles of the star. He anticipated all my surprises and ruined the evening. Never again! And mark you, the greatest author of all made no such mistake.[5]

When the Wonder Fades

If one does choose to define everything in purely mechanistic or random terms, there inevitably follows an accompanying loss of that childlike sense of wonder—and where there is a loss of wonder, there are three direct consequences. First, there is the inevitable reduction of all of life, and everything ultimately becomes chemical or molecular. The implications of this reduction transfer to our interpersonal relationships in society. In the turbulent days of racial riots, Dr. Martin Luther King Jr. pleaded with the nation to turn its back upon past hatred. In his acceptance of the Nobel Prize for Peace, Dr. King said, "I refuse to believe the notion that man is mere flotsam and jetsam in the river of life . . . unable to respond to the eternal oughtness that forever confronts him."

Dr. King clearly invokes a transcendent value to human life. In contrast, a materialist is forced to a theory of randomness and cannot avoid this reduction of man to flotsam and jetsam. Where there is the loss of wonder there is a natural tug toward a reductionistic view of everything aesthetic or virtuous. For that matter, all of life boils down to the rags of matter in chemical or physical reaction, and the strongest "reactions" win.

Man becomes another blip on the radar screen of time. The noblest is reduced to the lowest, and love is merely glandular. What a tragic philosophy the antitheist begets, for the higher up he scales the pinnacle of evolution the more he is reminded of his utter insignificance.

In Marxism the state-controlled bureaucracy erects gigantic government buildings to dwarf the individual. In the guise of academic and hedonistic freedom, we have erected educational and monetary edifices that have reduced the individual to matter and money. In both arenas the end result is the same—out of dust, nothing but dust.

"No, Thank You"

Second, with a loss of wonder there naturally follows a loss of gratitude, for there is no one to be grateful to. As the universe is "just there," so we in the universe are "just here." This is an intriguing phenomenon in the West, gaining momentum all the time. All over the world hundreds of millions of people wake up each morning grateful to God for life and strength. As you travel around you see heads bowed before a meal or even in the eye of a storm, thirty-seven thousand feet above the ground, reverently recognizing His sovereignty. But here, while we as a nation have traditionally set apart one day a year to say "Thank You," thanks to the skeptic, Thanksgiving Day has now been reduced to Turkey Day. That ironic caption may well be more descriptive than we ever intended.

We are living dangerously on this great continent, imagining that by our own power, our own will, and our own ingenious capacities we have built history's most modern nation. We think we ourselves have pulled ourselves up by our own economic and technological bootstraps. God says the nations are but a drop in the bucket and that it would be very easy for our national glory to be suddenly a thing of the past. All it would take is one giant catastrophe to bring any nation to its knees.

The loss of gratitude is a serious loss. If children are raised without a sense of gratitude toward those who gave them life and sustenance, they become potential enemies with terrifying possibilities.

To reinforce this connection between wonder, gratitude, and meaning, I borrow from two dramatic situations, both taking place several thousand feet in the air. Some years ago an Air Canada jet was on a flight from somewhere in the United States to Ottawa, Canada. Around the ten- to fifteen-thousand-foot mark, as I recall the incident, a fire broke out in the washroom of the plane. The pilot had only a few moments before the plane would be turned into a fireball in the sky. Immediately, he began a rapid descent to the nearest airport, which was Cincinnati. By this point the fire was moving out of control. He hit the runway so hard at touchdown that the wheels broke. The emergency crews began to work feverishly to rescue as many passengers as possible. However, once the doors had been opened, the inrushing oxygen had turned the plane into a violent blaze. Several passengers lost their lives, but the brave crew members were able to rescue most. The pilot himself, as a captain should, was the last to leave the burning aircraft, his own uniform in flames.

I have no doubt that as the last line was written on that tragic incident, the deaths of some notwithstanding, all accolades were showered upon the professional skill and behavior of the captain. If you or I had a loved one on that plane who owed his or her life to that captain, it would have been most reasonable for us to clasp his hand and say, "Thank you!" May I suggest the possibility that even had you lost a loved one you would still have wanted to say, "Thank you for trying."

Now turn your attention to another incident a short while later. An airplane from a major airline was en route to the Caribbean Islands when somewhere over the water it lost power in one engine. Through a strange series of incidents, one by one, all engines lost power. The quivering voice of the pilot came over the P.A. system to announce, "Ladies and gentlemen . . . ditching is inevitable." Suddenly, breaking the deathly silence on board the plane, one engine restarted and the pilot was able to gain enough power for the plane to limp back to safety. Whom do you thank then?

"I suppose it is like this," says G. K. Chesterton. "If my children wake up on Christmas morning and have somebody to thank for putting candy in their stocking, have I no one to thank for putting two feet in mine?"[6] Gratitude is a natural outworking of wonder, and wonder is cognizant of God Himself. Where there is no wonder there is no gratitude. Self-aggrandizement breeds a sense of entitlement. Entitlements unfulfilled give birth to catastrophic means of procurement—the ramifications are immense.

A Useless Passion

This leads me to the third consequence when wonder has been lost. Not only is there a reductionism and a loss of gratitude, but there is also an inevitable slide into emptiness. I think particularly of our present generation, which enjoys more sophisticated toys than ever before, yet each toy has a shorter thrill-span than the previous one. We are constantly wearied of our new inventions, and the expression "built-in obsolescence" has taken on a new twist, applying not only to the gadgets but to life itself.

H. L. Mencken said, "The problem with life is not that it's a tragedy, but that it's a bore." A child who is filled with wonder is also filled with a sense of enchantment, a sense of significance, a sense of meaning. When wonder ceases, boredom and emptiness begin to stalk existence.

A Necessary Demise

The unhappy reality is that at some time in a child's life the wonder evoked by balloons, twinkling lights, and fairy tales begins to pale. Though this transition is seen by the parents through nostalgic eyes, they would be rightly distraught if that stage in a child's experience never ended. What can replace the wonder, that will not be outgrown, and that will fill life with meaning?

It is to that which I now draw our attention, illustrating its great significance. In observing this stage of transition I want to focus not only on the "why" of it, but also to address what has undoubtedly concerned you during our excursion to fairyland. Once again I am indebted to Chesterton for this insight.

Imagine yourself unfolding a tale with all the appropriate emotion and gestures to three young children. I can easily identify with that scenario, for my wife and I have three children of our own—Sarah, Naomi, and Nathan. Enter into their world with me at ages seven, four, and one when they were independently told the same story. Let me invite you to listen in as the story is reaching its climax.

To Sarah I say, "Little Tommy got up, walked up to the door, and opened the door. Suddenly a dragon jumped in front of Tommy." Sarah's eyes get wide, remaining transfixed, until I assure her that Tommy whipped the dragon.

Next I narrate the same story to Naomi at age four. I say, "Nimmi, little Tommy got up and walked up to the door, and (with my voice hushed and the words spoken slowly and deliberately) . . . Tommy . . . opened . . . the . . . door!" Naomi's eyes widen as she tingles with the anticipation of what lies behind the door.

Now I am telling the story to Nathan at age one. You have to remember that his whole worldview is exhausted by one word—*cookie*. I say "Nate, little Tommy got up and . . . walked . . . up . . . to . . . the . . . door." Nathan's eyes are ready by this point to tear through his pudgy cheeks.

Do you understand what is happening here? At age seven, Sarah needed the dragon to evoke wonder. At age four the mere gesture of slowly opening the door struck that chord for Naomi. And for Nathan at age one it was a pretty big deal just to walk up to the door. I say to you with emphasis that the *older you get, the more it takes to fill your heart with wonder, and only God is big enough to do that.* Not only is He big enough, but in Christian terms He is also near enough.

This was the crowning discovery of that great mind and genius, the poet Francis Thompson. Many of you may recall his most enduring work "The Hound of Heaven." Thompson lived a very turbulent life. Having left home in conflict, he lived the life of a vagabond on the streets of London rather than go to college, wandering through two areas of the city. During the day he would satisfy his opium addiction, fitting in among the losers and the lost in London's Charing Cross district. At night he would saunter over to the River Thames and lie down to sleep by its banks. Periodically he would pick up a newspaper from the overflowing trash in the area and scrounge for a piece of paper on which he would write a letter to the editor of the newspaper in response to some article he had read. The editor became frustrated and at his wit's end because he recognized the genius of a Milton behind the writing but there was never a return address.

Throughout his constant and deliberate running from God, Thompson kept in touch with the Scriptures, and one passage began to haunt him— the story of Jacob, who spent most of his life on the run. The Scriptures tell of a dream Jacob had one night in which he saw a ladder between heaven and earth and the Lord Himself at the top of the ladder. When he awakened from that dream he said, "Surely the LORD is in this place, and I was not aware of it" (Gen. 28:16). As Francis Thompson continued to dwell on that story, something remarkable happened, and what can only be called a dramatic conversion of his life took place. Listen to these incredible words:

> O world invisible, we view thee,
> O world intangible, we touch thee,
> O world unknowable, we know thee,
> Inapprehensible, we clutch thee!
>
> Does the fish soar to find the ocean,
> The eagle plunge to find the air—
> Do we ask of the stars in motion
> If they have rumor of thee there?
>
> Not where the wheeling systems darken,
> And our benumbed conceiving soars!—
> The drift of pinions, would we hearken,
> Beats at our own clay-shuttered doors.
>
> The angels keep their ancient places;—
> Turn but a stone, and start a wing!
> 'Tis ye, 'tis your estranged faces,
> That miss the many-splendoured thing.
>
> But when so sad thou canst not sadder
> Cry—and upon thy so sore loss
> Shall shine the traffic of Jacob's ladder
> Pitched betwixt Heaven and Charing Cross.
> Yea, in the night, my Soul, my daughter,
> Cry—clinging Heaven by the hems;
> And lo, Christ walking on the water
> Not of Gennesaret, but Thames![7]

God met Francis Thompson where he was, restoring wonder and meaning to his life. Nietzsche said he went looking for God and couldn't find Him—nihilism was born. The psalmist David, who became known as the sweet singer of Israel, said in Psalm 139:7–8, "Where can I flee from your presence? . . . [Wherever I go] . . . you are there." Hope was born. Francis Thompson's writings tell of the wonder that filled his life when he stopped running from God—a relationship was born. The God who walked on Gennesaret and Thames is also within reach in Haight-Ashbury or on Pennsylvania Avenue.

How do you find that wonder? May I suggest to you, dear friend, that it is not in argument, nor is it in mere dogma. It is not even found in the church. There is a clue to meaning in our experiences—that clue is in relationships. The centerpiece of history, says the Bible, is Christ Himself, and you will find unending wonder in a relationship with Him. The historian Lecky reminds us that no one in history has effected such a change upon the moral fabric of society as Jesus Christ. The answer to the search for wonder is in a relationship with Christ. Jesus Christ went beyond fantasy: He pointed to the truth.

9

Truth—an Endangered Species

I N THE CHILDHOOD YEARS, wonder can be attained by dabbling in the world of fantasy. That is both the glory and the fragility of childhood. But as the years pass, wonder is eroded in the face of reality and in the recognition that life may not be lived in a fairy-tale world. A displacement is brought about by the ever-increasing demand of the mind, not just for the fantastic, but for the true. The search for truth then becomes all-pervasive, encompassing implications for the essence and destiny of life itself. Even if not overtly admitted, the search for truth is nevertheless hauntingly present, propelled by the need for incontrovertible answers to four inescapable questions, those dealing with origin, meaning, morality, and destiny. No thinking person can avoid this search, and it can only end when one is convinced that the answers espoused are true. Aristotle was right when he opined that all philosophy begins with wonder; but the journey, I suggest, can only progress through truth.

Cultural norms can often change and settle in precarious ways. Such shifts are currently underway, aided by an explosion of information, images, and technology that have left the mind assaulted by various enticements. In the dramatic displacements that we are witnessing, the question "What is truth?" must be answered if the essence of life is to be guarded.

Following an address I gave several years back at a gathering of sports executives from several parts of the world, I informally interacted with several of the delegates. For some of them, it was the first time in their lives they had the freedom to attend and experience a conference such as this. I recall in particular one delegate from what was formerly East Germany. Naturally I raised the subject of the radical transformation for that country with the dismantling of the Berlin Wall, and I asked him how the citizens were coping with this historic change. His answer was most surprising to me, although it came more from his context in sports. He spoke of the deep sense of betrayal felt by the East German athletes, betrayal by the political leadership that had led their country to bankruptcy, while boasting Olympic superiority. "We have been lied to" and "We have been used" were the most frequent comments this leader heard. "They lied to us about the past, about the present, and about the future. We sold ourselves to the service of the state, and now we see the exploitation to which we were subjected—carnage, corruption, and scheming were endemic to our system."

Such terrible experiments perpetrated upon humanity have exacted an irrecoverable cost in human life and suffering. Those of us who live with the great privilege of liberty can only shake our heads in sorrow for those who have paid the awful price of such experimentation.

But let us pause for a moment. To what lies have we been subjected? On every side I see the glare of billboards promising that happiness lies in the next car or the next house. Educators promise that if we only tell our children about sex we will reduce the rate of teen pregnancy and the threat of venereal disease. Social workers promise that drug education will remove this scourge from our continent if we will "just say no." Politicians promise that technology and communication will lead to a better understanding and to peace. Lawmakers promise that new laws will eradicate racial tensions. Now we are promised that if we would only get God out of education and get the Creator out of the scheme of things we will all be better for it.

But the duplicity that has emerged from political leaders, legal tacticians, and, for that matter, even from some purveyors of religion has left a generation of young people apathetic, cynical, and even fearful. To the question "What do you wish for most in your life?" asked of Canadian teens during a survey conducted a few years ago, the number-one answer, revealing our cultural tragedy, was "Somebody we can trust."

And so we move away from the twinkling-eyed response of a child in his or her world of fantasy to the harsh world of knowledge and truth—the latter now becoming an endangered species with no guarantee of protection.

Few incidents have revealed this poverty of truth more blatantly than the shooting down of Korean Airlines flight 007 a few years ago by the

Russian Air Force. To this day we wonder if we have heard the truth. You may recall that the Russian leaders immediately surrounded the story with statements and disclaimers, charts, and military personnel—medals weighing down their chests—to tell the world their version of the episode. One of the strongest claims they made in their own defense was that the navigation lights of the Korean airliner were off and were not turned on even when the pilot was ordered to do so.

Sometime later the recordings of the conversations in the cockpits were retrieved by another nation's intelligence network. In his evening program, American newscaster Ted Koppel along with syndicated columnist William Safire interviewed Vladimir Posner, from the Russian newspaper *Pravda*. As Safire and Posner began their exchange, Safire reminded Posner that the tape recording of the entire conversation was now on hand. Posner acknowledged that fact. The questioning ran as follows:

"Mr. Posner, your authorities have up to this time insisted that KAL 007 did not have its navigational lights on."

"That is right," said Posner.

"But in the recording we hear one of your pilots saying that the lights were indeed on."

"Oh yes," countered Posner, "the lights he is referring to are the lights of his other comrade who was also circling the Korean airliner."

With a prosecutor's glee William Safire shot back, "But the tape recording's exact wording says, 'Target's lights are on.' Since when does one of your pilots refer to his comrade's aircraft as 'target'?"

There was a conspicuous silence from Mr. Posner's side, followed by some mumbling that cleverly refocused the dialogue. As I listened to that exchange I reflected on the irony of it all, for *Pravda* means "truth." And, may I add, that with the changes in the geopolitical scene, in a strange turn Mr. Posner became, I understand, a media figure featured regularly on a news program alongside Phil Donahue. I shall refrain from further comment except to say that this may well be the ultimate illustration of media burlesque.

The chimera is no longer a monster in Greek mythology; the hybrid may well be giving us the news. It is little wonder that as a journalist Malcolm Muggeridge became the quintessential cynic, having witnessed the sheer hypocrisy and manipulation of people by the medium he came to know so well. His autobiography is subtitled *A Chronicle of Wasted*

Years. Listen to how he positioned the two worlds of totalitarianism and democracy, and the lies we have both believed.

> Yet even so, truth is very beautiful; more so, as I consider, than jus-
> tice—today's pursuit—which easily puts on a false face. In the nearly
> seven decades I have lived through, the world has overflowed with
> bloodshed and explosions whose dust has never had time to settle
> before others have erupted; all in purportedly just causes. The quest
> for justice continues, and the weapons and the hatred pile up; but
> truth was an early casualty. The lies on behalf of which our wars
> have been fought and our peace treaties concluded! The lies of revo-
> lution and of counter-revolution! The lies of advertising, of news, of
> salesmanship, of politics! The lies of the priest in the pulpit, the pro-
> fessor at his podium, the journalist at his typewriter! The lie stuck
> like a fish-bone in the throat of the microphone, the hand-held lies
> of the prowling cameraman! Ignazio Silone told me once how, when
> he was a member of the old Comintern, some stratagem was under
> discussion, and a delegate, a newcomer who had never attended
> before, made the extraordinary observation that if such and such
> a statement were to be put out, it wouldn't be true. There was a
> moment of dazed silence, and then everyone began to laugh. They
> laughed and laughed until tears ran down their cheeks and the
> Kremlin walls seemed to shake. The same laughter echoes in every
> council chamber and cabinet room, wherever two or more are gath-
> ered together to exercise authority. It is truth that has died, not God.[1]

Then followed an indictment of our side of the world with a critique even more graphic—though thankfully he hinted at a solution in the closing line.

> In this Sargasso Sea of fantasy and fraud, how can I or anyone else
> hope to swim unencumbered? How can I learn to see through, not
> with the eye? Take off my own motley, wash away the makeup,
> raise the iron shutter, put out the studio lights, silence the sound
> effects and put the cameras to sleep? Watch the sun rise on Sunset
> Boulevard, and set over Forest Lawn?
>   Find furniture in the studio props, silence in a discotheque, love
> in a strip tease? Read truth off an auto cue, catch it on a screen, chase
> it on the wings of muzak? View it in living color with the news, hear

it in living sound along the motorways? Not in the wind that rent the mountains and broke in pieces the rocks; not in the earthquake that followed, nor in the fire that followed the earthquake. In a still, small voice. Not in the screeching of tires, either, or in the grinding of brakes; not in the roar of jets or the whistle of sirens, or the howl of trombones, the rattle of drums, or the chanting of demo voices. Again, that still, small voice—if one could catch it.[2]

Muggeridge has touched the nerve of the problem here in addressing our search for meaning separated from truth. His description of the lie stuck like a fish-bone in the throat of the microphone is painful and descriptive. Differing political theories may grant us different standards of living, and I am not for one moment belittling that. However, I am saying that those differences can easily obscure some fundamental similarities, one being that of the essential human condition. If we do not understand this, we betray ourselves doubly. Jesus very poignantly draws our attention to the reason for this common ailment.

Judging Our Judgments

In the brief but significant conversation recorded between Jesus and Pontius Pilate, we read of Pilate asking Jesus, "Are you a king?" We can well imagine a sardonic grin planted on the face of this puppet in the hands of Caesar, inquiring into the kingship of this Jewish carpenter.

Jesus responded by questioning Pilate's question, asking, in essence, "Are you asking this on your own or has someone else set you up?" This method of questioning the question was repeatedly used by Jesus with very good reason because it compelled the questioner to open up within his own assumptions.

Pilate was somewhat exasperated by this seeming insolence. "Look," he answered, "I did not bring you here—your own people have done that."

Then Jesus answered, "My kingdom is not of this world. If it were, my servants would fight to prevent my arrest. But now my kingdom is from another place."

Pilate said, "Ah! So you are a king."

The response of Jesus discloses Pilate's real predicament. "You are right in saying I am a king. In fact, for this reason I was born, and for this I

97

came into the world, to testify to the truth. Everyone on the side of truth listens to me."

The answer is both subtle and daring. The fundamental problem Jesus was exposing to Pilate and to the world is not the paucity of available truth; it is more often the hypocrisy of our search. Truthfulness in the heart, said Jesus, precedes truth in the objective realm. *Intent is prior to content.* The most provocative statement Jesus made during that penetrating conversation was that the truthfulness or falsity of an individual's heart was revealed by that person's response to Him. The implication was uncompromising. He was, and is, the truth. What you do with Him reveals more about you than it does about Him.

Pilate served as a perfect illustration of Jesus' point. He muttered, "What is truth?" and never waited for the answer. I suspect he knew the answer but was a power-seeking slave to the system and to his own political ambition. Pilate really desired no solution—he merely sought an escape (see John 18:28–19:16).

Lost in the Interpretation

Let me address this whole issue of objective truth without and truthfulness within from a different angle. I come from India, and my wife is from Canada. One of the languages with which I was raised is Hindi. Language, of course, has that unique capacity to open a world of imagination and a wealth of memory. Even though I left India several years ago, there are some concepts the Hindi language captures for me that English cannot. So often when I am with some Indian friends, one of them may make a remark in Hindi that brings laughter to those of us who understand it.

My wife will invariably ask, "What did he say?" and I promptly make the translation, knowing very well her predictable reaction: no smile, not even a hint of it, and then she will utter, "But what was so funny?" Then immediately she adds, "I know. It loses something in the translation." Any of you who have ever had to do translation work well understand the problem.

Have you heard the folk story of the bandit José Rivera, who became notorious in several little towns in Texas for robbing their banks and businesses? Finally the townsfolk, weary of the constant plundering, hired a ranger to track down José Rivera in his hideout in Mexico and retrieve the money. The ranger at last arrived at a desolate, ramshackle cantina. At the counter he saw a young man enjoying his brew. At one of the tables, hands over his ample stomach, hat over his eyes, snored another patron. With much gusto, the ranger approached the young man at the bar and announced that he was on a mission to bring back José Rivera, dead or alive. "Can you help me find him?" he asked. The young man smiled, pointed to the other patron, and said, "That is José Rivera."

The ranger shifted his southern girth and ambled over to the sleeping bandit, tapping him on the shoulder. "Are you José Rivera?" he asked. The man mumbled, "No speak English." The ranger beckoned to the young man to help him communicate his mission.

The ensuing conversation was tedious. First the ranger spoke in English and the young man translated it into Spanish. José Rivera responded in Spanish, and the young man repeated the answer in English for the ranger.

Finally, the ranger warned José Rivera that he had two choices; the first was to let him know where all the loot he had stolen was hidden, in which case he could walk away a free man. The second choice was that if he would not reveal where the money was stashed, he would be shot dead instantly. The young man translated the ultimatum.

José Rivera pulled himself together and said to the young man, "Tell him to go out of the bar, turn to the right, go about a mile, and he will see a well. Near the well he will see a very tall tree. Beside the trunk of that tree is a large concrete slab. He will need help in removing it. Under the slab is a pit in the ground. If he carefully uncovers it he will find all the jewelry and most of the money I have taken."

The young man turned to the ranger, opened his mouth . . . swallowed . . . paused—and then said, "José Rivera says . . . José Rivera says . . . 'Go ahead and shoot!'"

Something was lost in the translation, wasn't it? It was not the absence of knowledge that evoked ignorance; it was the suppression of truth. I ask you, does anyone really need to tell our Hollywood elites that there is too much violence on the screen, glorifying the debased? Does anyone really need to alert our society to the danger of promiscuity? Yes and no. Yes, because the warning cries ever need to be sounded to keep our young alerted to the pitfalls of the moral squalor to which they are subjected. But no, because, for most, the truth does not really matter—it is the will that is wrong.

Images and Temples

It is this willful suppression of truth that results in an assault upon the sacred in the pursuit of the profane. Think with me for a moment on this issue. Of all the possibilities to which we have recourse in entertainment, why are sensuality and violence the two most often used to titillate? Why not more healthy laughter? Why not more moral impetus? Why not more normative illustrations of what a home could be and should be? Why not more creative and legitimate entertainment rather than that which is destructive and offensive? May I propose an answer?

God tells us we are created in His image. In the book of Genesis, He strongly requites the penalty for murder because murder is a direct attack upon the dignity of man, created in the image of God. When we look further into the Scriptures, Jesus reminded His followers that true worship is not in a building of bricks or stones. The human body itself is a temple.

These two truths—that humanity is made in God's image and that the body is the temple of God—are two of the cardinal teachings of Scripture. What else will entertainment do when it gets profane but attack the two principal teachings of human essence? Violence defaces the image of God, and sensuality profanes the temple of God. The image of God and the temple of God have both been violated and replaced with the gods and idols of our time. Thus, when former Vice President Dan Quayle reprimanded Hollywood for what it was doing, he was angrily castigated because he touched the idols of our age. And even though *Atlantic Monthly* ran the cover story "Dan Quayle Was Right" some months later, what difference does that confession make if nobody really cares what is true anymore? The loss of truth, like the loss of wonder, filters down into our day-to-day lives and takes its toll upon society.

Personal, Not Merely Propositional

Here again the Christian message is unique and brings a clue to help us break loose from this asphyxiating context. Just as wonder was found in a person, so the Scriptures claim and prove that truth is fully embodied in a person, the person of Jesus Christ. It is not merely that He has the answers to life's questions as much as that He is the answer. Once again we find the truth not merely in abstractions or creedal affirmations, but in knowing Him. When the apostle Thomas asked Jesus to show him the way to God, Jesus answered, "*I* am the way and the truth and the life. No one comes to the Father except through me" (John 14:6, emphasis mine).

Two very obvious deductions follow from this assertion that Jesus made: first, that truth is absolute, and second, that truth is knowable. Very basically stated, truth is simply what is. Falsehood is stating something to be so when it is not so. In fact, immediately preceding this conversation with Thomas, Jesus talked about the reality of heaven and said, "If it were not so, I would have told you." Everything Jesus affirms about reality corresponds to reality. Everything He denies about reality is because that denial corresponds to reality.[3]

To restate, Jesus' absolute claim that He is the way, the truth, and the life means categorically that anything that contradicts what He says is by definition false. I challenge you to have the courage to study His claims and His teaching, and you will find a message that beautifully unfolds, encompassing the breadth of human need and the depth of human intellect. It is the beauty of Jesus' life that children can understand Him, and yet, the staunchest of skeptics such as Paul can ultimately bend that knee and call Him Lord.

May I take the liberty of making a personal suggestion here? As discomforting as it is to admit, much of what the church has had to face by way of criticism has been deserved. Much wrong has been perpetrated in history by people supposedly acting in the name of Christ. In many parts of the world today the church has a poor name, and a look back at her track record in those settings often reveals valid reasons for that contempt. But this may also be falsely seen as all-encompassing, because the deviants often get more attention than do the normal. In our day, much of what is offered on Christian television programming leaves not only the skeptic bemused but also many Christians embarrassed. Those who have used the name of Christ for personal gain will stand accountable before God. But I point you not to them or to any man; rather, I point you to the person of Jesus Christ. Look at who He is and who He claims to be.

There is a magnificent story in Marie Chapian's book *Of Whom the World Was Not Worthy.*[4] The book told of the sufferings of the true church in Yugoslavia where so much wrong has been perpetrated by the politicized ecclesiastical hierarchy. That which has gone on in the name of

Christ for the enriching and empowering of corrupt church officials has been a terrible affront to decency.

One day an evangelist by the name of Jakov arrived in a certain village. He commiserated with an elderly man named Cimmerman on the tragedies he had experienced and talked to him of the love of Christ. Cimmerman abruptly interrupted Jakov and told him that he wished to have nothing to do with Christianity. He reminded Jakov of the dreadful history of the church in his town, a history replete with plundering, exploiting, and indeed with killing innocent people. "My own nephew was killed by them," he said and angrily rebuffed any effort on Jakov's part to talk about Christ. "They wear those elaborate coats and caps and crosses," he said, "signifying a heavenly commission, but their evil designs and lives I cannot ignore."

Jakov, looking for an occasion to get Cimmerman to change his line of thinking, said, "Cimmerman, can I ask you a question? Suppose I were to steal your coat, put it on, and break into a bank. Suppose further that the police sighted me running in the distance but could not catch up with me. One clue, however, put them onto your track; they recognized your coat. What would you say to them if they came to your house and accused you of breaking into the bank?"

"I would deny it," said Cimmerman.

"'Ah, but we saw your coat,' they would say," retorted Jakov. This analogy quite annoyed Cimmerman, who ordered Jakov to leave his home.

Jakov continued to return to the village periodically just to befriend Cimmerman, encourage him, and share the love of Christ with him. Finally one day Cimmerman asked, "How does one become a Christian?" and Jakov taught him the simple steps of repentance for sin and of trust in the work of Jesus Christ and gently pointed him to the Shepherd of his soul. Cimmerman bent his knee on the soil with his head bowed and surrendered his life to Christ. As he rose to his feet, wiping his tears, he embraced Jakov and said, "Thank you for being in my life." And then he pointed to the heavens and whispered, "You wear His coat very well."

Do yourself a favor and get your eyes off the shortcomings of institutions and people and history's dark spots. Level your scrutiny at the person of Christ, and you will see the One who wears His Father's coat very well. Pilate said of Him, "I find no fault in this man." The thief on the cross said, "We receive the due reward of our deeds, but this man has done nothing wrong." Jesus looked at His fiercest opponents and said, "Which of you convinces me of any sin?" That last challenge could not have been made by any other religious leader, founder, or prophet. The sinfulness of each one of them is readily visible and undeniable. Jesus alone stands without moral blemish. Fairy tales are merely fantastic; Jesus Christ is fantastically true.

By claiming to be the truth, Jesus implies that all He affirms is true and that nothing He says is false. If it is true that the foundational pursuit of life is meaning, then that meaning must be within the confines of truth, and that truth cannot be found apart from Jesus. In searching for ourselves, we can never know ourselves until we know Him. Jesus made a profound statement when He said that He had come to reveal the hearts of men. This impassioned search for ourselves culminates only when we find Him, whom to know is truth. Then and then alone, we are set free for the purposes of our Creator.

10
Love's Labor Won

I HAVE SO FAR PRESENTED two essential components for meaning—the pursuit of wonder and the knowledge of truth—and suggested that they are both fulfilled in a person. I now suggest that the third component essential to meaning is love. From the wonder of childhood to the search for truth in adolescence, we come to the consummation of love in young adulthood. Christopher Morley said, "If we all discovered that we had only five minutes left to say all that we wanted to say, every telephone booth would be occupied by people calling other people to stammer that we love them."[1]

None of us will deny the indispensable role love plays in filling our lives with meaning, which explains why there is such devastation when love is lost.

On love and marriage G. K. Chesterton made this poignant observation:

> They have invented a new phrase that is a black-and-white contra-
> diction in two words—"free love." As if a lover had been, or ever
> could be, free. It is the nature of love to bind itself, and the institu-
> tion of marriage merely paid the average man the compliment of
> taking him at his word.[2]

The statement that, for me, captures the concept of love so clearly and yet seems totally foreign to our "disposable" society is that "It is the nature of love to bind itself." Realistically, what passes for love today would be more aptly described as self-gratification, or indulgence. Once again, I have had in my own life the opportunity to study the contrasting cultural concepts and manifestations of what we human beings call love.

In the East, devotion, commitment, and role relations find a cultural emphasis. In the West, romance becomes the sum and substance of it all. Somewhere the two must be incorporated, for without romance, marriage is a drudgery, but without the will and commitment, marriage is a mockery.

But in both East and West there is something that happens in our young-adult years that probably brings one of the more radical transformations in the human experience. With the wonder of childhood gone and the search for truth continuing, the truthfulness of the heart's condition is then tested in love. This is where all our sentimentalities are forced to meet the test of character and genuineness. This is where those universalizable principles of Kant leave the ivory tower of philosophy and are personally tested in the bedrooms and living rooms of our homes.

All those God-censoring statements we make questioning His fairness are now placed alongside our own practice of truth and often reveal the patent incongruity between our words and our deeds. Anyone who will not be faithful to his or her own commitment to love can hardly be taken seriously when defending his or her deceit as provoked by the absence of an objective standard of truth. What is clearly absent is the integrity and character that are implicit within love. We talk of love's making the world go around when in reality it is the search for a faithful, cherished love that sends one traveling the world over.

Unfortunately, in the English language we have cheated ourselves by using the same epithet *love* to cover a wide variety of relationships. In the Greek language there were four different words, each describing a different kind of love. *Agape* refers to a pure love with particular reference to God. *Phileo* is the love of friendship. *Storge* describes the love of a parent. And *eros* is romantic love.

Note carefully that although only one of the loves is physically consummated, all of them involve commitment. However, in our culture when we say "love" it is most often physical love that is implied, and that devoid of commitment. How strange that we call the sexual act "making love" when in actuality, if that act is without commitment in real terms, it is a literal and figurative denuding of love in which the individual is degraded to an object. Love is not love when it has been manufactured for the moment. Love is the posture of the soul, and its entailments are binding. When love is shallow the heart is empty, but if the sacrifice of love is understood, one can drink deeply from its cup and be completely fulfilled.

Let me therefore shift the focus from the analogy of marital love to love in a parenting and providing context, for it is in the love of parents for their children that both East and West share a common heartbeat. From the jungles of Ecuador or New Guinea to the boardrooms of business transactions in Tokyo or New York or London, children are dearly valued. It is the love for our children that all segments of society have in common, from the lowest to the highest.

Many times I have seen this affection demonstrated in strange and sometimes unexpected settings. Anyone who has ever tried to move his car along inch by inch in one of India's crowded cities has been confronted with a very clever ploy used by "professional" beggars. Every few feet as the beggar follows along, the occupant of the car is confronted by an expression of dire need etched into the beggar's face, an expression that seems pitifully well rehearsed. But that pathos does not always guarantee generosity from the passerby. The final "hit" is therefore made when the beggar holds up a little child in the face of the potential benefactor in a last-ditch effort to provoke any vestige of human pity.

It is a natural and universal sensitivity within the human heart, whether king or beggar, to lavish love upon our young and to care for our children. It is still the minimal test for civility, and more often than not we proverbially refer to a mother's love as the ultimate love. That is why in an aircraft mothers are directly instructed to first cover their own faces with an oxygen mask before tending to their children. Natural instincts would reverse that.

Erma Bombeck remarked that she knew she had grown old when her daughter who was driving her somewhere had to suddenly apply the brakes and instinctively reached out to protect her mother. Love's sacrifice had wonderfully brought the generation a full circle.

Here I think we must pause to understand the point I am making. The unifying principle in both romantic love and parental love is the same—one of honor and fidelity. The care and impartation of love can only be communicated to our children if we teach them that it is the nature of love to honor its commitments—to bind itself. If we do not understand this, all we do is transfer a pathetic self-centeredness masquerading as love. Once true love is understood, the world is opened up to a heartwarming truth. Love and sacrifice go together, and in the spending of love is the enriching of the spirit. The more one consumes love selfishly, the more wretched and impoverished one becomes.

Climbing the Ladder to the Wrong Pinnacle

Let me present for your consideration two dramatically different stories, one factual and the other a parable. Reflecting upon the thoughts these two stories generate within us will provide another hint of our deep hunger that points beyond itself to the larger fulfillment that we seek. And what is more, if we are careful in analyzing why we feel the emotions we do upon hearing such narratives, the conclusions we draw could well unlock the treasure to meet one of our greatest needs. Each of these stories in its own way is tragic, but not without recourse. Many of you may recall the popular song "Cat's in the Cradle" sung by Harry Chapin. The words always bring a tear to my eye because I am a father, and over the years I have had to travel so much. The song unfolds as follows:

> My child arrived just the other day;
> He came to the world in the usual way,
> But there were planes to catch, and bills to pay,
> He learned to walk while I was away.
> And he was talkin' 'fore I knew it and as he grew,
> He'd say, "I'm gonna be like you, Dad.
> You know I'm gonna be like you."
>
> And the cat's in the cradle and the silver spoon,
> Little Boy Blue and the man in the moon.
> "When you comin' home, Dad?"
> "I don't know when, but we'll get together then;
> You know we'll have a good time then."
>
> My son turned ten just the other day.
> He said, "Thanks for the ball, Dad, come on, let's play.
> Can you teach me to throw?"
> I said, "No, not today,
> I got a lot to do."
> He said, "That's okay."
> And he walked away but his smile never dimmed.
> It said, "I'm gonna be like him, yeah,
> You know I'm gonna be like him. . . . "
>
> And he came from college just the other day;
> So much like a man I just had to say,

"Son, I'm proud of you, can you sit for a while?"
He shook his head and he said with a smile,
"What I'd really like, Dad, is to borrow the car keys.
See you later, can I have them please?"

I've long since retired, my son's moved away.
I called him up just the other day,
I said, "I'd like to see you, if you don't mind."
He said, "I'd love to, Dad, if I can find the time.
You see, my new job's a hassle, and the kids have the flu,
But it's sure nice talkin' to you, Dad,
It's been sure nice talkin' to you."

And as I hung up the phone
It occurred to me,
He'd grown up just like me,
My boy was just like me.

And the cat's in the cradle and the silver spoon,
Little Boy Blue and the man in the moon,
"When you comin' home, Son?"
"I don't know when, but we'll get together then, Dad.
We're gonna have a good time then." [3]

The melodrama of this song was played out in Chapin's own life almost like a self-fulfilling prophecy. I have been told that his wife, who
wrote the words of the song, asked him one day when he was going to
slow down the torrid pace of his life and give some time to their children.
His answer was, "At the end of this busy summer, I'll take some time to
be with them." That summer, ironically and tragically, Harry Chapin was
killed in a car accident.

It is not possible to read that postscript of Chapin's death and miss the
larger point—that something was known, believed, and even "preached,"
but never lived. When we chase manmade crowns and sacrifice the treasured relationships for which God has made us, life loses its meaning. Unquestionably the story elicits our sympathy, but a gnawing feeling within
us says that love was squandered as the spirit lost its battle to the flesh.

In a dramatically different setting, the parable that I share with you now
I first heard as a boy growing up in New Delhi, where much instruction

is passed on by way of proverbs and parables. This one is no exception in its rich melodrama and Eastern hyperbole, but it brings with it one of the most powerful truths. You will have to pardon the bluntness of the parabolic details, but that, too, is culturally reflective.

It is the story of a young man who lived in a village and fell in love with a woman from a neighboring village. His love for her was genuine, and he sought her hand in marriage. She, in turn, felt no such affection for him and only exploited his feelings to her own advantage. She made it a game, ever demanding more and more proof of his love for her.

At last, when all her ploys were exhausted, she demanded the unthinkable. "If you really love me," she said, "I would like to be confident that it is an unrivaled love. To prove that, I ask you to take your mother's life and bring her heart to me as a trophy of my victory over your love for her." The young man was left thoroughly confounded for weeks and grief-stricken at his option. Unable to withstand his "loss" any longer and seeing his mother alone, in a frenzied fit he killed her and took the heart out of her body. He ran as fast as he could to present this trophy to the girl he loved, all the while fleeing the guilt that tormented him. While running through a heavily wooded area he stumbled and fell, and the heart bounced out of his hand. As he attempted to rise to his feet, he frenetically rummaged through the undergrowth looking for her heart. Finally, he spotted it and picked it up, and as he dusted off his knees he heard a voice coming from the heart saying, "Son, are you hurt? . . . Son, are you hurt?"

From the first time I heard it, no one needed to explain this story to me. Its message of the undying love of a mother stood out clearly amid all the gory details that surrounded it. But let me ask you this: What is it about this love that wins our deepest admiration? Is it not because the greater has conquered the lesser, and that the spirit has triumphed over the flesh? In fact, let us go even deeper—where did such a concept of love come from in the first place? May I suggest that a sacrificial love as noble as that could not have come from mindless matter but was placed there by our Creator, God Himself. Augustine said it well: "You have made us for Yourself and our hearts are restless until they find their rest in Thee." Our capacity to *recognize* love comes from God, and therefore both the definitive terms of love and the sacrifice that love entails must also come from Him. The Bible tells us not only that God is love but also that God has demonstrated that love in an ultimate expression.

Dr. E. Stanley Jones, a famed and noted missionary to India who was respected and admired even by Mahatma Gandhi, used to tell the story of a man, a devout Hindu government official, to whom he was trying to explain the concept of the cross. The man kept reiterating to Dr. Jones that he could not possibly make sense of the cross and of the love of God. Their conversations on this subject were circular and seemingly unsolvable to his satisfaction.

One day, through a series of circumstances, the man involved himself in an extramarital affair that tormented his conscience. He could live with himself no longer, and finally, looking into the eyes of his devoted wife, he told her the heartrending story of his betrayal. The hours and days of anguish and pain became weeks of heaviness in her heart. Yet, as she weathered the early shock she confessed to him not only her deep sense of hurt but also the promise of her undying commitment and love.

Suddenly, almost like a flash of lightning illuminating the night sky and the landscape below, he found himself muttering, "Now I know what it means to see love crucified by sin." He bent his knee in worship of his Savior and embraced his wife anew with the solemnity of life's binding commitment. That overwhelming sense of God's great love is why the hymn writer wrote:

> O Love that will not let me go—
> I rest my weary soul in Thee,
> I give Thee back the life I owe
> That in life's ocean depths its flow may richer, fuller be.[4]

Love has its demands. Love requires sacrifice. But in our high-paced lives, our priorities get inverted and we squander the sacred to protect the profane. It is the love of Christ that challenges our priorities and addresses the need of the human heart to love and to be loved. He becomes the consummate expression of love, and in knowing Him we find that love which brings meaning.

But there is a snag. Earlier, I commented on D. H. Lawrence's strong assertion that there must be something more than love that fills the vacuum of the human heart, and here I would like to present that pivotal truth Christ gives to us that carries us beyond a merely relational concept of love.

If you were to seriously engage any religious philosopher in conversation on the concept of love in other religious teachings you would probably be surprised at what surfaces. In Buddhism the very founder, Gautama Buddha, renounced his wife and family in search of inner peace. In Hinduism the concept of love is more that of pity. In Islam, at best, submission is demanded to a compassionate god, but the more one reads the workings of this compassionate god the more *compassion* seems a vacuous term. Only in the Christian faith is life with God always portrayed as a relationship of love. However, in Christian terms, loves does not stand merely as an emotion or even as an expression. In a relationship with God it ultimately flowers to worship. All earthly relationships as we know them will someday end. It is in worship alone that wonder and truth coalesce and our hearts become enriched by His love. That enrichment that results from worship feeds all other relationships and helps us to hold sacred our commitments. This concept is far too profound to ignore and will merit careful attention in the third part of this book.

D. H. Lawrence was right when he said the deepest hunger of the human heart goes beyond love—Jesus called that "beyond" worship. And Wolfe was right; there is that sense of cosmic loneliness apart from God. Jesus said, "I have come that [you] may have life, and that [you] may have it more abundantly" (John 10:10 NKJV). In Christ that loneliness is conquered as the hungers of the human heart are met and the struggles of the intellect are answered.

Conceding, then, that the commitment of love is essential to meaning, it follows that the absence of love contributes to the absence of meaning. Jean-Paul Sartre once said that hell is other people. To Sartre, life was bearable until other people came along. In one of his books, Dostoevsky depicts a conversation between two of his characters discussing hell. "Hell," says one of them, "must be the inability to love." I would concur. And in that sense, all hell has broken loose upon our culture, for with all the talk of love, we witness more betrayal, and the breakup of the family now dominates our society. Unless this trend is reversed, we will completely disintegrate as a civilization, for meaninglessness will unleash violence even upon those we claim to love. The love of God is indispensable to meaning—that love is revealed in Christ and may be experienced personally.

11

Crossing the Bar

WE HAVE COME to the final factor necessary for bringing meaning to life—security. This is most earnestly sought after in the waning years of life, the tail end of Shakespeare's seven stages. Beginning with wonder in childhood, through the pursuit of truth in adolescence and the fulfillment of love in the adult years, we finally face in the end an old age that longs for security. The reason for this is that the wonder has faded with the breakdown of the body. Truth brings the reality of a terminus for earthly existence. Love will soon be a thing of the past if death is the end of all consciousness. Where, then, does one find the security that can regain the wonder, know the truth, and enjoy the love?

If there is no life beyond the grave, then life is defined only in terms of "What makes me happy," or "Do whatever you feel is right" since there is no "why" to life itself. On the other hand, if there is life beyond the grave, then life must be defined from that vantage point and the central question becomes "What is it right to feel?" On the basis of that knowledge, the doing ensues.

All major religions believe in an afterlife of one sort or another, but none except Christianity has provided the historical substantiation of it. The Christian faith, although it is a whole system, can be completely decimated in principle if one can fully establish that Jesus did not rise from the dead. Many have tried to do just that and have either turned to Christ themselves in the process or have abandoned their attempt at disproof as an utter failure. No one in history could have wanted to disprove the resurrection more than the temple authorities or the Roman hierarchy. In subsequent years, no force would have wanted to rob Christianity of that claim more than Islam did. Yet the truth stands tall.

I personally have found the whole debate on the Shroud of Turin to be fascinating. I do not believe for a moment that it ought to be used as evidence for Christ's resurrection because it will always remain moot, even if dated to that period. But what is intriguing is that it bears the semblance of a teaser that haunts even the skeptic and evokes deep questions.

In spite of the impressions of worldly success, fame, and adulation, we are sometimes alerted to stories of human interest that reveal that the objects of such adulation have the same longings as the rest of us. When Elvis Presley's body was found the morning following his death, his half-brother testified that he was lying prone on the floor with a Bible and a book on the Shroud of Turin open beneath him. Let me repeat that the longing within our hearts for life beyond the grave does not of itself establish that there is indeed life beyond the grave, but this hunger does speak of our need to know the truth about death because that would then define life and bring security. Jesus said, "I am the resurrection and the life. He who believes in me will live, even though he dies; and whoever lives and believes in me will never die" (John 11:25).

The promise of this hope has fueled the lives of millions. One of the principal agents of that message was Saul of Tarsus, who, breathing threat and slaughter, was on his way to eradicate the early church until he was felled on the Damascus road by a blinding light and the voice of the risen Christ. He was taken to a house on the Street called Straight. What a marvel it is to be in Damascus, as I have been, and walk on the Street called Straight. There is an old, small, dark house that is claimed to have belonged to Ananias, the man who helped Paul in the hour of his conversion. Whether or not it is his house we cannot be sure, but two thousand years after the event the name of the street has not changed, reminding the visitor of what took place here.

It was here that Saul of Tarsus received his divine commission to stand before leaders and princes on behalf of this risen Christ. Fearing nothing from that point on, he said, "Let no one cause me trouble, for I bear on my body the marks of Jesus" (Gal. 6:17). From being a terrorist and a persecutor of the followers of Christ, this young Jew, a Roman citizen living in a Greek city, touched the world with the message of the Christ who had triumphed over the grave. It is this message that brought him security and the knowledge that life is more than its threescore years and ten.

As I bring this part of the book to a close I remind you of the four essential components to meaning in life—wonder, truth, love, and security. When one claims to have found meaning, that meaning must coalesce these four elements. And all four are found in the person of Jesus Christ, who alone brings life meaning by meeting the test at every age of life. Not one of those tests provides the answer in isolation. But taken together they make perfect sense.

Many years ago I had the privilege of speaking across the length and breadth of the country of Vietnam. The year was 1971, and I was still an undergraduate in college when the invitation was extended to me to come and speak at the U.S. military bases and hospitals, as well as in other settings. It was an experience that changed my life. I recall numerous conversations with military personnel, and more often than not the conversation turned to the subject of death, and ultimately to God. Those conversations are deeply etched in my memory.

One of the memories of those years is a poem that was written by an American soldier and given to me. I have treasured it ever since and will summarize what he so painstakingly described with poetic beauty. He tells of a life-defining night when he was caught in the crossfire of a battle that raged around him and a war that he could not silence within him. The one, a conflict of ideology for which the weapons of warfare now thundered forth their fury; the other, a struggle of the heart and mind as they dealt with matters of the soul. It was to that inner embattlement he directed his attention.

The deafening noise of exploding shells and the sound of the signal to fight what could well have been his last battle did not daunt his yearning to settle that inner turmoil. Once again, within him he heard the voices of friends from the days of his youth who had convinced him of a mindless universe. But now, from his shellhole as he saw the starlit sky, he felt the skeptic had not called a spade a spade. In silence he peacefully surrendered to the Lord whose love he could resist no longer, and with the triumph of the soul, he said, "Now that I have met you I'm not afraid to die."

Ironically, several years later when I was in Syria, I heard a young officer testify to an identical struggle and to victory through Christ on a fateful night atop the Golan Heights. That battle, history records, exacted a terrible price in human life. Odd as it seems, such settings have settled wars of personal destiny for an astonishing number of soldiers. Victory over the grave puts every other battle in perspective.

Let me share those glorious words of Malcolm Muggeridge on his discovery of a personal relationship with Jesus Christ.

> I may, I suppose, regard myself as a relatively successful man. People occasionally stare at me in the streets, that's fame; I can fairly easily earn enough money to qualify for admission to the higher slopes of the Internal Revenue Service. That's success. Furnished with money and a little fame, even the elderly, if they care to, may partake of friendly diversions. That's pleasure. It might happen once in a while that something I said or wrote was sufficiently heeded for me to persuade myself that it represented a serious impact on our time. That's fulfillment. Yet, I say to you, and I beg you to believe me, multiply these tiny triumphs by millions, add them all up together, and they are nothing, less than nothing. Indeed, a positive impediment measured against one drop of that living water Christ offers to the spiritually thirsty, irrespective of who or what they are.[1]

We have moved from the world of a child to the sunset years of life in our pursuit for meaning, and we have seen how this search for meaning fails if our lives are lived without God. May I take the liberty now to tie it all together with this personal anecdote.

When our little boy Nathan was just a few years old, I saw him one Sunday morning utterly enthralled by the simple act of letting a helium balloon float to the ceiling and then climbing up on a sofa and pulling it down. He repeated that sequence more times than I cared to count. The rapturous expression upon his face was worthy of Milton's pen—letting the balloon go, chuckling to his heart's content, and bringing it down from atop the sofa.

G. K. Chesterton said something to the effect that God's infinite capacity is revealed in a child's propensity to exult in the monotonous. Which of us is not familiar with the sight of a little one being hurled into the air and caught, only to hear him or her say, "Do it again!" For one who lives with God, the exultant repetition is daily witnessed as we enjoy His creation—God says to the sun, "Do it again!" and to the moon, "Do it again!" and to the seasons, "Do it again!"

But alas! There came that first hint of boredom for the child and the inevitable departure from childhood. So, our little guy went out of the house and onto the driveway, where he let the balloon loose in the vaster expanse. I was a moment too late to stop him, and together we watched it go. As it painfully dawned on him that there was no sofa big enough to bring it down, he predictably burst into tears. Then, with a sudden hint of a glint in his eye, he stopped and said, "I know what, Daddy. The next time you are in a plane you can bring it back for me!" The most disappointing thing to him was to hear me say, "I'm sorry, son; I can't do that."

Somewhere and sometime, human enthrallment finds its limit, as does human capacity. God alone is the perpetual novelty—providing wonder, truth, love, and security.

Who am I? . . . Whoever I am, thou knowest, O God, I am thine.[2]

PART III

WHO IS JESUS (AND WHY DOES IT MATTER?)?

12

Getting to the Truth

I N SOME WAYS, to draw the conclusion that God alone is the perpetual novelty is to state the obvious. It cannot be denied that if, indeed, we can know with certainty that there is a God and that He has spoken, it follows ineluctably that He alone would be the perpetual novelty. It would then logically follow that to know Him—to live with Him—would be the supreme purpose and pleasure of life. But that is a big "if." How do we know if Christ really is the way and the truth and the life, as He claimed He was? In our consideration of that all-important issue, let us first examine one of the most controversial and castigated assertions of the Christian faith—its exclusive claim to truth.

Christianity is often scorned as the pariah among the religions of the world and considered by its detractors to be controversial because modern learning mocks the very notion of truth as absolute. The Christian faith is often castigated because the contemporary mind-set is infuriated by any claim to ideational elitism in a pluralistic society. How dare one idea be claimed as superior to another? After all, we are supposed to be a multicultural society: Should not truth also come in different dress?

One of the recurring elements in the Bible, especially in encounters involving Jesus, is the element of surprise. That surprise is not only contained in what Jesus said, but more often it is to whom He said those words that brings the surprise. Consider Jesus' claim, "I am the way and the truth and the life. No one comes to the Father except through me" (John 14:6). Jesus spoke these words to the apostle Thomas, the apostle whose name, even after two millennia, is synonymous with doubt. Thomas was the last to believe in the resurrection of Jesus because he did not want to trust to such a stupendous claim secondhand. He needed to see and to feel before he would bend his knee to the Christ he knew had been crucified.

Ironically, this Thomas, once he had seen and touched the resurrected Christ, went to India to preach the gospel—where the religious landscape boasted 330 million deities in its multifaceted pantheon, a number that was constantly increasing. Into this wide embrace, a mix between crude polytheism and evolving pantheism, Thomas proclaimed Jesus as the way, the truth, and the life. He paid the ultimate price of his own life, and if tradition holds true (for which there is sufficient evidence), he was martyred in Madras, the city of my birth.

Before us now is the task of justifying that extraordinary claim—the exclusivity and uniqueness of Jesus Christ. Who is He? Does it really matter two thousand years after He walked this earth? Obviously, once the first part of the question is answered, the latter part is a foregone conclusion. Let me set a model before you for determining truth, and then we will examine five distinct categories in which Christ's claim that He is the truth is sustained and is worthy of consideration and scrutiny.

The Humiliation of Truth

A serious casualty of our time that defies comprehension is the death of truth. By denying absolutes and eradicating all points of reference by which we test veracity, our civilization has entered *terra incognita* on matters of the greatest importance even for survival. We do business in the arena of values as though it were virgin terrain, never before tread upon by any knowledgeable explorer. Skepticism and cynicism have suddenly become the hallmarks of sophistication, and the knowledge of who we are has been left to the domain of the uneducated or unscientific (since they are the only ones naive enough to believe that truth is absolute). Pronouncements on life's essence are relegated to funeral parlors or psychiatric wards, but in the real world of stuff and academia, truth is now a vacuous word, a solipsist's refuge. At least, such is the posture taken by some of the so-called brightest minds of our time.

Historian Gertrude Himmelfarb, in a scholarly and incisive analysis of the academic impoverishment that now plagues us, mourns this loss of truth as a life-desecrating tragedy. She quotes one of America's leading philosophers, Richard Rorty, proudly debunking his own discipline of philosophy as mythological and insisting that any philosopher who thinks he or she can locate reality is "a real live metaphysical prig." Rorty bemoans, "There are to be sure such dudes left."

> You can still find philosophy professors who will solemnly tell you that they are seeking the truth, not just a story or a consensus but an honest-to-God, down-home, accurate representation of the way the world is. A few of them will even claim to write in a clear, precise, transparent way, priding themselves on manly straightforwardness, on abjuring "literary" devices.[1]

It is pathetic to hear such illogic—such arrant nonsense in the truest sense of the term—emanating from the pen of one who is supposed to be a thinker. All we need to ask of Rorty is whether his conclusion against the possibility of truth is itself true or merely another literary device. The fact is that each of us, either implicitly or explicitly, lives by certain pre-committed principles that are believed to be the nonnegotiables of life. We do not just arbitrarily believe everything we hear, but consciously or un-consciously, test propositions to determine their truth or falsehood. Once a proposition has been tested and proven to be true, we may choose to ig-nore the ramifications that follow, but we can no longer question its veracity.

The Truth about Truth

Prior to entering the core of Christian defense, the first step is to cross two major hurdles. The first one deals with the very method of how we arrive at the truth for any religion, and the second examines whether truth can indeed be exclusive. As dreary as this task may seem, it is a procedural necessity if we are to be fair to the question.

I suggest that there are three tests to which any system or statement that makes a claim to truth must be subjected as a preliminary requirement if that statement is to be considered meaningful for debate. Those tests are (1) logical consistency, (2) empirical adequacy, and (3) experiential relevance.

These three tests provide a high degree of confidence that as they are applied to a system of belief, truth or falsehood can be established. The truth claims of Christianity, Hinduism, Buddhism, Islam, or atheism must *all* meet these tests. Is there a logical consistency in what is stated? Is there empirical adequacy where its truth claims can be tested? Is there experiential relevance—does it apply meaningfully to my life?

There is, however, a potential shortcoming to this threefold test, and it has been addressed by philosopher Norman Geisler in his writings on epistemology. Dr. Geisler astutely points out that it is possible for some philosophical systems to meet these three tests and still be intrinsically false. For example, if one were to grant some of Hinduism's presuppositions, Hinduism can meet the three tests as stated. But when those presuppositions are scrutinized by other methods of truth-testing that fall outside the bounds of sheer logic, the presuppositions themselves are found to be indefensible. As an instance, one of the presuppositions of Hinduism is that the material world as we know it is not distinct from the ultimate, impersonal reality, Brahman. If we grant Hinduism that assumption, it meets the three tests for truth. On the other hand, if we can prove that assumption to be false, the edifice of pantheism collapses.

How may we demonstrate that falsity? Although I cannot go into great lengths in that pursuit here, I can highlight at least one significant flaw while remaining within the context of this book. Dr. Geisler helps us by bringing to our attention two tests that, in effect, negate pantheism. One is called the undeniability test; it is a test for truth. The other is the unaffirmability test, a test for falsehood.

Take, for example, the issue of my existence. While my own existence cannot be logically proven, it is nevertheless existentially undeniable. That means I cannot deny my existence without affirming it at the same time. I recall the classic interaction between a student and his professor. "How do I know I exist?" demanded the student in a philosophy lecture. "And whom shall I say is asking?" came the reply. Undeniability, therefore, is clearly a test for truth.

The unaffirmability test, on the other hand, is a test for falsehood. This basically means that just because something can be stated, it does not necessarily follow that the statement is true. "I cannot speak a word of English," may be passionately stated, but it cannot be affirmed at the same time. For while saying, "I cannot speak a word of English," I am actually speaking several words of English. Therefore, my statement is false. In Hinduism one has to say, in effect, "God exists, but I don't." It is an unaffirmable position. Unaffirmability, therefore, is a test for falsehood.

These two tests, added to the previous three tests of logical consistency, empirical adequacy, and experiential relevance, complete a very effective fivefold system for determining truth. Rather than get too far afield, may I recommend your own personal reading on this important subject?

All the angry, denouncing words of the Rortys of this world notwithstanding, these tests pertain. For anyone to take seriously the statement that there is no truth that corresponds to reality defeats the statement itself by implying that it is not reflective of reality. If a statement is not reflective of reality, why take it seriously? Truth as a category must exist even while one is denying its existence and must also afford the possibility of being known.

This establishes the first part of what I have deemed a procedural necessity. There is also a second prejudice that must be addressed.

The Hidden Truth about Exclusive Truth

One surprising illusion under which the modern critic of Christianity lives is the belief that Christianity is the only system of belief that is exclusivistic. This assumption reveals a significant ignorance of all of the major worldviews present today. In reality, every system is implicitly exclusivistic. Buddhism was born out of a repudiation of two cardinal doctrines of Hinduism. Gautama Buddha rejected the *Vedas* as the ultimate truth and denounced the caste system outrightly. The caste system, of course, was inextricably woven into the doctrine of reincarnation and hence, the nuance of difference in Buddhism's doctrine of transmigration.

Sikhism, in effect, rejected both Hinduism and Buddhism. And in a valiant attempt to pull everything together, Baha'ism, an attempt at religious universalism, deveined all of them and excluded the exclusivists. Even a cursory understanding of Islam conveys its radical exclusivism. Islam is not only exclusive theologically, it is also exclusive linguistically. According to Islamic teaching, the sole, sufficient, and consummate miracle in Islam is the Koran, which is only recognizable in the Arabic. Any translation diminishes the primary source and desacralizes the verbiage. And I might add that it is not merely an understanding of Arabic that is required but a sophisticated knowledge of it. As for antitheism, it rejects all theistic viewpoints and treats their beliefs as orphaned from reason. So let us be honest; let's remove this scar attributed by antitheists to Christianity that supposedly mars the otherwise beautiful countenance of religious or secular tolerance.

The issue, then, is not whether the belief system you espouse—monotheistic, atheistic, pantheistic, or otherwise—is exclusive. The issue is whether the answers to the four basic questions of life pertaining to origin, meaning, morality, and destiny within the context of each of these worldviews meet the tests of truth. Are they logically consistent, are they empirically adequate, and are they experientially relevant? Do they meet the tests of unaffirmability and undeniability? The answers to life's four questions must in each instance correspond to reality, and the sum of the answers must cohere as a system.

It is absolutely imperative to understand that when an antagonist of the Christian faith poses a question of the Christian, he or she must, in turn, be willing first to justify the question within the context of his or her own presuppositions. Second, he or she must also answer the question on the basis of those presuppositions. In other words, the questioner is also obliged to answer the same question. An attitude that says, "You can't answer my question, and therefore I can believe whatever I want to believe," is intellectual hypocrisy.

Let me therefore reiterate that *truth, by definition, will always be exclusive.* Indeed, Jesus claimed such exclusivity. Had He not made such an assertion, He would have been unreasonably implying that truth is all-inclusive, which it cannot be. The real question that remains is whether Jesus' claims to truth withstand the tests for truth and whether, in His person, He met those tests. Let me present to you a very significant illustration to prove my argument of truth's exclusivity.

Either/Or, Both/And

Sometime ago, when I was in California delivering a series of addresses on the Christian faith, a professor of philosophy who had been in the audience confronted me with a rather stern challenge. The situation was somewhat ironic and would have been quite humorous had it not involved some obvious irritation on the part of my antagonist. Flinging down the gauntlet, he dared me to speak the next night on the subject of "Why I Am Not a Hindu." I must confess I was rather taken aback, as this was an American gentleman who had adopted the Eastern

GETTING TO THE TRUTH

mystical worldview for himself and was most agitated that I, an Indian, had committed my life to Christ. I interacted with him for a few moments in order to get a feel for the levelheadedness of our discussion and then said I would rather not deal with a frontal attack on any issue so culturally sensitive in such a setting. "Besides," said I, "I have heard it said that when you throw mud at others, not only do you lose a lot of ground, you also get your hands dirty." He was neither persuaded nor amused.

He was insistent and continued to challenge me. "Go ahead, speak on that subject, and I will bring my philosophy class with me. They will take you apart after you are through." Without question, by his polemic stance he was waging a psychological war.

By this point quite a crowd had gathered to listen with gladitorial glee to this verbal slugfest. Unable to shake off this determined man, I finally made a counteroffer. I had been planning to speak one night on "Why I Am a Christian"; I suggested that perhaps that would provide sufficient material upon which his philosophical heavyweights could pounce. "I would be delighted," I said, "to respond to any challenge on that. After all, implicit in that presentation would be why I am not anything else." And so he agreed.

As the lecture unfolded I could sense his discomfort, for I was touching upon the nerve of his worldview—the basic laws of logic and how they apply to reality. I began by establishing the law of noncontradiction, which contends that if a statement is absolutely contradictory, without qualification, that statement cannot be true. I continued by demonstrating that in the myriad postulations of Hinduism there are numerous contradictions, a fact admitted to by even some of its leading proponents. If the law of noncontradiction applies to reality and Hinduism is plagued by contradiction, then I concluded that, as a system, Hinduism is false. To this very day, Hinduism lives with a titanic struggle between its two poles of theism (a belief in a personal deity) and monism (a belief in an impersonal, absolute reality). In fact, more and more, Hindus are prone to offer Hinduism not as a religion but as a culture because of its admixture of so many contrary strands.

Parenthetically, for those who are not familiar with this kind of thinking, and for whom philosophy is not part of the daily diet, the law of noncontradiction works something like this: Suppose my wife and I were walking together and you came by and said, "Hello, Mr. and Mrs. Zacharias. I hear you are expecting a baby." If, to your question, my wife answered "Yes" at the same time that I said "No," what would you think? You might conclude that an attempt at humor was being made, or that perhaps the woman accompanying me is not Mrs. Zacharias, or possibly that she has not yet broken the news to me. This is because the same question, at the same time, meaning the same thing cannot elicit two absolutely opposite answers. It is the simple clue to truth we use in the courtroom and at our workplace. It is the law of noncontradiction. This was the key issue that this professor was going to address in our discussion.

At the end of the lecture, he stormed to the front with his note takers and exploded, "You have done the greatest damage to Eastern philosophy I have ever seen anyone do, and the reason is that you don't understand the Eastern mind." Even his own students could not help but see the irony of a Westerner telling an Easterner that he did not understand the Eastern mind. This was indeed comical.

I decided the time had come to rescue this discussion from ridicule, so I asked him to meet me for lunch the next day where we could try and work through our disagreement. He accepted, and when we met, he wasted no time. He began with, "Your biggest problem is that you do not understand Eastern logic." I concluded it would be best to let him explain Eastern logic to me. His argument expounded on two kinds of logic, one the either/or logic and the other, the both/and logic. "The either/or logic," he said, "is built on the law of noncontradiction, meaning that if a statement is true, its opposite has to be false." So far I agreed with him.

As the professor waxed eloquent and expounded on the law of noncontradiction, he eventually drew his conclusion: "This is a Western way of looking at reality." I disagreed with that conclusion and asked him to cross it off his placemat where he had delineated his syllogisms. He refused, and I allowed him to proceed, knowing that sooner or later he would have to reject his conclusion.

His next major explanation was on the dialectical method. This is not either/or; this is both/and. G. W. F. Hegel used this in his dialectic between an idea (a thesis) and its opposite (an antithesis) to form the synthesis (finding a middle ground). Karl Marx used it to demonstrate history's inexorable move from the employer on one side and the employee on the other to a merger into a classless society. (Strangely, no one ever shows you a classless society.) My philosopher friend went to great lengths to establish the both/and logic as a superior way by which to establish truth.

"So, Dr. Zacharias," he said, "when you see one Hindu affirming that God is personal and another insisting that God is not personal, just because it is contradictory you should not see it as a problem. The real problem is that you are seeing that contradiction as a Westerner when you should be approaching it as an Easterner. The both/and is the Eastern way of viewing reality." Again I asked him to strike out the last line of his conclusion on the both/and system, but of course he did not.

After he had belabored these two ideas of either/or and both/and for some time and carried on his tirade that we ought not to study truth from a Western point of view but rather from an Eastern viewpoint, I finally asked if I could interrupt his unpunctuated train of thought and raise one question. He agreed and put down his pencil.

I said, "Sir, are you telling me that when I am studying Hinduism I *either* use the both/and system of logic *or* nothing else?"

There was pin-drop silence for what seemed an eternity. I repeated my question: "Are you telling me that when I am studying Hinduism I *either* use the both/and logic *or* nothing else? Have I got that right?"

He threw his head back and said, "The either/or does seem to emerge, doesn't it?"

"Indeed, it does emerge," I said. "And as a matter of fact, even in India we look both ways before we cross the street—it is either the bus or me, not both of us."

Do you see the mistake he was making? He was using the either/or logic in order to prove the both/and. The more you try to hammer the law of noncontradiction, the more it hammers you. (Another way to consider this discussion is to say that if the both/and logic is all you make it to be, why can't I use *both* the both/and *and* the either/or? Why just one of them?)

Now let me make two vitally, vitally important points here. This philosopher was partly right. In the East there is a popular tendency to *appear* accepting of all religions as just different facets of the same truth. Dr. Radhakrishnan (the noted Indian philosopher who taught at Oxford succeeding the renowned Dr. Zaehner and then went on to become India's president) made a staggering comment in his book *The Hindu View of Life.* He said that one can be a Muslim, a Christian, a Buddhist, and even an atheist—and still be a Hindu. Radhakrishnan was clearly equivocating. He himself confessed elsewhere that Hinduism had opened its arms

CAN MAN LIVE WITHOUT GOD

so wide to include so much that when the arms finally closed, Hinduism would be strangled by the embrace.

However, popular Hinduism is not classical Hinduism, and the whole method of teaching of the greatest Hindu philosopher Shankara was quite Socratic as he debated ideas not in a dialectical mode (both/and) but in a noncontradictory mode (either/or). He would challenge his antagonists to prove him wrong, and if not, to surrender to his view. The point, then, is not whether we use an Eastern logic or a Western logic. We use the logic that best reflects reality, and the law of noncontradiction is implicitly or explicitly implied by both the East and the West.

There is a second point that needs to be made about the law of noncontradiction. It is ultimately not a test for truth but for falsehood. A statement may be noncontradictory but nevertheless false. For example, there is nothing contradictory within the statement itself about my saying that there is a red car in the driveway, but I may still be telling you something that is false. On the other hand, if the statement is unqualifiedly contradictory—to wit, talking about square circles—it cannot be true. This is why I find atheism clearly false. Its theory and its injunctions are fraught with contradictions.

Now, if the law of noncontradiction applies to reality, and if the same question at the same time cannot elicit two opposite answers, both claiming to be true, you must submit to one conclusion: Jesus made a most reasonable statement when He claimed exclusivity. You may say He was wrong, but you must acknowledge that He was making a meaningful statement because truth by definition is exclusive. The inescapability of this fact is proven if you choose to challenge what I am saying. The moment you try to refute what I'm saying, you are employing the law of noncontradiction, implying that you are right and I am wrong. That is why Aristotle said, "I can prove that law to you. All you've got to do is open your mouth and say something." Even the Eastern mystic knew he could not escape the overarching law of noncontradiction. He therefore opted for silence by saying, "He who knows, does not speak; he who speaks, does not know." But he *spoke* to tell us that! Another sage said, "When the mouth opens, all are fools." Alas, his mouth opened to formulate that test.

You may as well try to describe a one-ended stick as to deny the law of noncontradiction. In effect, you are forced to say nothing, and Aristotle defined nothing as "that which rocks dream about."

We are left with either the dreams of rocks or the acceptance of the law of noncontradiction. Jesus claimed to be "the truth." Let us test His claims and teachings. If they are true, what He says matters more than anything else in life.

13
Humanity's Dilemma

I N THE FOLLOWING PAGES I hope to examine some of the principal teachings of Christ upon which the whole edifice of Christianity stands. First and foremost, let us consider Christ's careful and specific description of human nature. This is undoubtedly one of those thorny and distinguishing features between Christianity and all other religions or worldviews. The differences work themselves out in our political and cultural theories. As an example, consider the two following perspectives on the nature of man and witness how disparate the ramifications can be. I call to your attention the thoughts of Rousseau and Pascal on man's fundamental nature. Their thinking is destinies apart.

With his propensity for oracular and epigrammatic beginnings, Jean Jacques Rousseau opened the first chapter of *The Social Contract* with the words, "Man was born free; and everywhere is in chains." Rousseau's doctrine of man propounded a basic and inherent goodness; yet he saw that good did not prevail. His development of the politician theory of socialism came hand in hand with a plan for environmental engineering and with social contracts that would capitalize on this innate goodness and usher in an ideal state. That which he envisioned was never to be because his fundamental postulate on the nature of man was wrong. His notions were soon decimated, just as the utopian dreams of the rebirth of man anticipated by the Romantic poets of the early-nineteenth century were shattered by the Napoleonic Wars. Any philosophy that has built its social structure assuming an innate goodness finds its optimism ever disappointed. History belies that belief.

In contradistinction to these false assumptions of man's nature and to humanistic utopian hopes in man, by man, and for man, Blaise Pascal exposed the fundamental problem with such optimism.

It is in vain, oh men, that you seek within yourselves the cure for all
your miseries. All your insight has led to the knowledge that it is not
in yourselves that you discover the true and the good. The philosophers promised them to you, but they were not able to keep that
promise. They do not know what your true good is or what your
nature is. How should they have provided you with a cure for ills
which they have not even understood? Your principal maladies are
pride, which cuts you off from God, and sensuality, which binds
you to the earth. And they have done nothing but foster at least
one of these maladies. If they have given you God for your object,
it has been to pander to your pride. They have made you think you
were like him and resemble him by your nature. And those who
have grasped the vanity of such a pretension have cast you down in
the other abyss by making you believe that your nature is like that
of the beast of the field and have led you to seek your good in lust,
which is the lot of animals.[1]

Is Pascal right? How do we come to terms with what human nature
essentially is? Jesus taught unequivocally that the self-will within each life,
which seeks absolute autonomy and bends to no higher law than one of
its own, is rebellion of the highest order, inevitably descending to the
lowest level of indignity and indecency.

No good can come if the will is wrong. This teaching of Jesus is often
dismissed as doctrinaire and as an impediment to human creativity. Yet
in the proverbial wisdom of every culture it is sustained and proven again
and again, even in the form of tragicomedy. Let me share a couple of
humorous anecdotes to illustrate what I am saying.

Australia is an incredibly beautiful country in its geography and landscape, but each time I have visited there someone has invariably reminded
me that Australia was originally settled by criminals consigned from
Great Britain. On the heels of that reminder generally follows a cynical explanation of the present cultural condition in the light of its criminal
past. I therefore share this story as it was told by one of the Australian
speakers at a conference in Sydney in which I participated.

In the story, two Aussies appeared at the pearly gates of heaven, catch-
ing the doorman completely by surprise; he was certainly not expecting
any Australians in heaven. He asked them to please wait at the gates until
he could verify their credentials with Saint Peter (for some reason in our

folk humor Peter has been assigned all authority in heaven too). When Peter was informed of these applicants from "down under," he, too, was caught off guard and decided he would need to accompany the doorman back to the pearly gates to talk to these unexpected visitors. But when they arrived at the entrance, behold—the Australians were gone—and so were the pearly gates!

Is it not a revelation of our deepest beliefs over academic pretense when people can parody themselves and show their own duplicity, recognizing it as the bane of their common failing? In our educational sophistication and philosophical brazenness, we may mock the belief in the depravity of man as an antiquated idea, but it resurfaces every day, in every life, and in every culture, destroying civilization in its march.

I love to tell this second story, for it has a universal ring of authenticity. It is the story of two brothers, well known all about town for being as crooked in their business dealings as they could possibly be. That notwithstanding, they continued to progress from wealth to greater wealth until suddenly one of the brothers died. The surviving brother found himself in search of a minister who would be willing to put the finishing touches to the funeral. He finally made an offer to a minister that was hard for him to refuse. "I will pay you a great sum," he said, "if you will just do me one favor. In eulogizing my brother, I want you to call him a 'saint,' and if you do, I will give you a handsome reward." The minister, a shrewd pragmatist, agreed to comply. Why not? The money could help put a new roof on the church.

When the funeral service began, the sanctuary was filled by all the important business associates who had been swindled through the years by these two brothers. Unaware of the deal that had been made for the eulogy, they were expecting to be vindicated by the public exposure of the man's character.

At last the much-awaited moment arrived, and the minister spoke. "The man you see in the coffin was a vile and debauched individual. He was a liar, a thief, a deceiver, a manipulator, a reprobate, and a hedonist. He destroyed the fortunes, careers, and lives of countless people in this city, some of whom are here today. This man did every dirty, rotten, unconscionable thing you can think of. But compared to his brother here, *he was a saint.*"

I first told this story at a conference held in Amsterdam that was attended by ten thousand delegates from all over the world. When I later watched the response of the audience on video, every face was in up-roarious laughter. It was understood by every person present because, no matter what part of the world we come from or what strata of society we represent, we must all admit our own shortcoming—that we only feel exonerated when we gauge our level of saintliness in comparison to someone else of lesser esteem.

The point I am making is that any conclusion about the nature of man, only in human terms, remains circular when we use terms like *good* and *bad*. The Bible is very clear in its description of man's nature. The Greek word for *sin* used in Christian teaching conveys not just the idea of transgression or violation, which we connote in the English language, but includes the concept of missing the mark, of falling short of the goal. What is that mark? The Scripture writers state that it is the standard of God Himself.

For years we have fought this concept, calling it demeaning, con-demning, and morally snobbish, and repudiating it as a hangover from ideas that are now anachronistic. We wonder how modern men and women can possibly buy into this antiquated view that is propagated by a power-mongering church in order to keep people ever at her door. (Ted Turner has stated categorically, in his self-proclaimed role of spokes-man for optimistic humanism, that "people of this age shouldn't be told to do anything."[2]) But does not this very audacity only buttress the teaching of Christ on the nature of man—wishing to be accountable to nobody?

One of the most powerful stories I have ever heard on the nature of the human heart is told by Malcolm Muggeridge. Working as a journalist in India, he left his residence one evening to go to a nearby river for a swim. As he entered the water, across the river he saw an Indian woman from the nearby village who had come to have her bath. Muggeridge impul-sively felt the allurement of the moment, and temptation stormed into his mind. He had lived with this kind of struggle for years but had somehow fought it off in honor of his commitment to his wife, Kitty. On this occa-sion, however, he wondered if he could cross the line of marital fidelity. He struggled just for a moment and then swam furiously toward the woman, literally trying to outdistance his conscience. His mind fed him the fantasy that stolen waters would be sweet, and he swam the harder for it. Now he was just two or three feet away from her, and as he emerged from the water, any emotion that may have gripped him paled into insignificance when compared with the devastation that shattered him as he looked at her. "She was old and hideous . . . and her skin was wrinkled and, worst of all, she was a leper. . . . This creature grinned at me, showing a toothless mask." The experience left Muggeridge trembling and muttering under his breath, "What a dirty lecherous woman!" But then the rude shock of it dawned upon him—it was not the woman who was lecherous; it was his own heart.[3]

This is precisely the teaching of Christ's message. When we look into the human heart we see the lust, the greed, the hate, the pride, the anger, and the jealousies that are so destructive. This is at the heart of the human predicament, and the Scriptures call this condition sin.

We have learned so easily to trivialize our condition. In a recent profound article by one of the most knowledgeable historians on the Holocaust, every possible explanation was given some attention attempting to answer the question, "Why?" Germany's economy, the unfairness of the Versailles Treaty, the rise of a demagogue—all were presented, and numerous others, as possible answers to the question of why the Holocaust happened. The one thing the author did not mention is the very thing that Jesus talked about, that the heart of man is desperately wicked. Who can understand it?

G. K. Chesterton said that there are many, many angles at which one can fall but only one angle at which one can stand straight. If we do not understand sin, humanity will forever test the angles. The worst effect of sin, according to Christ, is manifested not in pain or poverty or bodily defacement but rather, in the discrowned faculties, the unworthy loves, the low ideals, the brutalized and enslaved spirit.

If you reject this concept of sin as a Christian imposition upon our freedom, unsustained by modern psychological theory, listen now to these surprising words from Professor Hobart Mowrer, one-time president of the American Psychological Association, who taught at both Harvard and Yale. In an article in the *American Psychologist* in 1960 he said:

> For several decades we psychologists looked upon the whole matter of sin and moral accountability as a great incubus and acclaimed our liberation from it as epoch making. But at length we have discovered that to be free in this sense, that is, to have the excuse of being sick

rather than sinful, is to court the danger of also becoming lost. This danger is, I believe, betokened by the widespread interest in existentialism, which we are presently witnessing. In becoming amoral, ethically neutral and free, we have cut the very roots of our being, lost our deepest sense of selfhood and identity, and with neurotics, themselves, we find ourselves asking, "Who am I, what is my deepest destiny, what does living mean?"

In reaction to the state of near limbo into which we have drifted, we have become suddenly aware, once again, of the problem of values and of their centrality in the human enterprise. This trend is clearly apparent in the programs at our recent professional meetings, in journal articles, and to some extent already in our elementary textbooks. Something very basic is obviously happening to psychologists and their self image.[4]

Mowrer then quotes Anna Russell in a psychiatric folk song:

> At three I had a feeling of
> Ambivalence toward my brothers,
> And so it follows naturally
> I poisoned all my lovers.
> But now I'm happy I have learned
> The lesson this has taught,
> That everything I do that's wrong
> Is someone else's fault.[5]

Can there be a clearer statement on the condition of the human heart? To be sure, Mowrer would not want to be perceived as espousing a biblical doctrine of sin. (Unfortunately, as many of you know, Mowrer's own life ended in suicide.) But he does confess outrightly that the humanistic trivializing of wrongdoing is utterly bankrupt and incapable of expressing our real human predicament. An admission such as this from one not sympathetic to Christianity signifies that the attempt to portray mankind without any transcendent accountability has inexorably contributed to our individual sense of loss and alienation. And once that feeling of estrangement is etched upon our consciences, we are alienated not only from God, but even from ourselves and ultimately, from our fellow human beings.

A Global Prejudice

The ramifications of Jesus' teaching on sin are many. Let me underscore just one because it is such a felt ache in our culture, and unless we learn to get to the root of this problem the future holds little promise.

As one who has spent half of my life in the East and the other half in the West, I know personally some of the anguish one feels amid racial tensions and intolerance. It is important to add that for some reason the West is often charged with being singularly guilty in this matter. That is a false notion. Even in a land like India, where tolerance is a key word, antipathy between the north and the south runs very deep, and color is a vital component in that prejudice. As we look across this globe today, there are few things that are as deeply troubling and volatile as this issue—the tragedy and the hell of racism. The pain of personal rejection by reason of birth alone is one of the deepest pains a human being can ever experience.

I do not know how many of you heard the tennis great Arthur Ashe interviewed when it first became public knowledge that he had contracted AIDS from a blood transfusion during heart surgery. This greatly admired and mild-mannered gentleman looked into the eyes of the small army of reporters interviewing him and said, "As painful as it is to know that I have this dread disease, nothing could be as painful as the rejection I have endured all my life by virtue of my color."

Think of the agony encased in those words. Think about it. That a man so respected, so talented, so gentlemanly could express that the pain of the disintegration of his body was secondary to the deep, emotional suffering he had endured over a lifetime of personal rejection because of his color—is very sobering.

But this is not a distinctively modern dilemma. Turn your attention with me to Jesus' interaction with a Samaritan woman by Jacob's Well two thousand years ago. I focus on this conversation of Jesus with this woman because it was not atypical of the encounters He had. He often talked with the rejects of His society. In this case, the woman was a Samaritan, a pejorative term in that culture for a mongrel tribe treated with contempt by the ethnically unadulterated. To add insult to her injury, she had been married, betrayed, and abandoned by five husbands. Everything about her life spoke of personal rejection. By virtue of her ethnicity, her gender, and her moral experience, she was one of society's outcasts. We can easily understand why she was so shocked and dumbfounded that this man, a rabbi, would engage her in a gracious conversation. That very gesture by Jesus implicitly restored dignity and respect to her. The range of emotions that swept through her mind prompted her to say, "Why are you even asking me to give you some water to drink?" The reason she was puzzled that He would talk to her is obvious; she was ethnically "unclean," a victim of prejudice. Jesus brought about an incredible life transformation, and she was never again to see herself—or anyone else—in the same way, God had done a work in her heart. Her inward look and her outward look were changed by first changing her upward look. That sequence is the only way to bring about real change in human intercourse. Our relationships to God dictate our relationships one to another.

But in our own day we have tried to do away with prejudice apart from God, seeking solutions by writing new laws and rewriting old ones, by re-educating ourselves and our young. Yet, who among us can say that we have succeded in eliminating the victimization of people? If anything, our society constantly stands at the brink of conflagration as violence between rival groups erupts suddenly and ruthlessly if there is even a hint of a discriminatory judgment. Oh, we rewrote the law books in India too. Yet one theory still asserts that the Hindu who assassinated Mahatma Gandhi did so to remove the Gandhian ideal that sought to obliterate the caste system. Whether or not this theory is true, India's discriminatory struggle continues.

I am convinced that all our attempts to change the letter of the law and to reeducate people have been, and are, merely band-aid solutions for a fatal hemorrhage. The system will never change because our starting point is flawed. The secular view of man can neither give the grandeur that God alone can give, nor can it see the evil within the human heart that God alone can reveal and cure, for atheism implicitly denudes each individual of the grand image God has imprinted upon His creation.

Two contemporary cosmologists make the terrifying comment, "Ultimately it is not human beings that are important, it's DNA." From those words one may infer that prejudice is not personal; it is merely an aversion for certain DNAs. Is this not the inevitable slide of an antitheistic view of man, even though counterintuitively and in practical terms such a bizarre conclusion is incongruent with life itself, where personal loves and concerns outweigh all other considerations? Can we just reduce people to chemicals?

Ted Turner, who is not afraid of tackling anything difficult, was once asked on a program with David Frost whether he had any deep regrets along the way to his trophy-studded life. There was a sudden melancholic expression on his face, an evident twinge in his emotions, and somberly Turner said, "Yes, the way I treated my first wife." He caught the interviewer off guard with his emotion. I admire that candor. But we must ask, Why feel such remorse if it is only the rejection of a certain DNA? Life becomes unlivable and our emotions unexplainable, if personhood is not given value beyond the material.

Invested Dignity

So where does human dignity come from? There is no way to contrive it or to enforce it; human dignity must be essential. Here, the Christian teaching is unique. Professor Peter Kreeft of Boston College has lucidly pointed out this difference between Christianity and secular thought. In the economy of God's creation, there was intended an egalitarianism among human beings; that is, each person was equal in essence and dignity. On the other hand, there was to be an elitism in ideas, meaning that not all ideas are equal—some ideas are clearly superior to others.

Antitheistic thinking has inverted that economy—indeed, it is compelled to—because its starting point leads to the opposite conclusion; people have been rendered elite, and ideas are egalitarian. As a result, we exalt some individuals or races while rejecting others and at the same time foolishly argue that all ideas are equal.[6] If the scourge of racism is ever to die, it will only do so on the biblical basis of who we are as human beings as we learn to respect each person in his or her distinctive and essential splendor—granted by virtue of creation. Ironically, in rejecting any part of humanity we essentially reject ourselves.

The scriptural teaching is that man is created in the image of God. The literal translation of David in Psalm 8:4 is "You have made man with just a little of God lacking in him." This dignity may not be conjured up or legalized by decree. This is our essential splendor, the splendor of people of *all* races and colors. We all share that equal glory, *but* having rejected God we find that glory marred by sin, which engenders hate. The glory can only be restored by dealing with that sin. We are in need of a heart transplant, but the more we refuse to acknowledge our wretched condition, the more the solution evades us, and people continue to live undignified lives. Jesus went to the core of the problem when He said, "You refuse to come to me to have life" (John 5:40). How desperately evil the heart of man is (see Mark 7:21)! Our problem is not an inadequate education. It is a rebellious heart.

The Faceless Mirror

G. K. Chesterton once remarked that to disbelieve in God would be like waking up in the morning, looking into the mirror, and seeing nothing. There would be nothing to reveal your appearance.

That is what the Bible contends is the effect of sin; it robs us of our true nature and denies us the vision of who we really are. Let me explain this a little more because so much of this vital Christian concept is misunderstood or misrepresented.

A well-known figure who has come under public scrutiny in recent times is John DeLorean. Once the fair-haired boy of the automotive world, DeLorean suddenly found himself in a court of law accused of drug dealing and having to fight for what was left of his empire. In his book, he narrated the pivotal moment in his trial, a moment that to him was like a sudden dawn breaking upon his bleak darkness. DeLorean described his emotions as a key government witness and paid informer testified against him, piling lie upon lie and building a completely fabricated series of conversations. *Why is he doing this? To what end is he building this totally false story?* puzzled the frantic and uncontrollably angry DeLorean.

All at once, he realized that what was happening in the courtroom was a mirror image of what had happened in his own life. "I had a moment of déjà vu. I came face to face with the old John DeLorean in all his prideful pursuit of fame, power, and glory." Watching the self-serving zeal with which this lying witness trampled underfoot all that was decent and honorable, DeLorean saw that it was no different to the blind ambition that had driven him to chase his own dream of an automobile company; for in his pursuit he, himself, had trampled underfoot what he had once treasured. This inward look that led him to humble himself before God paved the way for a dramatic transformation in DeLorean's life as he sought forgiveness before a merciful God. It was a hard step for him, but repentance is always difficult.[7]

Jesus talked about the great gain each of us realizes when we recognize our own spiritual poverty, the lecherousness of our own hearts, and turn to God for deliverance from ourselves. Humbling and humiliation are not the same thing. Only God humbles us without humiliating us and elevates us without flattering us. Pascal said, "All of man's miseries are a reflection of his grandeur."

This same point of recognition also awakened the slumbering spirit of journalist Terry Anderson, who had been held captive by terrorists in Lebanon. Anderson said that during his captivity he saw much in his captors that he hated and despised. The more he saw them and talked to them, the more he was repelled by them. "Yet," he added, "in a strange way there was nothing in them I had not now also seen in myself."

Until we come to that point of recognizing our own spiritual impoverishment, our enslavement is greater than if we were merely physically shackled. If we, in our world, are to be rescued from the hell of intolerance and prejudice, we need to see its cause and cure. We are made in the image of God, but it is our sin that drives us to oppression and hate. That human condition is corrected only by a humble return to the One who created us. We cannot be humble in a life lived without God.

Bent for Greatness

There is a classic Old Testament passage in Genesis 32, the point of which often eludes even the careful reader. It is the narrative describing Jacob's returning home after a long absence. Years before he had fled from home because he stole the blessing that belonged to his older brother, Esau. While Esau was out on a hunt, Jacob, in a sinister move, impersonated Esau, and kneeling before his blind father, Isaac, asked Isaac to bless him with the birthright that rightly belonged to Esau. The father was thoroughly puzzled, for the voice sounded like Jacob's, and so he said, "You are not Esau—how can I give you the blessing?" Jacob offered him some fresh game for food, saying he had just brought this from his hunt. Hesitantly, Isaac blessed Jacob, thinking him to be Esau, and gave him the privilege of a birthright that wasn't really his. Because of his brother's resulting wrath, Jacob had to flee, and he had been on the run for all these years. During the intervening years, his mother, who had conspired with him, eventually died, and Jacob decided to return home, hoping his brother's anger had subsided.

Now the moment of confrontation had arrived. Their paths were closing in on each other, and Jacob was to meet with Esau the next morning. Jacob feared for his life and did the only thing left to do—he fell on his face before God. The Scriptures tell us that Jacob wrestled with God throughout the night, crying out, "I will not let you go except you bless me." It was the cry of a desperate man, not knowing what ominous fate awaited him the next day.

God responded with an extraordinary challenge to Jacob: "What is your name?" This is an incredible question from an omniscient being! Why would God ask Jacob for his name? Think of all that God could have said by way of reprimand. Instead He merely asks for Jacob's name. God's purpose in raising this question contains a lesson for all of us, too profound to ignore. In fact, it dramatically altered Old Testament history. In asking for the blessing from God, Jacob was compelled by God's question to relive the last time he had asked for a blessing, the one he had stolen from his brother.

The last time Jacob was asked for his name, the question had come from his earthly father. Jacob had lied on that occasion and said, "I am Esau," and stole the blessing. Now he found himself, after many wasted years of running through life looking over his shoulder, before an all-knowing, all-seeing heavenly Father, once more seeking a blessing. Jacob fully understood the reason and the indictment behind God's question, and he answered, "My name is Jacob."

"You have spoken the truth," God said, "and you know very well what your name signifies. You have been a duplicitous man, deceiving everyone everywhere you went. But now that you acknowledge the real you I can change you, and I will make a great nation out of you."

Greatness in the eyes of God is always preceded by humility before Him. There is no way for you or me or anyone else to attain greatness until we have come to Him. Self-exoneration and self-exaltation come easily when we compare ourselves against the lesser standard of another, but the result is inevitably alienation both from ourselves and from each other. Conviction of sin comes when we measure ourselves before God. A consciousness of one's own need is the beginning of purpose and the beginning of character. Jesus' description of our hearts is in clear correspondence with our universal experience; a denial of this description flies in the face of reality and breeds contempt one for another. God alone can bring the kind of change we need. G. K. Chesterton correctly remarked that the problem with Christianity is not that it has been tried and found wanting but that it has been found difficult and left untried. In response to an article in *The Times* of London entitled "What's Wrong with the World?" Chesterton replied, "I am. Yours truly, G. K. Chesterton." That is precisely Jesus' point—we are wrong with the world.

14

The Philosopher's Quest

T HE SECOND DEFENSE of Christ's teachings is that He alone answers the
determined philosophical quest for unity in diversity. From the
earliest days of Greek philosophy and the time of Thales, the question of
unity and diversity has haunted philosophy. In the beginning of a philosophical education, students are often asked this question: What was it
that existed after 585 B.C., but not before, and began at the ridiculous
hour of 6:13 P.M.? Part of the answer is that there occurred an eclipse of
the sun. But everyone knows eclipses had taken place before 585 B.C.
The unique phenomenon the question refers to is that Thales had predicted this one. It was Thales's speculations and his love for ordered
knowledge that gave birth to philosophy.

But Thales fervently sought the answer to another question. He knew
the world was made of an infinite variety of things—plants, animals,
clouds, etc. What, he wondered, was the one basic element that pulled
it all together, out of what had come such diversity? Thales thought that
element must be water, but his students went on to expand the underlying reality to include four elements—earth, air, water, and fire. From
then until now the quest for the philosopher has been to find unity in
diversity. Many of us may not realize all the implications of this quest, but
in simple ways it has made inroads into our language and culture.

For example, the word *quintessence* literally means "the fifth essence."
What was the fifth essence—the *quintessence* or ultimate essence—that
would unite the other four essences and explain unity in diversity?
Every American coin reads *E Pluribus Unum*—out of the many, one.
Out of diversity, unity. And the very word *university* means to find unity
in diversity.

At one point in history, theology was considered the queen of the disciplines, bringing a unified worldview to the diversity of mental pursuits. With the expulsion of God, unity has also been jettisoned, and a disjointedness follows. There is no coherence left in education. Modern-day university graduates are really graduating from pluraversity, where the various disciples do not connect. In effect, universities are not living up to their mandate.

From language to coinage to education, the search for unity in diversity has left its mark. Today this search for unity is even more important because as specializations increase there is a greater fragmentation of knowledge. Without unity of essence, the diversity of substance and knowledge will only continue to alienate us one from the other. Antitheists and theists agree on one thing: In this world of effect, diversity is present but unity is sought. The question is, How did diversity come about, and how do we locate or identify the unity?

Atheistic evolutionary theory is hard pressed to explain how the diversity that exists could ever have come about from the unity of primordial slime. Nor can Hinduism, Islam, and Buddhism make a sufficient explanation. Apart from all the physical diversities that exist in our world, within human intercourse three vitally important realities pertain—personality, communication, and love. These, too, speak of diversity, particularly in the realm of personality. Only in the Christian faith can these diversities be explained, for in the Christian faith alone there is unity and diversity in the effect of existence because there is unity and diversity in the first cause of our being. That unity and diversity are found in the community of the Trinity. In the Trinity before the creation of man, personhood, love, and communication existed in the Godhead. An important deduction pertains because in the Trinity there is implicit a hierarchy of roles within the Godhead that does not vitiate an equality of essence. A proper understanding of the Trinity not only gives us a key to understanding unity in diversity, but also brings us a unique answer to the great struggle we face between races, cultures, and—for that matter—even genders.

The Trinity provides us with a model for a community of love and essential dignity without mitigating personality, individuality, and diversity. Indeed, the Trinity entails a mystery, but as one of the great philosophers and legal scholars of our times, Mortimer Adler, noted, any knowledge of God would be expected to bring both rudimentary clarity and legitimate mystery. Adler's scrutinizing and legal mind led him to his own conversion to Christ.

Obviously, a very legitimate question may be raised as to how there can be a "three-ness" and a "one-ness" without equivocation. We must bear in mind that when referring to God as a personality there has to be a dimension where, by analogy, we understand how He can transcend finitude and yet be personal. C. S. Lewis said of the Trinity that it is either the most farcical doctrine invented by the early disciples or the most profound and thrilling mystery revealed by the Creator Himself, giving us a grand intimation of reality. Lewis does a masterful job in helping us approach this mystery of divine personality by the use of analogy.

> A good many people nowadays say, "I believe in a God, but not in a personal God." They feel that the mysterious something which is behind all other things must be more than a person. Now the Christians quite agree. But the Christians are the only people who offer any idea of what a being that is beyond personality could be like. All the other people, though they say that God is beyond personality, really think of Him as something impersonal: that is, as something less than personal. If you are looking for something super-personal, something more than a person, then it isn't a question of choosing between the Christian idea and the other ideas. The Christian idea is the only one on the market.
>
> You know that in space you can move in three ways—to left or right, backwards or forwards, up or down. Every direction is either one of these three or a compromise between them. They are called the three Dimensions. Now notice this. If you're using only one dimension, you could draw only a straight line. If you're using two, you could draw a figure: say, a square. And a square is made up of four straight lines. Now a step further. If you have three dimensions, you can then build what we call a solid body: say, a cube—a thing like a dice or a lump of sugar. And a cube is made up of six squares.
>
> Do you see the point? A world of one dimension would be a world of straight lines. In a two-dimensional world, you still get straight lines, but many lines make one figure. In a three-dimensional world, you still get figures but many figures make one solid body. In other words, as you advance to more real and more complicated levels, you don't leave behind you the things you found on the simpler levels; you still have them, but combined in new ways—in ways you couldn't imagine if you knew only the simpler levels.[1]

This helps us get a meaningful, albeit slender, grasp on how the concept of personhood, when transcending our finitude, can contain a complexity yet retain a meaningful simplicity. (One may also use the illustration of light in its wave and particle properties nevertheless held in tension—transcending, not violating, normal categories.)

In rigorously practical terms this concept of unity and diversity has fascinating implications for life. The Trinity may well be the most important teaching of Christ in this context of unity in diversity. The Trinity provides a blueprint for the love and communication we can share with our fellow human beings, retaining a wonderful diversity but brought together by a spiritual unity.

Since unity in diversity is a significant pursuit for all of life, it must address some very basic issues about how we live as individuals within ourselves. For even individually, we live with a diversity of desires in search of a unity in purpose. Once more, the Christian message addresses this philosophical question. Let me explain further.

The Coalescence of Worship

One of the great longings of the human heart is to worship; yet, within that very disposition there are tugs in many directions that clearly contradict the essence of worship. This fragmentation, which tends to break up the unity, is felt in every life. But there is a further complication. The idea of worship itself is not monolithic, or uniform, when you get a glimpse of the different kinds of worship in which people engage.

The thirst for worship or for the sacred across cultures and across time is ineradicable among the educated and the uneducated, the young and the old. During my days as a student at the University of New Delhi, I well remember students seated all around me with colored ash smeared on their foreheads, having visited the temple on their way to school. All over the world, churches, temples, mosques, and tabernacles abound. Sacred books still line the shelves of seekers after truth—the Gita, the Koran, the Grant Sahib, the Tri-Pitakas, the Bible, and more. Religious ceremonies are performed and prayers are invoked in life's most significant moments. Even a cursory look at the record of human history reveals a fervent pursuit of things spiritual.

Jesus was very much aware of this bent within the human spirit. That is why He said worship ought not to be only in spirit, but also in *truth*. Unguarded by truth there is no limit to the depth of superstition and deception into which the human mind can descend, albeit in the name of religion. Worship alone cannot justify itself; it needs the constraints of truth, and that truth is in the person and character of God. As an individual makes that commitment to God, not only is his or her life unified for God's glory, but also the moral and definitive impetus is given for all other pursuits and relationships.

In other words, worship must not only be deliberate; it must also be defined. Worship has been defined by God as something that must be directed to Him alone; it is not to be reduced to mere ceremony. In creating us, God created us to worship, and no degree of academic progress will ever replace that need.

I believe worship is important because it brings each life into cohesiveness within itself and into harmony with others in community. The famed Archbishop William Temple defined worship in these terms:

> Worship is the submission of all of our nature to God. It is the quickening of conscience by His holiness, nourishment of mind by His truth, purifying of imagination by His beauty, opening of the heart to His love, and submission of will to His purpose. All this gathered up in adoration is the greatest of all expressions of which we are capable.[2]

A careful examination of every phrase here is worthy of our attention. We humans are not a collection of isolated and unrelated senses. Putting it differently, when we give vent to contradicting impulses, the internal alienation that results is deep and destructive. In all of the situations life offers, the individual must have a commitment with a unified vision to a singular goal. When that is not the case, discord and estrangement await at every turn. Worship that is true and spiritual coalesces conscience, mind, imagination, heart, and will in one direction, creating a tapestry that bespeaks beauty and a life that is in harmony with ultimate good. Worship permeates every aspect of life, bringing unity to diversity within an individual life. That unity within expresses itself in all of life's pursuits and provides meaning for life itself, else there would be only diversity that could be a euphemism for contradiction.

Track and Altar

Once unity is procured within, it affects every aspect of life. A great illustration of the all-encompassing impetus of true worship comes to us from the film *Chariots of Fire,* which featured the lives of two determined runners in the 1924 Olympics in France. Each ran with equal passion but with diametrically different goals. Harold Abrahams ran for personal glory, personal recognition, and "a will to power." Eric Liddell, the Scotsman, ran out of his Christian commitment to excellence for God's sake.

Earlier in the story, Abrahams and a friend shared their thoughts on the theme of winning and losing, and the friend asked Abrahams how he handled losing. "I don't know," Abrahams said. "I've never lost." That told the story of a man confident and possessed with a passion to win. Nothing else mattered but being number one. Now, moments before his Olympic run for which Abrahams had spent years training, the moment of truth was upon him, and as he converses with his friend, Abrahams makes the most perceptive confession of all. "You know, I used to be afraid to lose. But now I am afraid to win. I have ten seconds in which to prove the reason for my existence, and even then, I am not sure I will." The words reveal extraordinary insight, for that is how most personal glory is sought but when procured, leaves the possessor empty.

By contrast, at one point in the film Eric Liddell is reprimanded by his sister for trying too hard in his effort to win the gold medal, thus neglecting things of greater importance. His answer to her reveals the profound connection of all of life's pursuits for him. He says, "Jenny, God has made me for a purpose—for China. But He has also made me fast. And when I run, I feel His pleasure."

If we can understand the difference between these two admissions, I am confident it will open up the two different worlds. The world of personal glory moves from triumph to emptiness because it can never deliver fulfillment of the spirit. It only sets a greater goal for the next time. In spite of the pathetic reports of drug addiction and artificially induced escapes among those who have experienced that personal glory, we in the West refuse to admit that the sheer winning of accolades cannot deliver what we say it will. There are, in fact, even biological factors that give us a powerful clue to the downside of our thrill-addicted lifestyle. Medical studies reveal that during physical or emotional exhilaration the body artificially generates adrenaline-like chemicals that are more potent than morphine and that generate a "high," or a euphoria, not felt when the body returns to the normal state. When life does return to normalcy, the absence of a high, or the downward swing, by contrast, is of depressive proportions. As a result, the individual who lives in the fast lane soon finds normal life unmanageable, necessitating an altered state of consciousness. Modern-day high-energy entertainers will do well to take note of this.

And so it was that Abrahams walked away amid thundering applause after winning the gold medal in the one hundred meters—but with a silence of despondency within. The downward tug was already underway. This perspective is not intended in any way to diminish the thrill of victory; it is only to say that all these accomplishments notwithstanding, a life can still remain fragmented and unmanaged, and victories can remain anticlimactic.

By contrast, Eric Liddell ran the four hundred meters and won. But more than that, he packed his bags and went on to China as a missionary to a cause greater than himself—the gold medal was put in its place, and his heart was completely at peace.

Crossing Boundaries

The unity in diversity brought by Christian worship takes us a step further. That is a difficult step because it deals with the demands of living in a community. How does the sacredness within translate to a diversity without? All around us we hear injunctions for behavior, such as "community standards," that are utterly senseless if taken at face value. We think that by coining such nomenclature we have solved the ubiquitous dilemma of right and wrong. The problem is that none of us lives in only one community, to say nothing of the ever-fluctuating standards of that one community. From the time I wake up until the time I go to bed, I have crossed several community lines. How does one make personal choices when the standards constantly change within and across communities? It is only the commitment of worship that brings undergirding unity to the diversity of life's inescapable challenges. Life cannot be sensibly lived, wafted by the winds of community changes.

Jesus Christ clearly pointed out that worship is coextensive with life. A follower of Christ does not go to a temple on the Lord's day as much as he takes the temple with him. The body is the temple. Victor Hugo said, "The world was made for the body, the body for the soul, and the soul made for God." The Trappist monk Thomas Merton put it differently: "Man is not at peace with his fellow man because he is not at peace with himself. He is not at peace with himself because he is not at peace with God."

Worship alone brings that peace, that unity in diversity. The application is clear. Your game on the tennis court, your role in a play, your giftedness in the arts, your brilliance in your studies, your relationship with your family, the exhilaration of success—all can be expressions of your worship when undergirded as you live your life with God. That coalescence is what Jesus drew attention to when He said, "True worshippers shall worship the Father in spirit and in truth: for the Father seeketh such to worship him" (John 4:23 KJV) and Paul said, "Whatsoever ye do, do all to the glory of God" (1 Cor. 10:31 KJV).

This concept of worship, by the way, is drastically different from Islam or any of the pantheistic worldviews such as Hinduism and Buddhism.

As a postscript, I would like to add that atheistic evolution is the most bankrupt of all worldviews in providing an answer for unity in diversity. An antitheist will ever be at the mercy of a thrill-addicted lifestyle, and as he constantly lives across community lines he becomes more akin to a chameleon, changing himself to blend in with the surroundings.

To sum up, worship provides the unity within for life's diversities. It provides the moral impetus in every level of relationship and across all lines. It is coextensive with life and gives to life the spiritual undergirding that is necessary for ultimate fulfillment. It bridges the diversities of our cultures by providing dignity to each individual and truth to the practice of worship and conduct. The pattern for this unity in diversity is the Trinity. Without any doubt, the search of philosophy and religion for the answer to unity in diversity is satisfied here by Christ.

15

The Historian's Centerpiece

W E COME NOW to the third consideration that is distinctive in Jesus' teaching. We have seen a glimpse of His teaching on the nature of man and on the nature of reality; now we come to the nature of history.

Listen carefully to the great contrasts that abound on this matter. The basic impetus for life in the existential worldview is to live with a passion for the now, to make a choice in the face of despair. Truth is subjectivity. Existence precedes essence. What you do determines who you are. Finding yourself hurled into existence, take life by the throat and authenticate yourself. Now! Passionately! Engage the present!

The utopianist or futurist, on the other hand, lives for the future. The word *utopia* was coined by the "Renaissance man," Sir Thomas More, that man for all seasons. In its historical drift, Marxist philosophy looks to the future, that utopia where there is no lion of an employer and no lamb of an employee—where all are equal.

The traditionalist, in distinction to both, lives for the past. The Hebrew mind-set was clearly traditionalistic. The play *Fiddler on the Roof* humorously resonates this propensity with the solo appearance of Tevye on stage at the play's beginning to monologue a description of his unsettled existence. The only way for his family to cope with the strains and demands of their mortal existence was to find a point of reference that would bring harmony and balance. It was only in "tradition" that they found such an anchor. Without that tradition, life would be as tenuous as a fiddler on the roof.

So there you have it. The existentialist lives for the now; the utopianist, for the future; and the traditionalist, for the past.

Hours before his death, Jesus saw these worlds in collision on the faces of His disciples. They had lived by their traditions; they had great hopes in Him for the future. But it was all beginning to fall apart in the now, and they would soon be looking back at the cross as having shattered all their utopian dreams. Jesus "broke bread," gave it to them, and said, "As often as you eat of this bread and drink of this cup [now] you proclaim the Lord's death [in the past] until he comes [in the future]" (see 1 Cor. 11:26). He fused all of history with meaning. There was a trans-temporal significance in the incarnation of Christ.

Again, this was and is clearly distinct from the other religions and secular worldviews. The gospel message speaks against the temptation to politicize religion or to try to usher in a future utopia by the sword. The gospel message does not render the past irrelevant. The gospel message delivers one from being overwhelmed by the present.

For the Christian, there is a critical engagement with all of history that permeates the Scriptures. It is for this reason that the prophetic writers were so involved in interpreting the times. Hundreds of years before the birth of Christ, they prophesied the manner and the place of His birth. Further, they talked not only of proximate history as it would unfold but also of the distant future.

One of the great prophecies, written more than five hundred years before Christ, comes to us from the book of Daniel. Daniel spoke prophetically of a dominant ruler who was yet to come, whose military ambition would be to conquer the world. His emergence upon the historical landscape and his departure would be equally sudden. Daniel said that after his demise his kingdom would be divided into four. These four would later converge into two and ultimately merge into one. So specific is this prophecy of Daniel's that liberal critics for years were terribly troubled by its exactness.

When you study the life of Alexander the Great you clearly see him, two centuries after Daniel, fitting that prophetic fulfillment. His life was cut short suddenly, and after he died his kingdom was divided into four. Those four, in turn, coalesced into the Ptolemaic and Seleucid empires; they later merged into a single power, the Roman Empire. Such specific prophecy is very hard to just dismiss with a shrug as merely coincidental, although it could be, if taken in isolation. However, add to this one prophecy the hundreds of other prophecies, and study this phenomenon along with the philosophical and historical aspects of the Christian faith, and you are presented with a compelling apologetic without equal.

The Scripture writers went beyond their immediate future. They expostulated in detail on distant history. They spoke of the "latter days" when there would be wars and rumors of wars, and catastrophic events would proliferate. They described warfare when the very elements would melt with fervent heat. This kind of imagery was very foreign to the crude military capability of two millennia ago. All of these prophecies ultimately led to the focus of Christ as the centerpiece of history.

Eight hundred years before the event, the prophet Isaiah said of Christ's birth, "For to us a child is born, to us a son is given" (Isa. 9:6). This carries emotionally tender terminology, but again it is stated with exactitude. The Child is born, not the Son. The Son is given. The Son eternally existed, the Child was born—the incarnation is vivid.

Let me put this in even sharper context because we must understand how seriously the prophetic office was taken and tested. The book of Deuteronomy tells us that if a single prophecy did not come true, its prophet was not God-appointed and, therefore, he should be shunned. The prophetic office was not the frivolous pursuit of some eccentric individuals in the midst of a gullible, unthinking people.

Amid all the specific foretelling, think of this surprising answer from Jesus that works as a silent apologetic from the converse side of prophecy. When asked when He would return, Jesus said, "No one knows about that day or hour, not even the angels in heaven, nor the Son, but only the Father" (Matt. 24:36). That does not sound like some power-hungry pragmatist who could have easily prognosticated some distant date when He would not have been present to face the embarrassment. In His willing submission even unto death, self-aggrandizement would have been a natural temptation. But He never yielded.

The Bible is replete with evidence of the supernatural elements that were testable, and also of God's pervading involvement with history past, present, and future. (By the way, let me interject that Islam does not lend itself to such empirical testing in history. As has already been stated, Mohammed's only miracle, Muslims dogmatically assert, was the Koran—nothing else was needed. And that miracle, I repeat, according to Islamic teaching, can only be understood and appreciated by sophisticates in the Arabic language.)

According to Christ's teaching, history is not just one event after another. Not only the present moment, nor only the past, nor only the future, but all of time is important to God. That is why the genuine Christian does not take it upon himself or herself to avenge the past. That is why the genuine Christian does not make this earthly kingdom into God's kingdom by way of the sword. That is why the genuine Christian transcends present disaster or immediate success. For him or for her, history is the arena in which God unfolds His plan and the individual is the microcosm in whom God does His work.

I suggest that if you contrast this with every other worldview, you will see the striking difference in Christianity. What reassurance this brings to every individual life—yours and mine—to know that God is involved with us personally! The ultimate coherence that God brings is not only in the history that we see within our threescore and ten years, but for life beyond the grave itself. It is to that which we now turn.

The Individual's Longing

Albert Camus once said that death was philosophy's only problem, and anyone who has watched a loved one die understands that philosophical problem well. I point to the answer of Jesus Christ as He responds to death and relates that to the nature of our destiny. We have looked briefly at Him as the answer to humanity's struggle, to the philosopher's quest, and as the historian's centerpiece. Now we come to see Him as the answer to the individual's longing.

The apostle Paul, who became a leading voice in early church history, said unequivocally, "If . . . Christ has not been raised. . . . [And] if only for this life we have hope in Christ, we are to be pitied more than all men" (1 Cor. 15:17, 19). Paul was not a pushover for any newfangled romantic notion. He was not one of those who ignored allegiances or veracity. He was willing to put his life on the line for what he believed, and he committed himself to the eradication of what he then considered the "myth" of the gospel. His Damascus Road encounter is now proverbial, signifying a radical change. Again, the easy way out for cynics and skeptics is to make a sweeping generalization and, with the wave of a hand, dismiss the historical facts. But to this very day, on Mars Hill in Athens stands the message etched in stone that Paul delivered before a crowd whose philosophical bent was equally proverbial. The message Paul brought was literally and figuratively a message of life and death. In the world of academia and commerce it is very popular to ignore such issues, but that may belie the hypocrisy more of that world than it does the world of day-to-day living and dying.

In the West, when responding to death we hold two postures. Our public decorum is distinct from our private pain. No culture on earth does more to dress up death while at the same time reducing it to a "ho-hum" reality in the workplace. However, our hypocritical indifference to death is turned to unbridled rage if the dead or the dying are in any way seen as victims of some imperialist power at whose door the blame can be laid.

This "What shall we do with death?" question is not only the private concern of the religious; it has drawn attention in the strangest of settings and pleads for a response. During one of Alfred North Whitehead's seminars at Harvard a student interrupted Whitehead and asked, "What has all this to do with death?" The student could well have been representing Heidegger or Nietzsche or Sartre or Camus or Kierkegaard or Jaspers. The concern with death's inescapability prompted not only their discussions, but sometimes the very title of their writings. While Kierkegaard and Camus, among others, stated the concern boldly, Heidegger's book bore the lifeless title of *The Possible Being—Whole of Being—There and Being—Toward—Death*. (I shall refrain from responding to Heidegger on the subject for obvious reasons!)

It was Freud who most pointedly, even humorously, portrayed our schizophrenia; he described how war has changed the way we viewed death.

[War has disturbed] our previous relation to death. This relation was not sincere. If one listened to us, we were, of course, ready to declare that death is the necessary end of all life, that every one of us owed nature his own death and must be prepared to pay this debt—in short, that death is natural, undeniable, and unavoidable. In reality, however, we used to behave as if it were different. We have shown the unmistakable tendency to push death aside, to eliminate it from life. We have tried to keep a deadly silence about death: after all, we even have a proverb to the effect that one thinks about something as one thinks about death. One's own, of course. After all, one's own death is beyond imagining, and whenever we try to imagine it we can see that we really survive as spectators. Thus the dictum could be dared in the psychoanalytic school: at bottom nobody believes in his own death. Or, and this is the same in his unconscious, every one of us is convinced of his immortality. As for the death of others, a cultured man will carefully avoid speaking of this possibility if the person fated to die can hear him. Only children ignore this rule. . . . We regularly emphasize the accidental cause of death, the mishap, the disease, the infection, the advanced age, and thus betray our eagerness to demote death from a necessity to a mere accident. Toward the deceased himself we behave in a special way, almost as if we were full of admiration for someone who has accomplished something very difficult. We suspend criticism of him, forgive him any injustice, pronounce the motto, *de mortuis nil nisi bene,* and consider it justified that in the funeral sermon and on the gravestone the most advantageous things are said about him. Consideration for the dead, who no longer needs it, we place higher than truth—and most of us certainly also higher than consideration for the living.[1]

Freud is correct in unveiling the forked-tongue approach we take at such moments in life. Academic and technological advancement have only increased this double-dealing. The truisms pronounced in reverential tones belie the mind's contempt for such beliefs. In wedding ceremonies, the clergyman pronounces the daring words, "If anyone has a good reason why these two should not be joined together . . ." with such confident tones, never waiting for any response—as if to convey that an objection is not possible. I have often wondered what would happen at funerals if a similar challenge were presented. Imagine the shock upon hearing the eulogist say, "If anyone disagrees with the description herein given of the deceased or challenges the destiny to which we have committed our trust . . . " And imagine further what would happen should a hand go up in the chapel!

"What has this got to do with death?" may not have been an appropriate question during Whitehead's lecture, but there is every reason to raise that question in reference to Jesus Christ. His claim to be the way, the truth, and the life is no small claim; and since death has much to do with life, His answer to death—His resurrection—provides the key to life itself.

Hope and Its Reason

There really are two questions that have relevance on this matter of Jesus' resurrection. The first is, "Did Jesus, indeed, rise from the dead?" The second is the equally emphatic: "So what?"

In terms of the first, no event in history has been so subjected to scrutiny and analysis as this claim of Jesus. This focus alone is an indicator of the importance of the event. So many ingenious ways have been concocted to falsify this cardinal truth of the Christian faith—from the swoon theory to the disciples' self-delusion—that it almost brings humor into the situation. I have often been amazed at the lengths to which scholars have been willing to go in an attempt to debunk the resurrection while scores of other religious figures (such as Krishna, Buddha, or Mohammed) have been left totally unstudied. An average student in India, for example, does not even know when Krishna was born or if indeed he ever was. At the same time, he or she has theorized about Jesus quite a bit.

This is a strange and ironic phenomenon, for even today while religious conversation in the workplace is being vociferously discouraged, the name of Jesus is still probably mentioned more than any other name—to be sure with profane exclamation, but nevertheless He is mentioned. In fact, our very calendar is positioned by the birth of Jesus. Of all His claims, His promise of His resurrection and its fulfillment was understandably the most controversial, but it was the ultimate justification of His message.

The issue of the resurrection naturally evokes interest. Did it really happen? May I suggest for your careful reading the debate on this subject that most thoroughly examines the evidence. The protagonist was historian Gary Habermas and the antagonist, Anthony Flew. The arguments and evidences marshaled by Professor Habermas left Flew on the run for most of the debate. The fundamental problem for the resurrection that Flew presented was really the same one that has been set forth by Rudolf Bultmann, one of the most influential critical theologians of this century—and a leading exponent in "demythologizing" the Scriptures. Bultmann rejected the resurrection *a priori*—just as his personal assumption. To his obviously prejudicial disposing of this historical event, Professor Jon MacQuarrie said:

> And here we must take Bultmann to task for what appears to be an entirely arbitrary dismissal of the possibility of understanding the resurrection as an objective-historical event. . . . The fallacy of such reasoning is obvious. The one valid way in which we can ascertain whether a certain event took place or not is not by bringing in some

sweeping assumption to show that it could not have taken place, but to consider the historical evidence available, and decide on that.[2]

MacQuarrie goes on to say that "Bultmann does not take the trouble to examine what evidence could be addressed to show that the resurrection was an objective-historical event. He assumes that it is a myth."[3]

In effect, the facts are unblushingly ignored. This is the precise prejudice with which much of liberal scholarship has treated the resurrection. In real terms, the New Testament is easily the best attested ancient writing in terms of the sheer number of documents, the time span between the event and the document, and the variety of documents available to sustain or contradict it. There is nothing in ancient manuscript evidence to match such textual availability and integrity. As the noted scholar Giza Vermes has said, "It should not be beyond the capabilities of an educated man to sit down and with a mind empty of prejudice read the account of Mark, Matthew, and Luke as though for the first time."[4]

When an honest reader looks at the affirmations that are made and the substantiations that are provided, the following deductions ensue:

1. Jesus Christ Himself talked of His resurrection on repeated occasions. Both His enemies and His followers were told to expect it. Those who sought to smother His teaching took elaborate steps to counter the possibility of His claim, including the placement of a Roman guard at the door to the tomb.

2. Although His supporters basically understood His promise to rise from the dead and had even witnessed His raising of Lazarus, they did not really believe that He meant it literally until after the fact. Therefore, they could not be accused of creating the scenario for this deception.

3. It was the postresurrection appearance that made the ultimate difference to the skeptical mind of Thomas and the resistant will of Paul.

4. The transformation of the disciples from a terrified bunch of individuals who felt themselves betrayed into a fearless group ready to proclaim the message to Rome and to the rest of the world cannot be explained with a mere shrug of the shoulder.

5. Had the Roman authorities wanted to eradicate Jesus' teaching once and for all, they would have only needed to present His dead body—but they could not. There is something often missed here. If the disciples were fabricators of an ideal, they could have merely posited a spiritual resurrection, which could have been done even with the presence of a dead body. Instead, they went the hard way, by talking of the resurrection of the actual physical body, which, if not true, was an enormous risk to take should the body have ever been detected. No, they believed in a literal resurrection because they had witnessed it. This is a very telling piece of evidence in light of the fact that Rome, itself, once diametrically opposed to the gospel, was later won over to Jesus' message. The religious leaders wanted nothing more than they wanted to stifle Christianity. And in fact, Jesus' own brother James was not a believer until after the resurrection.

6. One other very interesting factor to bring to our attention is from non-Christian sources. Even the Koran, which is hardly in favor of the Christian message, attests to Jesus' virgin birth and credits Him with the unique power to raise the dead, a most interesting notation often forgotten by the Muslims themselves.

In summary, it was Jesus' victory over the grave that provided the grand impetus for the early church to tell the world that God had spoken and, indeed, had done so in a dramatic and incontrovertible manner. All this transpired in history and is open to the historian's scrutiny.

The Illusion of Neutrality

But that brings us to the second question: "So what?" The reason for this question is not hard to understand. The resurrection by itself may not be self-explicating. It could be argued a few other ways that this "just happened," so why not treat it, then, as an aberration? But the resurrection of Jesus is not an isolated or vacuous event. It comes on the heels of a series of other events and teachings that have to be taken as a whole. Devoid of a context, the resurrection can be ignored, but positioned as it is with the birth, life, and death of one so unique, so without peer, so exclusive in His claims and instruction on life's nature and destiny, it would be foolhardy to dismiss the resurrection with "So what?" Robert Browning captured the choice we face very well.

> If Christ, as thou affirmest, be of men
> Mere man, the first and best but nothing more—
> Account Him, for reward of what He was
> Now and for ever, wretchedest of all.
> For see: Himself conceived of life as love,
> Conceived of love as what must enter in,
> Fill up, make one with His each soul He loved.
>
> See if, for every finger of thy hands
> There be not found, that day the world shall end,
> Hundreds of souls, each holding by Christ's word
> That He will grow incorporate with all,
> Groom for each bride. Can a mere man do this?
> Yet Christ saith, this He lived and died to do.
> Call Christ, then, the illimitable God,
> Or lost![5]

Christ—He is either the illimitable God or one dreadfully lost. There is no room for a theory that says He was "merely a good man." Study His life with unyielding honesty and the answer is evident. It is this hope He brings that grants us hope for each individual, for our communities, and for our world. Without this hope of life beyond the grave, every question from love to justice becomes a mockery of the mind.

Billy Graham on one occasion told of a meeting he had with German Chancellor Konrad Adenauer, at one time mayor of Cologne, imprisoned by Hitler for his opposition to the Nazi regime, and later chancellor of the West German Federal Republic from 1949 to 1963. Adenauer truly deserves the title of "statesman" as he picked up the broken pieces of his country and helped to rebuild it in a fractured world. On this occasion, he looked the evangelist in the eye and said, "Mr. Graham, do you believe in the resurrection of Jesus Christ from the dead?" Graham, somewhat surprised by the pointedness of the question answered, "Of course I do." To that confident reply Chancellor Adenauer said, "Mr. Graham, outside of the resurrection of Jesus, I do not know of any other hope for this world."

I have found this same sentiment echoed in two of the nations of our world that have experienced drastic transition. I refer to an occasion when I had been invited to deliver a series of lectures at the Lenin Military Academy and to participate in a round-table discussion at the Center for Geopolitical Strategy in Moscow. Present at the discussion were my wife, a colleague, and myself, and six Russian generals—all but one, atheists. The one-and-a-half-hour interaction we had was a momentous occasion in my own life. As we entered this imposing building, eight stories above the ground and four stories below, I was aware that I was in a historic setting; for out of this grand structure had been graduated all of the previous general secretaries of the USSR. In the welcoming hall, we were introduced to the great heroes of Russian warfare—Peter the Great and Kutusov as well as modern-day geniuses in geopolitical maneuvering. Every facet of the building was pompous and stately, intended not accidentally I am sure, to make the individual feel small and insignificant.

Here, in its inner chambers, our discussion began. As the conversation unfolded from early unease through robust argumentation all the way to our very warm and amiable conclusion, something incredible happened. One by one, each of these generals conceded that Russia was now in a pathetic state, not just economically but morally. As the men stood up to bid us good-bye, the senior-ranking general grasped my hand and said, "Dr. Zacharias, I believe what you have brought us is the truth. But it is so hard to change after seventy years of believing a lie." Outside of God, they, too, saw no other hope.

That same sentiment was again echoed by some of the framers of the Peace Accord after I finished a series of talks in Johannesburg, South Africa.

As I reflect on that, the leaders' confession and the words of the Russian general are haunting. *After seventy years of believing a lie, it is hard to change.* We stand at a moment in history where once-Marxist nations admit to a dastardly experiment that has failed, an experiment that demonstrates beyond any doubt the dire consequences that are reaped when God is eliminated from the framework of life's choices. Yet strangely enough, we in the West are now moving toward that same ideological base, unwilling to believe what stares us in the face. In Russia, in the name of equality, the individual was offered at the altar of the state. Here, in the name of humanism, human beings are steadily being denuded and offered up at the altar of economic and hedonistic gains. What a contrast this is to the value Christ places upon each individual life, when every facet of life and its context is given significance.

Many years ago, while he was a professor of philosophy at Princeton, the German scholar and distinguished Harvard graduate Walter Kaufmann wrote a book, *The Faith of a Heretic.* It was the American equivalent of Bishop John A. T. Robinson's book, *Honest to God.* As Kaufmann brought his book to a climax, he said this:

> That there are about a hundred million galaxies within range of our telescopes, and that our own galaxy alone contains hundreds of thousands of planets which may well support life and beings like ourselves seems strange to those brought up on the Bible, but not necessarily strange to Oriental believers.
>
> For those not familiar with the sacred books of the East, the contrast may come to life as they compare Renaissance and Chinese paintings: here [in the Renaissance] the human figures dominate the picture, and the landscape serves as a background; there [in the Chinese paintings] the landscape is the picture, and the human beings in it have to be sought out. Here man seems all-important; there his cosmic insignificance is beautifully represented.
>
> Modern science suggests that in important respects the Oriental religions were probably closer to the facts than the Old Testament or the New. It does not follow that we ought to accept the Buddha's counsel of resignation and detachment, falling out of love with the world. Nor need we emulate Lao-tze's wonderful whimsy and his wise mockery of reason, culture, and human effort. There are many possibilities: I say with Shakespeare, "All the world's a stage." Man seems to play a very insignificant part in the universe, and my part is negligible. The question confronting me is not, except perhaps in idle moments, what part might be more amusing, but what I wish to make of my part. And what I want to do and would advise others to do is to make the most of it: put into it all you have got, and live, and, if possible, die with some measure of nobility.[6]

I beg to differ with this fine scholar, but I have to wonder whether he has understood either Christianity or the Eastern religions; for that matter, his equivocation of the Christian message as synonymous with the Renaissance is at best tendentious, if not pathetic, for it is humanism that is built on the Renaissance, not Christianity. But his farcical conclusion of "make the best of it" is most betrayed by his words extolling the oriental genius, "[Man's] cosmic insignificance is beautifully represented." This is equivalent to our bloodletting and hate-filled films' issuing the all-comforting disclaimer at the end, "No animals were harmed in the making of this film." Nothing is said about any harm that may have been done to the people during the making of the film or to the innocent public who viewed it. But Kaufmann can be forgiven for this oxymoronic conclusion. He defined philosophy in his first line of the book as "a chaos of abstruse ideas"!

To tell us to die with nobility when there is no hope beyond the grave is farcical at best. All of Kaufmann's philosophizing on this matter is an attempt to smother that irrepressible longing, the longing for life beyond the grave, which, in his scheme of things, is neither explained nor satisfied. Contrast this with the fact of Christ's resurrection, which both justifies this longing and satisfies with fulfillment. In reality, when one denies the possibility of life beyond the grave—when one tries to live without God—the greatest problem for the skeptic still remains, the problem of life's suffering. It is to answer that question now in a broader context that I turn to Jesus' teaching on the nature of suffering.

16

The Believer's Treasure

THE WRITERS OF SCRIPTURE do not avoid the problem of suffering. They deal most profoundly with life's deepest hurts—with pain, starvation, death, bereavement, crime, exploitation, prejudice, hopelessness, etc. This problem of suffering, as I have said, is a problem all philosophies need to deal with.

Recently *Forbes* magazine invited several scholars from around the world to contribute to its seventy-fifth anniversary issue, addressing, of all themes, the question "Why are we so unhappy?" These scholars, including writer Saul Bellow, historian Paul Johnson, and others of international renown, approached the topic from their own various backgrounds and perspectives. In a memorable collection of articles from so diverse a group, they all agreed on one point; we are a troubled civilization because of the loss of a moral and spiritual center.

Perhaps that is why the issue of pain and suffering is even more of an enigma in our time (considering the gains that medicine and medical technology have made to minimize physical hurts) than ever before in history. Our pain is aggravated by the naive hope that all of our problems can somehow be solved by progress in the field of scientific advancement.

I recall attending, some years ago, a heavily advertised lecture delivered by Stephen Hawking at Cambridge University. I had eagerly awaited that afternoon for the opportunity to hear him address the announced subject: "Is man determined or free?" A theme with which the antitheistic pen has struggled, the subject is of great significance because the behavioral sciences can deduce any bizarre theory if the pure sciences posit a theory of our origins from matter alone. Hawking, as a scientist, needed to address the implications of determinism.

Is man determined by the random and mindless processes of time, matter, and chance in interplay, or is there a transcendence to which man can rise above the fatalism that would seem inescapable on humanistic grounds? The best of minds have tackled this question, and the stranglehold of determinism seems to get tighter for a life lived without God.

When Stephen Hawking speaks, scientists and philosophers listen. Severely impaired by Lou Gehrig's disease, Hawking spoke through a speech synthesizer (in an American accent, I might add, because the technology was developed in the United States). Developing his carefully measured argument, he contrasted the philosophical struggle with determinism or free will. Finally yielding to science as the consummate discipline, in the closing moments of his talk he presented his conclusion: "Is man determined? Yes! But since we do not know what is determined, he may as well not be." There was pin-drop silence. No one moved or whispered. The audience clearly felt let down, for no one was left any wiser than before Hawking had spoken. Then Hawking added this troubling postscript. He said he feared that since the evolutionary process had worked through the dialectic of determinism and aggression, our long-term survival and any hope for our species was in question. "However," he added, "if we can keep from destroying each other for the next one hundred years, sufficient technology will have been developed to distribute humanity to various planets, and then no one tragedy or atrocity will eradicate us all at the same time."

Hawking was unavoidably caught on the horns of a dilemma. On the one hand, if there is no God he could feel with full force the inexorable hold of determinism from which evolutionary theory could not escape—out of flux, nothing but flux. What followed from that deduction was even more troubling, for on the other hand, if evolution held true he could not further ignore the aggression and violence through which man has evolved. In Tennysonian terms, nature was "red in tooth and claw." Therefore, Hawking offered that mankind's only hope in his violent, evolutionary process was in the machines we could invent that would help stave off the atrocities of his fellow man. The savior of technology would come riding on the wings of science to rescue us from the clasping teeth of determinism. In short, the antitheist's answer to pain is technology.

I shuddered at the hollowness of our man-made solutions and could not help but remember C. S. Lewis's comment that technology and magic had something in common with, while separating them from, the wisdom of the ancients. To the ancient, the question was, "How do I conform the soul to reality?" The answer was, "by virtue and discipline." To the modern, the question is, "How can I reconfigure reality to accommodate my passions?" And the answer is, "by technique or technology." This is still our undying hope. Whether old or new, myths die hard.

At the Crossroads

There is something very emotionally transforming about the process of growing older. The more we see the unconscionable ends to which the human spirit can descend when it is determined to remain autonomous, the more our confidence in human methods diminishes. Into this kind of self-centered, earthly kingdom, Jesus brought a different and dramatic—albeit radical—response to pain and suffering. His answer was a stumbling block then, and it is a stumbling block now. But only if it is properly and seriously understood can its beauty be seen amid its obvious pain and hatred. I refer to the cross of Christ. The cross stands as a mystery because it is foreign to everything we exalt—self over principle, power over meekness, the quick fix over the long haul, cover-up over confession, escapism over confrontation, comfort over sacrifice, feeling over commitment, legality over justice, the body over the spirit, anger over forgiveness, man over God.

In his book *The Kingdom of God in America*, Reinhold Niebuhr said, "We want a God without wrath who took man without sin into a kingdom without justice through the ministrations of a Christ without a cross." In keeping with this sentiment, I quote Malcolm Muggeridge's words penned in the waning years of his life:

> Contrary to what might be expected, I look back on experiences that at that time seemed especially desolating and painful. I now look back upon them with particular satisfaction. Indeed, I can say with complete truthfulness that everything I have learned in my seventy-five years in this world, everything that has truly enhanced and enlightened my existence has been through affliction and not through happiness whether pursued or attained. In other words, I say this, if it were to be possible to eliminate affliction from our

earthly existence by means of some drug or other medical mumbo-
jumbo, the result would not be to make life delectable, but to make
it too banal and trivial to be endurable. This, of course, is what the
cross signifies and it is the cross, more than anything else, that has
called me inexorably to Christ.[1]

"The cross more than anything else." Why would a septuagenarian,
a one-time cynic, even utter such words when his life was ebbing to its
close? I believe it is because in the cross alone, pain and evil meet in consummate conflict. In the cross alone are integrated love and justice, the
twin foundations upon which we may build our moral and spiritual
home, individually and nationally. It is theoretically and practically impossible to build any community apart from love and justice. If only one
of these two is focused upon, an inevitable extremism and perversion
follow. Throughout history, mankind has shouted its ideals of liberty,
equality, and justice; yet the ideologies that have risen, supposedly in the
pursuit of human progress, have left in their wake some very dastardly
experiments that echo with the whimpering sounds of man, like a trapped
animal. Rising above the cry of liberty, equality, and justice is the more
rending plea for that sense of belonging we call love. And love unbounded
by any sense of right or wrong is not love but self-centeredness and au-
tocracy. In the cross of Jesus Christ, the demands of the law were satisfied,
and the generosity of love was expressed.

Let me briefly summarize the three great answers the cross brings to
the problem of suffering.

First, I see in the cross the expression of my own heart, for it was the
heart's rebellion against God and the will's disposition that vented its fury
upon the One who was and is the gospel. The cross symbolizes the anger
of man hurled toward the good, even toward God Himself. There is no
limit to how far any one of us can go when rebellion reigns unchecked,
as documented by historian Christopher Browning in his book on the
Holocaust, hauntingly titled *Ordinary Men*. Responding to the book, one
critic said, "The most frightening aspect of Christopher Browning's essential book is the knowledge it conveys to us that it was not a few brutes,
but many good and ordinary men, who committed murder for Hitler."[2]

But lest we think of wrong merely in quantitative terms, let me underscore a caution. During the Nuremberg trials of the Nazi judges who took

part in the Holocaust, the only judge willing to accept some responsibility for his role in the death camps tried to mitigate his guilt by saying, "I never intended it to go so far." To that exculpatory qualifier, one of the members of the tribunal pointedly responded, "The first time you knowingly condemned an innocent person you went too far." It was not the volume of sin that sent Christ to the cross; it was the fact of sin.

The human condition at birth places each one of us on a slippery slope, and nothing can stop our downward slide to absolute autonomy. In the cross, I see the ultimate rebellion—the shame and the pain of the human will when it brutally rejects even our Creator—the City of Man operating against the City of God. The irony of that brutality is that it was spearheaded by the religious leaders. Power is insidious when it is unanchored by goodness.

Second, in the cross of Jesus Christ, I see the marvel of forgiveness as a starting point for rebuilding one's own life. This is a simple truth, yet again unique to the Christian faith. Hear the words of an elementary schoolteacher:

> He came to my desk with a quivering lip,
>   the lesson was done.
> "Have you a new sheet for me, dear teacher?
>   I've spoiled this one."
> I took his sheet, all soiled and blotted
>   and gave him a new one all unspotted.
> And into his tired heart I cried,
>   "Do better now, my child."
>
> I went to the throne with a trembling heart,
>   the day was done.
> "Have you a new day for me, dear Master?
>   I've spoiled this one."
> He took my day, all soiled and blotted
>   and gave me a new one all unspotted.
> And into my tired heart he cried,
>   "Do better now, my child."[3]

If you would like to put forgiveness in perspective, look at the logic of unforgiveness, to which Bosnia provides a most graphic example. The wholesale slaughter of people in Bosnia and Rwanda is a bloody reminder of human vengeance and of life without the cross. The cross does not minimize evil; rather, it shows evil at its ugliest, even while offering a new beginning in the most profound sense of the term. But the grace of forgiveness, because God Himself has paid the price, is a Christian distinctive and stands splendidly against our hate-filled, unforgiving world. God's forgiveness gives us a fresh start.

Finally, the cross sounds forth the message that God is not distant from pain and suffering; He has done something about it. Not only has He done something about evil, He transformed that evil in the cross to counter it with good and to define the solution to evil. James Stewart of Scotland states this so succinctly, based on the biblical phrase describing Jesus' triumph in the words of the apostle Paul, quoting from Psalm 68:18, "He led captivity captive."

> It is a glorious phrase—"He led captivity captive." The very triumphs of His foes, it means, He used for their defeat. He compelled their dark achievements to subserve His ends, not theirs. They nailed Him to the tree, not knowing that by that very act they were bringing the world to His feet. They gave Him a cross, not guessing that He would make it a throne. They flung Him outside the gates to die, not knowing that in that very moment they were lifting up all the gates of the universe, to let the King come in. They thought to root out His doctrines, not understanding that they were implanting imperishably in the hearts of men the very name they intended to destroy. They thought they had God with His back to the wall, pinned and helpless and defeated: they did not know that it was God Himself who had tracked them down. He did not conquer *in spite of* the dark mystery of evil. He conquered through it.[4]

A short while ago I was speaking at a series of meetings in Belgium. One night my interpreter, Wilfred, was driving me to my engagement in the city of Genk at the border of Germany, very near the now well-known city of Maastricht, where the historic treaty was signed for European unity. I really did not know Wilfred well, so our initial communication was introductory and general. There was something about his demeanor, however, that endeared him to me as a gentle individual who had experienced some of life's pains and who had been scarred by carrying its heavier burdens. The hour was late, and the darkness of the night created a setting of stillness and aloneness that was perfect for a memorable interchange. We came from two different parts of the world—he from a small country that would have fit into one of India's smaller cities, I from a country too vast to measure by any typical ways of generalization. He came from a country still remembering the sounds of Nazi feet on its sidewalks; I came from one where the warfare has been more of the soul. With all that separated us, the next few moments would dramatically bring incredible closeness of heart and mind.

He began to tell me how it was that he came to commit his life to the person of Jesus Christ and how extremely this commitment had been tested. The many pauses during the narrative and the moving tone of his voice revealed how intensely he felt about what he was saying. He told of how he had been attending a conference in a rather Edenic setting somewhere in Switzerland some years ago. He described the unfolding events of one fateful day: "The hymns resounded all day on the reality of heaven, and the speakers expounded on it. I was basking in the greatness of this hope and enjoying the promise of such a destiny. Quite unexpectedly, my name was called during the meeting to go immediately to the office as there was an urgent call awaiting me. I did just that and picked up the phone to hear the somber and sobbing voice of my wife, Faith, informing me that our nine-month-old baby had, without warning, died in his crib a short while ago."

He recounted that the news brought him to the lowest point in his life. The devastation defied description. The anguish and anger built up within his heart to volcanic proportions, threatening to spew out his uncontainable grief. A cry within him wanted to sue God for contempt of human life—so ran the litany of emotions that spelled one basic feeling, that of absolute bewilderment. He packed his bags, bought himself a train ticket, and sat alone in his seat looking out through the window where nothing seemed to ease the ache.

Across the aisle from him sat a man reading his Bible, opposite whom sat two young people who did not try to hide their disdain toward so-called religious books. Their taunts were finally responded to by the man holding the Bible, and their discussion took on some heavy philosophical jousting. Finally, one of the young men, anger unmasked, leaned over and said to the man, "If your God is as loving and kind as you say He is, tell me why He lets the innocent suffer? Why does He permit so much warfare? Why does He allow little children to die? What kind of love is that?"

The questions, especially the last two, stabbed Wilfred in a way he had never felt before, and he caught himself on the verge of blurting out, "Yes, you religious zealot! Answer them and me, and tell us why He lets children die. What sort of love is that?" But a strange mental transformation took place in Wilfred's own mind. He awaited the other man's answer, and then he looked at the two young men and found himself saying, "Do you mind if I enter into your conversation? I'll tell you how much God loves you; He gave His only Son to die for you."

The young men abruptly interrupted him and argued that it was easy for Wilfred to make such platonic pronouncements disconnected from the concrete world of death and desolation.

Wilfred waited for the appropriate moment because he needed every ounce of courage and conviction to say it once, but to say it clearly. "No, no, no, my dear friends," he said. "I am not distanced from the real world of pain and death. In fact, the reason I am on this train is because I am heading home for the funeral of my nine-month-old son. He died just a few hours ago, and it has given the cross a whole new meaning for me. Now I know what kind of a God it is who loves me, a God who willfully gave His Son for me."

The cross uniquely reveals not a God who is taciturn and disengaged from the human scene but a God who is right in the middle of our conflicts and struggles. This is not the Buddhist notion of retreating from the real world through monastic self-renunciation or of counteracting with good to offset the ever-present evil. This is not the Hindu notion of a pantheon of gods whose lives so transcend this earthly domain as to be wedded to myth inextricably. Nor is this the Islamic concept that endeavors to build an earthly kingdom by whatever means it takes, even the sword. *This is the very incarnation, the embodiment of the Everlasting One,* to communicate to a world that hungers for relational bliss and that yearns for a love so supreme that all else may be expelled—and yet a world that convulses with fractured kinships. Contrast the two images that follow, and witness the Christian distinctive to such a reality:

> For they lie beside the nectar, and the bolts are hurl'd
> Far below them in the valleys, and the clouds are lightly curled

Round their golden houses, girdled with the gleaming world;
Where they smile in secret, looking over wasted lands,
Blight and famine, plague and earthquake, roaring deeps and
     fiery sands,
Clanging fights, and flaming towns, and sinking ships, and
     praying hands.[5]

That portrays the mythologies, old and new, where the gods are totally removed from the plight of man, even as beseeching hands reach
out to them. How different from the description of Jesus in the following passage.

The Incarnation

Who, being in very nature God,
     did not consider equality with God something
          to be grasped,
but made himself nothing,
     taking the very nature of a servant,
     being made in human likeness.
And being found in appearance as a man,
     he humbled himself
     and became obedient to death
          even death on a cross!
Therefore God exalted him to the highest place.
     and gave him the name that is above every name,
that at the name of Jesus every knee should bow,
     in heaven and on earth and under the earth,
and every tongue confess that Jesus Christ is Lord,
     to the glory of God the Father.

Philippians 2:6–11

Christ's arms are outstretched toward the stubborn will of humanity. Yet
the Bible itself says the cross is a laughingstock to some and a stumbling
block to others, even though its fact and message may be the only ways to
understand life's great struggle. Greed, power, and indulgence will always
find sacrifice, humility, and virtue to be repugnant, for they stand in the
way of self-aggrandizement. So we in the West have found a way to give
Nobel prizes to those like Mother Teresa and Martin Luther King Jr.

while privately distancing ourselves from the very reason that has made such lives so magnificent. It is somewhat akin to dropping a coin in the hat to get rid of the beggar so we can continue to make our speeches about the poor.

There is nothing in history like the cross that deals with the heart of man in such graphic and effective terms, notwithstanding Bertrand Russell, Swinburne, and their ilk, and all the educated and media elites of our time who seem to take delight in debunking the sacred. It is the cross that invites us to die to self that the life of Christ may live in us fully. Without the cross there is no glory in man. *The difference between man-made utopias and a God-made heaven is the cross.* That is why the former can never be.

One of the most profound books on the message of the gospel was written by John Bunyan, an ordinary tinker. In his book *The Pilgrim's Progress,* in allegorical fashion, you meet Pilgrim trying to journey with a burden-laden back to the Celestial City. Many opportunities have come along the way for him to be sidetracked and disencumbered. The greatest of all deceptions comes when Pilgrim is invited to the House of Morality, where Mr. Legality waxes eloquent on how to find the easy way out of his arduous journey. Pilgrim is nearly seduced and sweet-talked into unburdening his bent back at the House of Morality. Yet something does not ring true, and as he leaves, the wise instructor meets up with him and alerts him to the essential, unalterable dictum that there is no other way but to come by Calvary—the cross. It is only there that Pilgrim's burden could be lifted.

This simple, yet extremely resisted, truth ought to be a powerful reminder that any culture that ultimately anchors its morality in politics reveals both its philosophical bankruptcy and its palpable ignorance of history. "Politically correct" is at best circular—and at worst an oxymoron. Is it not terrifying that we, as a society, have already gone on record that we do not trust the arena of politics because it lends itself to such abuse, and yet we turn around and look to that institution to anchor our values? An Indian proverb says it is like roasting fish and then asking a fox to guard it for us. Morality will always be bent to suit the one whose will is being tested. That is why the cross stands supreme; here the will is surrendered and truth triumphs with love and justice as its handmaidens.

I am absolutely convinced that meaninglessness does not come from being weary of pain; meaninglessness comes from being weary of pleasure. And that is why we find ourselves emptied of meaning with our pantries still full. The cross stands above all this, redefining life itself. The cross stands as the central feature of the Christian explanation and as the answer to the problem of pain. The cross smacks against everything we think of as life. It may be time for us to reexamine with candor why this historic event has such defining power for life and death.

As I attempt to bring this all to a conclusion, let me state these words in summary. When man lives apart from God, chaos is the norm. When man lives with God, as revealed in the incarnation of Jesus Christ, the hungers of the mind and heart find their fulfillment. For in Christ we find coherence and consolation as He reveals to us, in the most verifiable terms of truth and experience, the nature of man, the nature of reality, the nature of history, the nature of our destiny, and the nature of suffering. Obviously, there is much more that can be said, and much has been written on the subject. But I want to challenge you to weigh, with an honest mind, the evidence that is there.

I think it appropriate to present this thought-provoking quotation from G. K. Chesterton in closing:

> Our civilization has decided, and very justly decided, that determining the guilt or innocence of men is a thing too important to be trusted to trained men. If it wishes for light upon that awful matter, it asks men who know no more law than I know, but who can feel the things that I felt in the jury box. When it wants a library catalogued, or the solar system discovered, or any trifle of that kind, it uses up its specialists. But when it wishes anything done which is really serious, it collects twelve of the ordinary men standing round. The same thing was done, if I remember right, by the Founder of Christianity.[6]

You be the judge. The jury has already recorded its conclusion in the pages of the Bible.

Appendix A
Questions and Answers
on Atheism and Theism

These questions and answers are taken from the Veritas lectures at Harvard University, upon which parts of this book are based.

FIRST QUESTIONER: My question is: Isn't it rather unrealistic and self-centered for God to condemn a bunch of atheists who don't believe in Him when He hasn't given them a convincing reason to?

R. Z.: It will take me about five to ten minutes, so you might want to have a seat.

I remember once when I was responding to a doctrinal questionnaire. The first question was: God is perfect—explain. I jokingly quipped to my wife that "the only more difficult question I can think of is to say: Define God and give two examples." As you can appreciate, some questions are thorny.

Your question, sir, is a very good one, but first let me point out to you some of the assumptions of your question that you will first have to defend before the question is even valid and that are vitally important for you to bear in mind.

You have invoked a moral law in raising the question, a moral law that basically says: It would be immoral of God to do this without giving sufficient evidence to condemn somebody. Is that not the presupposition of your question?

FIRST QUESTIONER: I guess that seems to be my assumption.

R. Z.: Not only seems, it has to be or the question self-destructs. The issue you have raised really points to a larger question on the fairness or moral legitimacy of all that God does. That is why I would like to deal with it in its larger indictment, which if satisfactorily dealt with, automatically addresses the particular issue too. And since this is the most often raised obstacle that honest skeptics present as a barrier to their belief in God, it is worthy of special attention.

Let me narrate an interaction I had with a student at the University of Nottingham in England. As soon as I finished one of my lectures, he shot up from his seat and blurted out rather angrily, "There is too much evil in this world; therefore, there cannot be a God." I asked him to remain standing and answer a few questions for me. I said, "If there is such a thing as evil, aren't you assuming there is such a thing as good?" He paused, reflected, and said, "I guess so." "If there is such a thing as good," I countered, "you must affirm a moral law on the basis of which to differentiate between good and evil."

I reminded him of the debate between the philosopher Frederick Copleston and the atheist Bertrand Russell. At one point in the debate, Copleston said, "Mr. Russell, you do believe in good and bad, don't you?" Russell answered, "Yes, I do." "How do you differentiate between them?" challenged Copleston. Russell shrugged his shoulders as he was wont to do in philosophical dead ends for him and said, "The same way I differentiate between yellow and blue." Copleston graciously responded and said, "But Mr. Russell, you differentiate between yellow and blue by seeing, don't you? How do you differentiate between good and bad?" Russell, with all of his genius still within reach, gave the most vapid answer he could have given: "On the basis of feeling—what else?" I must confess, Mr. Copleston was a kindlier gentleman than many others. The appropriate "logical kill" for the moment would have been, "Mr. Russell, in some cultures they love their neighbors; in other cultures they eat them, both on the basis of feeling. Do you have any preference?"

So I returned to my questioning student in Nottingham: "When you say there is evil, aren't you admitting there is good? When you accept the existence of goodness, you must affirm a moral law on the basis of which to differentiate between good and evil. But when you admit to a moral law, you must posit a moral lawgiver. That, however, is who you are trying to disprove and not prove. For if there is no moral lawgiver, there is no moral law. If there is no moral law, there is no good. If there is no good, there is no evil. What, then, is your question?"

There was a conspicuous pause that was broken when he said rather sheepishly, "What, then, am I asking you?" There's the rub, I might add.

Now, I do not doubt for a moment that philosophers have tried to arrive at a moral law apart from the positing of God, but their efforts are either contradictory in their assumptions or conclusions. I might say this is particularly true of David Hume. More on that later. I have gone to great lengths to use this illustration from the Copleston-Russell debate because your question, sir, was an echo of Russell's philosophical attack upon theism. When someone said to him, "What will you do, Mr. Russell, if after you die you find out there is a God? What will you say to Him?" Russell said, "I will tell Him He just did not give me enough evidence." Russell, in stating that, took a position diametrically opposed to scriptural teaching. The Scriptures teach that the problem with human unbelief is not the absence of evidence; rather, it is the suppression of it. "Nothing good can come," said Professor Richard Weaver, "if the will is wrong. If the disposition is wrong, reason increases maleficence." George MacDonald rightly argued that "to explain truth to him who loves it not is to give more plentiful material for misinterpretation."

Let me summarize:

1. To justify the question, God must remain in the paradigm; without God, the question self-destructs.

2. God has created us in His image. Part of that image is the privilege of self-determination.

3. The greatest of all virtues is love.

4. God, in His love, has created us, and in response, love from us has to be a choice. Where there is no choice, it is coercion, which means it is not love. In the Christian message alone, love precedes life; in every other worldview, life precedes love. Therefore, in the Christian framework, love has a point of reference, God Himself.

5. God communicates to mankind in a variety of ways:
   a. Reason (philosophical),
   b. Experience (existential),
   c. History (empirical),
   d. Emotions (relational),
   e. The Scriptures (propositional), and
   f. Incarnation (personal).

Take these six areas that are open to serious critical thinking, and you will find that the problem is not the absence of evidence; rather it's the suppression of it. May I add that it was in this very school that Simon Greenleaf, professor of jurisprudence, said of the documents of the New Testament, "You may choose to say I do not believe it all, but you may not say there is not enough evidence."

MODERATOR: Let me ask you a few questions that have been handed in because I think they are related:

First, it is true that the absence of meaning in pain and death and life is terrible. That doesn't mean that atheism is false.

Second, does it take as much faith to be an atheist as it does to believe in God? If yes, what kind of faith?

R. Z.: Oh, my! Those are two different questions. Let's take the first one. It is absolutely true that if meaninglessness reigns supreme, especially in terms of pain and suffering, and if there is no answer for it in atheism, that does not necessarily mean that atheism is false. In fact, if you recall, I even stated that just because a religious system claims to have support and hope in times of pain and death does not automatically grant that system a corner on truth in all that it affirms. The test for truth goes beyond that. What, then, is the breakdown point for atheism in its confession that it has no answer or hope for human suffering?

Your question as posed assumes to be a meaningful one and the answer you seek, I assume, will be tested for meaning also. Meaningfulness, then, becomes central to this very dialogue. I well recall a back-and-forth discussion I had once on the campus of the University of the Philippines in Manila. A student from the audience shouted out that everything in life was meaningless. I responded by saying, "You do not believe that."

He promptly retorted, "Yes, I do," to which I automatically countered, "No, you don't."

Exasperated, he said, "I most certainly do; who are you to tell me I don't?"

"Then please repeat your statement for me," I requested.

"Everything in life is meaningless," he stated again without qualification.

I said to him, "Please remain standing; this will only take a moment. I assume that you assume that your statement is meaningful. If your statement is meaningful, then everything is not meaningless. On the other hand, if everything is meaningless, then what you have just said is meaningless too. So, in effect, you have said nothing." The young man was startled for a moment and even as I left the auditorium, he was pacing the back of the floor muttering, "If everything is meaningless then . . ." So it went.

I bring that analogy to point out a similar mistake you are making. You are logically arguing for an existential struggle. By that I mean you have framed the question logically, but your complaint is an existential one. And the reason you are looking for a meaningful answer to your question is that you believe life to have meaning. But if pain, suffering, and death have no reasonable explanation at all, even though they are universally experienced, then life itself has no meaning. Why should you be looking for a meaningful answer to the question? That is a blatant contradiction between your logic and your experience, which, when propositionalized, becomes illogical.

Let me take this a few steps further. Why is it that you can subscribe to a worldview that has no explanation to the central features of human experience and see no illogic to it, but at the same time you debunk the theistic worldview because you say it is incoherent with the dilemma of suffering?

As if that were not far enough, let us go even further. If pain and suffering are no longer moral problems for the atheistic mind, should one who inflicts pain and suffering be considered an immoral person? If the answer is yes, try explaining that in a transculturally satisfying manner. If no, what does that do to our judicial system? As a matter of fact, it is plausible to argue that if death is the end of all things and life ceases to be anything after one dies, then the logic of unforgiveness and the logic of avenging any wrong becomes a very attractive option to many. May I suggest to you that this is precisely the logic of groups or countries that desire "ethnic cleansing." It is also the logic of the terrorist who blows up a plane in the air, inflicting pain on some innocent families because "their government" (i.e. the government of the families blown up) "supported our enemies," they argue, "and our families were victimized."

In effect, to just posit that "because we do not have an answer for pain and suffering does not mean the belief system is invalid" is rather simplistic. The link of pain, suffering, and death joins the link of morality on the one side and of meaning on the other. It does not stand as an isolated piece. To use a different analogy, it is part of a larger puzzle.

Contrastingly, G. K. Chesterton, the English philosopher, presented a very powerful idea. He argued that for the Christian, joy is the central feature of life, and sorrow is peripheral because the fundamental questions of life are answered and the peripheral ones are relatively unanswered. For the antitheist, sorrow is central and joy peripheral because only the peripheral questions are answered and the central ones remain unanswered. Your question moves the existential dilemma to a logical one of incoherence.

SECOND QUESTIONER: Well, I can just tell you, I've heard all of this said before . . . I'm not miserable.

R. Z.: I never said you were.

SECOND QUESTIONER: No, but you are trying to make me. It isn't working.

R. Z.: No, I wish I had tried.

SECOND QUESTIONER: I also want to make a point that you use the straw man version of atheism, which I have encountered before. Many philosophers say that atheism does not necessarily mean a dogmatic assertion that God does not exist. It is my view that I am an atheist because I lack theistic evidence.

R. Z.: But why aren't you a pantheist?

SECOND QUESTIONER: Because there is no evidence for pantheism either.

R. Z.: Oh, so all . . .

SECOND QUESTIONER: . . . lack sufficient evidence.

R. Z.: All right. What, then, is your question?

SECOND QUESTIONER: Why is it that despite the fact that Michael Martin and George Smith and many other humanist philosophers continue to correct you on the philosophy of atheism, you continue to present this version of atheism where it is a dogma?

R. Z.: All right, thank you. Your information is both misleading and escapist; your question, therefore, is wrongheaded. I deliberately quoted my definition from a primary source, the renowned *Encyclopedia of Philosophy*, edited by Paul Edwards. Of course there are some like Martin, and for that matter Huxley, who like to hide behind a softer version of atheism (just as Russell did in his debate) because they know the philosophical decimation they would experience in trying to defend the absolute negative—There is no God. Their soft position that there is not sufficient evidence for theism commits three logical blunders.

First, to move to atheism by default is hardly an academically credible switch to make when there are myriad other options.

Second, to say that there is insufficient evidence for theism and therefore I am an atheist implies a logically satisfactory defense of atheism that they do not have. After all, why else would they hold to it if it is logically indefensible, when their very reason for denying theism is that it is logically indefensible?

Third, it is purely an admission that atheism cannot be defended, even though they have tried, hence the softer version of agnosticism. Let us look at the words themselves.

The word *atheism* comes from the Greek, which has two words conjoined. The *alpha* is the negative, and *theos* means "God." The atheistic position, whether you like it or not, posits the negation of God. Having quickly recognized the inherent contradiction of affirming God's nonexistence, which absolutely would at the same time presuppose infinite knowledge on the part of the one doing the denying, a philosophically convenient switch was made to agnosticism. But *agnostic* has an even more embarrassing connotation. The *alpha* means the negative, and *ginosko* is from the Greek "to know." An agnostic is one who doesn't know. It sounds quite congenial and sophisticated at the same time, but the Latin uncomplimentary equivalent is "ignoramus." That is why the agnostic does not feel lauded in this category either but dresses up the concept, manufacturing a certain aura not inherent in the word while smuggling in atheism for all functional purposes. So I say to you, the charge is not against the apologists; that is to dislocate the problem. The hat pin is in the heart of the atheistic position, which could not live with itself. Let me add that an honest agnostic should be open to the evidence.

THIRD QUESTIONER: In your talk, you seem to be saying that we should turn to God and religion as it would show us a way to deal with pain. Does this mean that the criterion for choosing a worldview is what is going to make us happy or satisfies our needs? And if so, why choose Christianity over a number of other religions that help us deal with pain?

R. Z.: Absolutely not. In fact, I clearly stated in my lecture that this does not necessarily follow. What I *am* saying is that if Christianity is true, it will help you deal with pain and suffering; but it is not true just because it deals with your pain and suffering. That would be like the vacuous leap of existentialism.

The real question, of course, is whether Christianity and the exclusive claims of Christ are true, as opposed to other religions. That can be clearly and convincingly demonstrated as I have done in some other lectures and writings. Obviously we cannot explore that issue and make all the comparisons required just here. My next lecture does present a defense of Christianity. If demonstrably true, then the answer to pain follows. Conversely, just because a belief alleviates pain does not make the belief as a system true.

FOURTH QUESTIONER: You show that Nietzsche's rejection of God was out of his own existential experience, his pain, but your answer to his position is based on logic. Doesn't that mean that his position is just as good as yours but that you are just going in one direction and Nietzsche in another?

R. Z.: My challenge to Nietzsche's position is based on his own existential grounds and on a logical critique and on history. But since his starting point is an existential leap and my starting point is historical and philosophical, one position is not as good as the other. If our starting points were the same, then our positions might be equally good or bad.

Nietzsche's criticism of Christianity is an emotional tirade. His biggest argument is based on a morally self-stultifying argument. My challenge has been to show that self-stultification. If you point that out in the position I have presented, then you have a valid critique.

FIFTH QUESTIONER: You argue against Nietzsche in part because his position produced evils such as Hitler. But what about evils that Christianity has produced, such as its persecution of unbelievers during the Crusades?

R. Z.: That is a very good question, but there is an important difference. I thought I already answered that in the lecture. On the one hand, the evils of atheism are a direct outgrowth of the teachings of atheism. This is a most awkward and painful reality for atheists to admit. First, let me state clearly what I am not saying. I am not saying that atheism equals killing. I am not saying that all atheists are "evil." To infer those conclusions, which I am denying, is merely to misunderstand or misrepresent the logical problem. I am saying that violence is a logically deducible path from atheism, and may I recommend for your reading that Darwin himself categorically stated this in *A World of Natural Selection*. Tennyson, in pre-Darwinian poetic postulation, described nature "red in tooth and claw." Where antitheism has been the reigning ideology, blood has flowed without restraint—China, Russia, and Nazi Germany provide the gruesome tale of the tape. On the other hand, it is plain to see that where Christianity has wielded the sword and ground out pain upon people or ridden the political horse in triumph, it has only steered abysmally away from the path that Christ laid before His followers. The politicization of religion in history has more the fury of hell than the grace of heaven. Dostoevsky's Grand Inquisitor was not the first religious leader to drive Jesus out of the temple. Jesus said, "My kingdom is not of this world else would my servants fight." Jesus never commended the exploitation of people or the philosophy of violence. The use or abuse of Christianity in contradiction to the very message of the gospel reveals not the gospel for what it is, but the heart of man. That is why atheism is so bankrupt as a view of life, for it miserably fails to deal with the human condition as it really is.

AUTHOR'S NOTE: One of the questions that is frequently asked challenges that Christians leap from atheism to Christianity without first establishing that there is a God. It is indeed a very valid question. Just because an argument can effectively decimate the philosophy of atheism does not necessarily mean that Christianity is therefore true. When that challenge is presented to the Christian, there are really two major steps to be taken in dealing with it.

The first step is to demonstrate that God exists. The second is to defend the Christian message as the system that best explains who this God is.

In the format I have adopted because of time constraints in the lecture-ship, I have presented the uniqueness of Christ in an effort to work back to theism. By defending the person and the teaching of Jesus Christ, I have considered theism itself implicitly defended. For clearly Jesus taught the existence of God, and He taught that in His person He was God Incarnate, the self-disclosure of God Himself.

However, to be philosophically correct, it is true that theism has to be established before Christianity can be legitimately defended. In light of that, I delineate briefly the argument for God's existence.

Anyone who has ever dealt with a textbook on the philosophy of religion or studied apologetics knows that the subject can easily become tedious. Through the process of the argumentation, words, concepts, and names appear that often leave the serious thinker quite overwhelmed. How is it that something as basic as the first cause of the universe can be so obscure and elusive? G. K. Chesterton once said that it was the reading of the atheists that led him to God as he considered their arguments vapid and thoroughly unconvincing. In like manner, if one is not careful, tedious argumentation for the existence of God can be counterproductive and can sidetrack the reader from the very purpose of the argument.

I would merely like to touch on the fringe of this issue in order to at least defuse the criticism of a huge leap taken to get from atheism to Christ. To appeal to both the detailed thinker and the one who desires just the hub of the argument, I am presenting two approaches. I would like to suggest that the reader pursue these in greater depth if desired by turning to the primary sources.

Although in classical apologetics arguments such as the teleological (from design) and the moral (from morality) are often used independently, in actuality they are offshoots of a larger argument known as the cosmological (arguing from causality). The teleological argument, for example, demonstrates design and argues from that to a designer. The moral argument moves from the direction of effect to cause. Therefore the cosmological argument is the parent form of the classical proofs since it seeks to establish the very principle of causality as necessary. I will present the outline briefly before moving to a simpler format for a theistic proof.

Philosopher Norman Geisler is, in my estimation, the leading and most able exponent of the cosmological argument, having defended it against its staunchest critics.[1] Dr. Geisler develops his defense of theism through ten steps, each one well anticipating the critic's questions. The following is his outline:

1. Some things undeniably exist.
2. My nonexistence is possible.
3. Whatever has the possibility not to exist is currently caused to exist by another.
4. There cannot be an infinite regress of current causes of existence.
5. Therefore, a first uncaused cause of my current existence exists.
6. This uncaused cause must be infinite, unchanging, all-powerful, all-knowing, and all-perfect.
7. This infinitely perfect being is appropriately called "God."
8. Therefore, God exists.
9. This God who exists is identical to the God described in the Christian Scriptures.
10. Therefore the God described in the Bible exists.

I commend Dr. Geisler's writings for your study. In his defense of these postulates, and especially of the sixth step, it is vital that you follow his tightly woven argumentation.

There is a simpler form of a theistic defense provided by Professor Dallas Willard of the School of Philosophy (which he at one time directed) at the University of Southern California. He delineates three stages of evidence for God's existence. These, he believes, provide a framework that lead him to his theistic deductions.[2]

Stage one is his argument from the physical world. "However concrete physical reality is sectioned, the result will be a state of affairs which owes its being to something other than itself." Willard gives a detailed demonstration that for anything to exist, all preconditions necessary for its existence must have been completed in order for that particular thing to exist. In that series of causes there has to be at least one state of being which itself exists but does not derive its existence from anything else. It is self-existent, i.e., uncaused.

Professor Willard responds to those who would argue that this uncaused entity itself could be just another physical reality:

It will be objected by some that, though the series of causes for any physical state is finite, the first physical event or state in the series could have come into existence without a cause—could have, in short, originated "from nothing." Many discussions today seem to treat the "Big Bang" in this way, though of course that would make it totally unlike any other "bang" of which we have any knowledge. "Big Bang" mysticism is primarily attractive, I think, just because "the bang" has stepped into a traditional role of God, which gives it a nimbus and seems to rule out the normal questions we would ask about any physical event. *That* "bang" is often treated as if it were not quite or not just a physical event, as indeed it could not be. But what, then, could it be? Enter "scientific mysticism." And we must at least point out that an eternally self-subsistent being is no more improbable than a self-subsisted event emerging from no cause. As C. S. Lewis pointed out, "An egg which came from no bird is no more natural than a bird which had existed from all eternity." (C. S. Lewis, *God in the Dock,* p. 211)[3]

Arguments against causality as a philosophical principle have been raised by David Hume, as well as others. Willard entertains all these criticisms and counters with superb answers. The whole idea of the universe "popping out," or of something coming from nothing, would in effect violate the system of law which governs the origin of things of its type. *The probability of something physical coming from nothing is zero, and not a single physical state or event being observed or otherwise known is known to originate from nothing.*

We have, then, an "ontologically haunted" universe—an uncaused reality that exists which is unlike any other physical reality that we know. This has to be something more than physical. There has to be something more than physical or "natural," something quite different in character from which or from whom this physical universe derives its existence. Clearly this at least provides for the possibility of God, giving a "spiritual" uncaused entity some "breathing room." A strictly physical or natural explanation is not provable by the laws that govern a physical or natural universe. In short, the tests of nature for nature establish that naturalism as a first cause is indefensible. Something beyond a physical reality is needed to explain this universe.

Stage two is Willard's argument in the form of the teleological argument, but he underscores the fact that it is not an argument *from* design as much as it is an argument *to* design. That is a pivotal distinction. Evolution as a theory cannot logically be a theory of *ultimate* origins, precisely because its operation presupposes a text of design within a context of facilitating that actualization. In other words, not *all* order has evolved. The being from order that the evolutionists argue for did not come from being without order. The dimensions are of a stupendous magnitude; they are both diachronic and synchronic.

After establishing that not all order has evolved, the theist can then demonstrate that in our human experience, before any order is imparted to our physical creations, order first existed in our minds. Design in mind precedes design in kind. Once again there is breathing room for God, for nothing in our experience that is designed has come to be, apart from the coalescing of entities conducive to design, in circumstances complementing that capability; existing first in the mind.

Dallas Willard ends stage two with this challenge to the antitheist:

> At the first stage we said that the probability, relative to our data, of something (in the physical universe at least) originating from nothing was zero, and we invited the atheist to find one case of this actually happening, to revise the probability a bit above zero. Now we urge him to find one case of ordered being—or just being, for, whatever it is, it will certainly be ordered—originating from being without order.[4]

In *stage three,* Willard presents the argument for God from the course of human events—historical, social, and individual—within the context of a demonstrated extranaturalism (stage one), and of a quite plausible cosmic intellectualism (stage two). "This human life is to be interpreted within the ontological space of the actualities, with their attendant possibilities hewn out in stages one and two."

If nothing cannot create something, this allows, indeed, demands, that a nonphysical reality be the first cause. Further, if the text to design within a context of complementariness sustains the conclusion that order has never come from disorder, the argument for an intelligent cause is again supported. And if history and human experience reveal realities that can only be explained in the realm of a transcendent reality, one can compellingly argue for the existence of an intelligent first cause we call God. Willard powerfully ends his summary by quoting the skeptic, David Hume:

> The most natural sentiment, which a well disposed mind will feel on this occasion, is a longing desire and expectation that heaven would be pleased to dissipate, at least alleviate, this profound ignorance, by affording some more particular revelation to mankind, and making discoveries of the nature, attributes, and operations of the divine object of our faith.[5]

I wholeheartedly concur with Professor Willard when he says, "Possibly this prayer has already been answered."

Appendix B
Mentors to the Skeptic

René Descartes (1596–1650)

Descartes has been called the "father of modern philosophy." He was educated in a Jesuit college in France, and while serving in the army in Germany he recorded that he received divine instruction to develop a unified system of reality based on mathematical principles. Descartes argued that there is nothing so far removed from us as to be beyond our reach, or so hidden that we cannot discover it through reasoning. As a mathematician, he desired to establish truth claims without merely presupposing such propositions to be certain or self-evident. Such an idea was a radical departure from traditional scientific theory, which was founded on probabilities. Descartes wrote several books, including *Meditations on First Philosophy*.

Descartes's now famous statement—"I think, therefore, I am"—was the starting point of his philosophical inquiry. His skepticism led him to question his own existence, but having doubted, he concluded that he thought, and in thinking, he existed. He applied the same paradigm in determining God's existence. Descartes basically proposed two proofs for the existence of God.

First, he argued from the idea of God in his own mind: Since the human mind is imperfect, the concept of a perfect mind could not have been born in an imperfect mind. Therefore, said Descartes, the idea of a perfect mind must have been planted in the imperfect mind by the perfect mind itself—which has to have been God.

His second proof was in the tradition of Anselm. Basically, he argued that just as a triangle by definition must have three sides, so a necessary being—God—would necessarily have to exist, else He would not be a necessary being. Therefore, God exists.

One can readily see the vulnerability of these proofs. First, the move from thought to reality is not a valid move. Just because it is possible to think of something as possible does not grant it existence in actuality. In fact, could not the very fact of the imperfection of the human mind result in imperfect thinking even about the existence of perfection?

Second, the rationally inescapable is not always the real. We agree that a triangle must have three sides, but this does not prove that a triangle exists. It only proves that *if* a triangle existed it would have three sides.

Finally, if Descartes is trying to establish that only that which is rationally necessary can be admitted with absolute certainty, he falls a victim to his own sword because at the same time he admits to some first principles that themselves are not proven as rationally necessary.[1]

Let us try to understand a little of who Descartes was, what his context was, and the shortcomings in his philosophy.

Descartes lived at a time when the philosophy of skepticism was fast spreading through the writings of Rabelais (1492–1533), Montaigne (1533–1592), and Francis Bacon (1561–1626). Hailing from a family of attorneys and businessmen, argument and mathematics were natural gifts of his genius. Although known for several works, at one stage he wanted to pull it all together in a *magnum opus* with the incredible title of *Project for a Universal Science Designed to Elevate Human Nature to Its Highest Perfection.* Interestingly he gave up that effort because he felt it unwise to encroach upon the domain of revealed religion.

Descartes's principal aim was to acquire knowledge in a certain and trustworthy way transcending the skepticism of his time. Striving for mathematical certainty, in a sense he displaced metaphysics and thereby God, who would gradually be elbowed out into being more an innate idea rather than a rationally defendable entity. Again, it is important to note that *Descartes was not doing away with the certainty of God but methodologically moving God to a different "way of knowing."*

In his *Meditations on First Philosophy* (IV) he said:

> And when I consider, I doubt, that is to say, that I am an incomplete and dependent being, the idea of a Being that is complete and independent, that is, of God, presents itself to my mind with so much distinctness and clearness—and from the fact alone that this idea is found in me, or that I possess this idea, I conclude so cer-

tainly that God exists, and my existence depends entirely upon Him in every moment of my life—that I do not think that the human mind is capable of knowing anything with more evidence and certitude.

Although Descartes made this statement, he did put the knowledge of God on the road to skepticism. Since he reduced God to an innate idea, coupled with his skepticism of the senses, Descartes would not have agreed with the apostle Paul—"For since the creation of the world God's invisible qualities—His eternal power and divine nature—have been clearly seen, being clearly understood from what has been made." He had a unique response to sense perception. Since he could only be certain of that which existed in his mind, he made an extrapolational leap, saying that "Since God would not deceive my senses," the existence of an eternal world of bodies is actual.

Gradually, the God of Descartes became more like the God of the deists. His interest lies more in the study of the cosmos than in the study of its Creator. Christian philosophy is displaced by mathematical certainty, and God is only brought into the picture for matters his philosophy cannot explain. His thinking set the stage for his disciple Spinoza, who has rightly been called the metaphysician of modern atheism. Philosophers Ronda Chervin and Eugene Kevane clearly point this out, and Descartes's own words affirm this sentiment:

> I am a Catholic, I wish to remain one, and I have faith in the teaching of the Church. But I simply bracket all that out: It is in the realm of religious sentiment and emotion, whereas my universal science is in the realm of reason and knowledge.[2]

This introduces that cardinal principle of Descartes's method—the separation of religion, faith, and theology on the one hand from philosophy and the empirical sciences on the other hand. Philosophy suddenly loses its internal relationship to revealed religion and is well on its way toward becoming separated as a secular subject, the step that Spinoza will complete.

The warning from Descartes is obvious. It is not only one's initial conclusions about God that are important, but also the very process by which one comes to know and understand that God. If the method is flawed and God is relegated to the nonrational, "bracketed out" from reason, it is only a step away from self-deification and the irrational.

David Hume (1711–1776)

David Hume was admitted to Edinburgh University when he was twelve years old, but he left before completing his degree because, he said, he had "an insurmountable aversion to everything but the pursuits of philosophy and general learning."[3] At twenty-three he began writing his first book, *A Treatise of Human Nature,* in which he established the empirical argument that facts cannot be proved by *a priori* reason but are discovered or inferred from experience. Hence, God's existence, the origin of the world, and other subjects that transcend our finite human experience are unverifiable and meaningless. Hume tutored students and served a post as a librarian, but he gave himself chiefly to writing. Among his other works are *Enquiry Concerning Human Understanding* (1748), *History of Great Britain* (1754–1762, six volumes), and *Dialogues Concerning Natural Religion* (1779). He spent many years in France associating with the men of the Enlightenment. At one stage he served as secretary to the British ambassador in Paris. Hume's name is associated with empiricism and skepticism.

We may examine Hume's thinking in three different areas. First, by way of knowledge and certainty—what can you know, and how can you know it? In his *Enquiry Concerning Human Understanding* he says:

> When we go through a library, persuaded of the truth of our philosophy, what havoc we will cause there! If we take off the shelf for example a volume of theology or metaphysics, we must ask ourselves: Does it contain reasonings or quantity or number? The answer is, No! Does it then contain experimental reasonings based on questions of fact? No! Away with it, then, and cast it into the flames! For it contains nothing but sophisms and illusions.[4]

With these words, Hume presents both his starting point and his point of collapse. Hume believed that all of our knowledge comes to us through our senses and by reflecting on the ideas that come through the senses to the mind. According to Hume, nothing is in the mind that was not first in the senses. To test the validity of an idea, one must ask what sensory impressions brought it about. There is no light of intelligence to pierce through this "sense-delivered" impression that will lead to an essential understanding of the things that exist. Man is reduced to a physical object to be studied, the same way other physical objects are studied. Further, he adds that since man is all matter and substance, the soul is effectively banished.

He adds three other vitally important ideas. First, that all the ideas that are present in the mind are nothing more than collections of particular ideas, all sensations are "loose and separate," and all that we experience is a series of unconnected and separate sensations. We do not, in fact, even have direct knowledge of ourselves. All we know of ourselves is a disconnected bundle of sense impressions.

A second idea that directly attacked one of the classical proofs of God's existence is Hume's philosophy on causality. Philosopher Norman Geisler words this Humean position very forcefully:

> The idea [says Hume] of a causal relation appears in the mind only after there has been an observation of constant conjunction in experience. That is, only when we observe death to occur after holding another head under water for five minutes do we assume a causal connection. Once one event is observed to happen after another repeatedly, we begin to form the idea that one event happens *because* of the other. In brief, the idea of causality is based on custom. . . . There is always the possibility of the *post hoc* fallacy—namely, that things happen after other events (even repeatedly) but are not really caused by them. For example, the sun rises regularly after the rooster crows, but certainly not because the rooster crows.[5]

This inability to determine the cause of the world—and therefore the uncertainty of predicting the future—leads to skepticism. The principle of causality, then, according to Hume, is nothing but an association of successive impressions. Through habit and custom we expect that the succession will take place; in reality there is no necessary connection. In short, nothing authorizes even science to formulate universal and necessary laws.

The third of Hume's ideas that I would like to summarize is on ethics. Morality, he taught, is not based upon reason or matters of fact, but upon feelings. A moral judgment is born within, dependent on whether you find a sense of approval or disapproval following an action. This moral judgment is the result of feeling, not of reason. Vice and virtue may be compared to sounds, colors, heat, or cold. (We can now understand where Bertrand Russell was coming from when he said he differentiated between good and evil the same way he differentiated between colors.)

One can readily see by Hume's analogy how such a philosophy could pave the way for a totalitarian state where society is programmed to feel as the powers that be desire it to feel. (On an aside, it is noteworthy that Hume brought Jean Jacques Rousseau to England with him for an extended stay. It is Rousseau's educational theory—"state-controlled value impartation"—that we now live with.)

To sum up Hume's thinking, there is a clear animosity against revealed religion, against the miraculous, and against God. He effectively furnished the model for the atheistic mind and laid the foundations for some of the greatest tyrannies upon humanity. A brief critique of Hume follows:

1. Hume's contention that, in order to be meaningful, all statements should either be a relation to ideas, i.e., mathematical or quantity, or else should be of experimental reasoning based on questions of facts is itself based neither on mathematical fact nor on experimentally established fact. Therefore, his very definition of a meaningful statement, on his own terms, is meaningless.

2. Hume's assertion that all events are entirely loose, separate, and unconnected is unsustainable. His very statement implies a unity and connection, else there would be no way to make that statement. In other words, he assumes a unified self while denying a unity.

3. Hume's skeptical deduction that all judgment about reality be suspended is self-defeating because that call to suspend judgment is in itself a judgment about reality.

4. Hume's argument against miracles is equally flawed, as are some of his other critiques of God that we have touched upon. The argument runs something like this: Since a miracle is a violation or exception to a law of nature, by definition it is based on the

lower degree of probability. A wise man, says Hume, will always base his belief on the highest degree of probability; therefore, a wise man will disbelieve in miracles.

Hume's argument is somewhat strained once again. For example, the possibility of this world happening, even according to the strongest antitheist, is as close to zero as one can get. Therefore, the wise man should deny the existence of the world. His argument is dreadfully circular: He first assumes that miracles can never happen and then concludes that they have never occurred. The real wise man, to counter Hume, would be one who would make his conclusion based on the evidence.

Considering Hume's positions, it is not surprising that he concludes, "I am affrighted and confounded with that forlorn solitude in which I am placed by my philosophy."[6] He may have spoken better than he knew. The damage his philosophy has done by the removal of the intellect as a way to reason God's truth has, in effect, marred an essential aspect of the very image of God in man, removing the foundation of education and culture.

Immanuel Kant (1724–1804)

Immanuel Kant was born in 1724 in the city of Konigsberg, East Prussia, now a part of Russia and renamed Kaliningrad. His father was a saddler, but Kant himself was to work more with the abstract ideas of life, becoming one of the greatest philosophers of all time, ranked alongside the "big three"—Socrates, Plato, and Aristotle.

After his graduation from university in the city of his birth, he became a private tutor to Prussian families and, ultimately, professor of logic and metaphysics at the University of Konigsberg in 1770. Kant lived a very quiet and orderly life, traveling very little. He remained a bachelor all his life and was proverbially renowned for his absolute punctuality. A highly respected man, his interests touched the lives of people then and for centuries since. One of his students wrote that "nothing worth knowing was indifferent to him."

Many of Kant's one-liners filter down into the philosophical classroom to this very day. It was Kant who said that David Hume was the one who "first interrupted my dogmatic slumber." He also made the statement that two things forever held him in awe—"the starry hosts above and the moral law within." It would take volumes of study to fully comprehend those simple statements.

At this time in the development of philosophy, there was quite a struggle under way between the Continental allegiance to rational thought and the British espousal of sense experience. That struggle manifests itself even today and is most clearly seen in the different ways that Europe, Britain, and the United States treat the subject of apologetics—the defense of the Christian faith. The reason for the difference is the divergent value each places upon the method of arriving at truth.

Kant attempted a synthesis between the empiricism of the English mind and the rationalism of the Continental mind. The empiricists claimed that our sense experience is the source of all belief. Kant recognized that but did not go along with the skeptical conclusion that those beliefs fell outside of experience and therefore could not be justified. At the same time, he rejected the rationalist's claims that factual truths about what does and does not exist can be exclusively established by the use of reason alone. He sought to discover whether it was possible to have metaphysical knowledge, that is, knowledge on such matters as the existence of God, the immortality of the soul, and whether human beings have free wills. His conclusions are recorded in his *Critique of Pure Reason*.

In many ways, Kant is the single progenitor of modern man's confidence in the power of reason to grapple with material things and its incompetence to deal with anything beyond the material. All that is manifestly real is rationally justifiable, and all that is ultimate is rationally indefensible.

Obviously Kant's sophisticated and detailed ideas cannot be presented in this context. The ramifications of his philosophy, however, are far-reaching because of his theory of knowledge. Professor Colin Brown sums up that theory at its core.

> Kant's view of knowledge may be summed up by saying that its raw material consists of the outside world perceived by the senses (the synthetic element), but that this is inevitably processed by the human mind (the *a priori* element). In perceiving the raw material the mind employs the Forms of Intuition of time and space. It also makes use of Categories or the Pure Concepts of the Understanding, such as

quantity and quality. The result is that the mind does not actually perceive things as they are in themselves. For "while much can be said *a priori* as regards the form of appearances, nothing whatsoever can be asserted of the thing in itself, which may underlie these appearances." It is as though we look at everything through rose-tinted spectacles. We see things, but they are always colored. Just so, Kant argued, the mind looks at everything through its Forms of Intuition and Categories of Understanding. Inevitably, the mind conditions everything that it encounters.

This doctrine has far-reaching consequences. It was intended to be a safeguard against Hume's skepticism, but the price that it paid for this defence was further skepticism. It has often been remarked that Hume gave Kant the problem of Knowledge and Kant gave it back as if it were the solution.[7]

Kant's agnosticism on ultimate reality is self-defeating. It is not possible to posit anything about ultimate reality unless one knows something about ultimate reality. To say, as Kant did, that one cannot cross the line of appearances is to cross the line in order to say it. In other words, it is not possible to know the difference between the appearance and reality unless one knows enough about both to distinguish between them.

It is this very attempt in Eastern philosophy that led to absolute silence. Some readers may recall that in the last wordless communication between Buddha and his disciple, Ananda, Buddha kept stripping the petals from a flower as Ananda watched. Finally Buddha looked at Ananda and smiled, and Ananda smiled in return. That was it. When Ananda was asked what it all meant he answered (irresistibly), "I now know." If he were pushed to answer what he knew, he would have said, "I now know that I know." Ultimate reality in the Kantian system is unknowable, but Kant's exposition of its unknowability is, therefore, self-stultifying.

Elsewhere I have already dealt with the shortcomings of Kant's ethical theory. In a philosophical sense, he became the ocean into which many divergent philosophers have converged and from which many lesser seas or rivers of thought emerge.

Sören Kierkegaard (1813–1855)

If Bertrand Russell's life is aptly described as one of contradiction, Kierkegaard was the embodiment of conflict. His entire life—from childhood to death—was one emotional roller coaster. Raised in a home where melancholy pervaded the household, he came by this mind-set quite naturally. His father lived a life of tormenting guilt for one reason or another. The senior Kierkegaard had been unfaithful to his first wife, who died at childbirth. He was sure that God was "getting back" at him because not only did he lose her, he also lost five of his seven children. On one occasion he clenched his fist at the heavens and swore at God, a memory that was never to leave him or his son. That guilt also haunted the elder Kierkegaard throughout his life.

The youngest of the seven children, Sören was born in 1813 and died at the age of forty-two. In a very unique sense, philosophers are a product of their times, and just as Immanuel Kant can be better understood if one first understands David Hume, so also Kierkegaard's philosophy is better understood as an intense reaction to Hegel.

According to the Hegelian view, the individual is subsumed by the unfolding of ideas in a dialectical process. Concepts and abstractions are more important than what is actual and particular. Mind and ideas are supreme, and there is clearly a loss of personality and individuality in the process. It is fascinating to see the disagreements among commentators on Hegel— some branding him atheistic, some branding him theistic, and still others branding him pantheistic or even panentheistic (all things in the universe are parts of God but God, by virtue of being the whole, is greater than the sum of the parts). In that context, if the ultimate reality is mind, then the particular manifestations are secondary. Hegel loses the value of the individual.

In reaction to this, Kierkegaard "restored" individual worth. For the want of a better term, his philosophy was the individuation of religion. He maintained that the individual human will and ability to choose are of supreme importance. A choice is not made by invoking certain criteria; rather, it is a "leap of faith" that affirms the incarnation of God while recognizing it as an intellectual absurdity. This affirmation must be made without reference to others as an affirmation of one's own individuality. Religious commitment in these terms is purely and exclusively a matter of individual faith.

One of the keys to understanding Kierkegaard is to be able to capture what he stated to be the three stages of life—the aesthetic, the ethical, and the religious. Each stage is spanned by a leap of faith. However, when progressing from one stage to the next one, he does not so much abandon the previous stage as relegate it to a place that is secondary to the subsequent stage. In the aesthetic stage, an escape from boredom is sought by the romantic pursuit of a whole range of pleasures. But the desired result is not achieved, and the end of this stage is despair. From here, the leap is made to the ethical stage, where one responds to objective morality by a call to duty. This, too, fails to validate individual existence, and the third leap, in recognition of one's mortality and sinfulness, is to the religious stage. This final leap is not "once and for all" but a repetitive act.

In his book *Fear and Trembling*, Kierkegaard focuses on the story in Genesis 22 of Abraham offering up Isaac. He considers this to be the sublime illustration of the religious transcending the ethical—knowing the universal moral law not to kill, Abraham nevertheless is propelled by his religious personal faith in God to "kill" his son. Thus, the individual is elevated above the universal.

An entry from Kierkegaard's journal sums up this utterly subjective way of truth: "The thing is to find a truth which is true for me, to find the idea for which I can live and die."[8] To Kierkegaard, the content and the extent of biblical truth was quite insignificant. He stated that if biblical writers had only left us one sentence—"We believe that in such and such a year God appeared among us in the humble form of a servant; that He lived and taught in our community and finally died"—it would have been sufficient. The historical and rational are clearly irrelevant. Kierkegaard's influence on theologians and philosophers has been quite extensive, including Barth, Heidegger, Jaspers, and others.

The shortcomings of Kierkegaard's philosophy ought to be quite clear. First and foremost, he fails to provide a truth test for contrary religious belief. If God exists in reality, His character and person exist apart from my choice to believe in Him. The nature and content of the term *God*, apart from truth, are open to any choice if reason and history are not criteria for my decision.

Second, Kierkegaard would have to admit that he was either making a truth claim or he was not. If indeed he was, then he would have to provide a truth test apart from a "leap of faith."

Third, Kierkegaard has no rational basis on which to engage the antitheist. For before one can enjoin a belief in God, one must demonstrate that there is a God.

Friedrich W. Nietzshe (1844–1900)

When Friedrich Nietzsche was born on October 15, 1844, the church bells were ringing, and that was considered a good omen. It happened to be the birthday of the Prussian king, Friedrich Wilhelm, hence, the ringing of the church bells and the very name with which Nietzsche was christened.

Nietzsche's father was a Lutheran pastor, and both of his grandfathers were in Christian ministry. He lost his father when he was only five years old, necessitating a move to Naumburg, where he grew up in a home with his mother, his sister, his grandmother, and two maiden aunts.

He was educated at the Schulpforta, a famous school established during the Reformation in a former Cistercian monastery. Nietzsche was considered an exemplary student and went on to study at the University of Bonn and the University of Leipzig. At the age of twenty-five he was appointed to a professorship at the University of Basel, Switzerland, and in 1872 he took up Swiss citizenship.

Among those who had a profound influence on Nietzsche were the philosopher Arthur Schopenhauer (who has been called the philosopher with an obsession for the will) and the musician Richard Wagner. The latter friendship was to end in a bitter breakup, brought about by Wagner's overwhelming arrogance and unashamed anti-Semitism.

Nietzsche suffered with very poor health and as a result had to resign from his teaching position after just ten years. During the next ten years he was to write copiously in spite of his debilitating condition. The last twelve years or so of his life, he was insane and was cared for by his sister, Elizabeth. She herself is not looked upon too kindly by scholars (which is an understatement) because she took charge of all of his manuscripts, apparently suppressing, modifying, and disseminating them as she chose, often distorting their emphases and meanings. Her biography is interestingly titled *Zarathustra's Sister.* She herself regarded Hitler to be the embodiment of the *Ubermensch,* or Superman, eulogized by Nietzsche.

Nietzsche's literary productions began with *The Birth of Tragedy* (1872), an attempt to interpret art and drama in the light of Schopenhauer's philosophy. *Untimely Meditations* (1873–1876) was dedicated to Schopenhauer and Wagner. Others to follow included *The Gay Science* (1882), *Thus Spake Zarathustra* (1882–1885), *Beyond Good and Evil* (1886), *Genealogy of Morals* (1887), *The Twilight of the Idols* (1889), and the posthumously published *Antichrist* and *Ecce Homo.*

If there is one word to sum up Nietzsche's life it would be *irony*. His style of writing was rich in irony instanced by the denunciation of morality through the mouth of the moralist Zarathustra. But that irony played itself out in his own life. He talked of a universal madness and tragically went insane himself. He spoke of the supremacy of the Superman who by the power of his will would dominate, yet of his own life he said, "I have been more of a battlefield than a man." He spurned Christian moralizing, yet it was an immoral tryst that evidently resulted in his syphilis and ultimately his insanity. He wrote in confident tones, yet he described himself as the "philosopher of the hazardous 'perhaps?'" His poetry bespoke an artistic mind, yet his life was one of dissipation and chaos. Everything in life, he thought, could be reduced to the will for self-assertion, yet in his latter years he was in effect a prisoner to his sister's will. In a strange way he admired Jesus, yet he did much to destroy the gospel message. In his comment upon the Gospels he saw only one noble figure—Pontius Pilate—for asking his disdainful question "What is truth?"

One of Nietzsche's greatest admirers was Adolf Hitler, who visited the Weimar Nietzsche archives several times. Elizabeth (Nietzsche's sister) congratulated Mussolini on the occasion of his fiftieth birthday for being the "noblest disciple of Zarathustra." In that sense, Nietzsche's philosophy was made to serve one of history's bloodiest experiments.

There is a terrible sadness to Nietzsche's life, and it is very difficult not to feel a deep regret for a life made so pathetic and for a genius so squandered. There is sadness, also, as one sees the lives of those around him. In the year that he died, his sister, Elizabeth, also saw her husband commit suicide. His mother, Franziska, was a devoted Christian woman who nursed Nietzsche for eight of the eleven years of his insanity until she herself died in 1897. In a letter she wrote to a friend, she expressed surprise at how much Scripture Nietzsche knew and quoted in his last days. She said, "Again and again my soul is filled with gratitude to our dear God that I can now care for this child of my heart." It must have crushed her to see this pitiful-looking man often remain silent for a month or more at a time. For most of those years he did not know who he was, where he was, or what century he lived in.

But if Nietzsche's definition of a Superman is evaluated, in an ironic sense he fulfilled it. Nietzsche defined the Superman as one who realizes the human predicament but who nevertheless creates his own values and in the face of anguish or deprivation is nevertheless able to build his life in triumph over it. Much of what he predicted man would see in the twentieth century has turned out to be so—the bloodiest century in history. One of his friends who spoke at his funeral closed with the words, "Peace be with thy ashes! Holy be thy name to all future generations!" Ironically, in *Ecce Homo,* not yet published at his death, Nietzsche had written, "I have a terrible fear that one day I shall be pronounced 'holy.'" This, too, he had foreseen.

Bertrand Russell (1872–1970)

Called "Bertie" by those in his inner circle, Bertrand Russell is one of the more colorful personalities in philosophy. Toward Russell one would find it very hard to remain neutral. Having lived to the ripe old age of ninety-eight, his life spanned a very critical period of political, social, philosophical, and religious upheaval. And in keeping with his affinity for controversy, he strode into all four arenas with fists flailing.

Russell was a prolific writer for whom writing came very easily. He wrote approximately seventy books on themes as varied as China, morals, mysticism, logic, Bolshevism, marriage, education, geometry, science, philosophy, mathematics, social reconstruction, nuclear disarmament, communism, capitalism, religion, and scores of others. Some of his magazine articles included his views on the use of lipstick, choosing cigars, and wife-beating. Russell had a broad reach of ideas and a penetrating mind in argumentation. He was merciless in his criticism of views he abhorred, and his personal attacks were scathing. Historian Paul Johnson says that no intellectual in history offered advice to humanity over so long a period as Bertrand Russell. He was far better at relating to ideas than he was at relating to people: "I like mathematics because it is not human," he said.

Russell's whole life can best be summarized by the word *contradiction.* Publicly, he fought for peace in the world, yet privately he fomented hatred toward people he disliked. In his speeches, he argued for disarmament and was a pacifist, but on numerous occasions he expressed the wish that America would militarily preempt the burgeoning power of the Soviet Union. He wrote some of the most vilifying articles against Marxism but later in life wrote with equal anger against the United States and capitalism. In one instance, he branded John Kennedy and Harold Macmillan as possibly more evil than Hitler. He delivered papers on the rights of women yet privately belittled their intellectual capacities. He berated his brother for leaving his wife yet his four marriages were marred by infidelities. He would get incensed when he was lied to but was often trapped in his own deceit.

Not only was there such contradiction and duplicity in his life, he changed his philosophical views on numerous occasions. The philosopher Charlie Broad, professor of moral philosophy at Cambridge from 1933 to 1953, remarked that Russell produced a brand-new philosophy every few years.

All this notwithstanding, Bertrand Russell was a genius, and it is terribly unfortunate that a mind as capable as his sank into frivolous arguments revealing more his prejudices than his intellect. For example, he stated in his diatribe against Christianity that as far as he knew Christianity had only produced two good things: first, the calendar, and second, that it was an Egyptian priest who first noted the lunar eclipse. "Other than that," he said, "I see no good having come out of Christianity." That became more and more typical of the outbursts he would make on religion. Russell was an able debater and had a knack for reducing the issue to a tantalizing paradox from which he would emerge by establishing a theory he had wanted to defend.

One of Russell's famous paradoxes he articulated in a set theory. The subject is far too complicated to enter into here, but it was formulated out of a recognition of the need for a theory of the infinite. This is how he laid out the problem: Some sets (classes or collections) are members of themselves and some are not. For example, the set of dogs is not a member of itself since it is a set and not a dog, whereas the set of non-dogs is a member of itself since it is not a dog, and it is dealing with non-dogs. This is how Russell then phrased his paradox: Is the set of all sets that are not members of themselves a member of itself? If it is, then it is not. If it is not, then it is. A nonphilosophically minded student would be amazed at the profound influence this had on the development of set theory.

Russell used this same approach in many of his arguments against God. The way he dealt with the meaninglessness of statements was by raising similar questions and forcing equivocating options. One of his principal arguments against God and a moral law went something like this:

If there is a moral law, as is contended by theists, "Then," said Russell, "it either results from God's fiat (decision or decree) or else it does not."

If it is the former—God's fiat—then it is purely arbitrary, and goodness is just another way of saying "because God said so." On that basis God could pronounce anything He chose to and thereby it would be good or bad. On the other hand, if God is subject to some goodness beyond Himself, then He Himself is not ultimate. The choice Russell places before the theist is that either God is merely arbitrary or else He is not ultimate.

The dilemma Bertrand Russell brought forward is not only false; it is also falsely placed. The question he raised needed to be raised of himself, not of God: Is Bertrand Russell arbitrary in his moral choices or subordinate to another? If he is being arbitrary then why all his vilifying of America during the Vietnam War and his branding of John Kennedy and Harold Macmillan as evil? From whence does he get his moral units of measurement? On the other hand, if he is not being arbitrary, there must be a moral law above him. That, however, he does not want. So Russell fells himself by the same argument he places upon God.

Conversely, if God is demonstrated to be the entity that the Christian Scriptures affirm Him to be—infinite, all powerful, holy, and loving—is it not possible that the moral law is an outflow of God's immutable nature? Thus, God is not arbitrary, nor is the moral law superior to God—it is intrinsic to His person. The moral law has to be positioned somewhere. When applied to a human being, it raises an extraordinary dilemma if at the same time that finite individual denies God. However, when it is positioned in an infinite, uncaused being—God Himself—it is intrinsic.

The difficulty Bertrand Russell expresses here points to a larger problem in his very understanding of personality and knowing. Russell actually came to the conclusion that we are not directly acquainted with a self but are able to be acquainted with mental facts such as willing, believing, and wishing. He carried this over to his belief that *God* was a meaningless word because it had no point of reference. Evidently, the personality of God is something that, by his presuppositions, Russell dismisses, and he judges the person of Christ in history even more severely. It is these presuppositions and dichotomies that drove Russell to live his own life amid constant contradiction and to reduce people to numbers and quantities.

Jean-Paul Sartre (1905–1980)

Jean-Paul Sartre, a French philosopher and novelist, came under the influence of some sophisticated thinkers such as Edmund Husserl and

Martin Heidegger. Sartre became a leading exponent of atheistic existentialism. At the end of the Second World War, he was a leader of left-wing French intellectuals and cofounded the radical journal *Les Temps Modernes*. In his later years, he moved somewhat away from existentialism and more toward his own style of Marxist sociology. He did, however, maintain that Marxism and existentialism are complementary in their critique of society and in their avowed pursuit of expression in political liberty and the freedom inherent in human nature.

Sartre had a very acerbic pen, and his harsh castigation of those he did not like was common fare. He was considered by those who knew him to be a supreme egoist. His father died when Sartre was only fifteen months old, and he seemed to go out of his way to speak unkindly of his father's legacy. "If he had lived, my father would have laid down and crushed me. . . . The dead man meant so little to me." A slightly built man (five feet, two and a half inches), Sartre cast a gigantic shadow upon the rebellious university student in the 1960s.

Sartre is known for his rather loose-living lifestyle and for his strong revolutionary political theories. What Heidegger became to the Nazi ideology Sartre became to the Marxist cause. He himself said that his credo was "Travel, polygamy, and transparency"—a credo that may well be the script for modern-day tabloid journalism. René Descartes once said that there was nothing so absurd or incredible that it has not been asserted by one philosopher or another. Sartre perfectly fit that description and often made the most outlandish statements. Few incidents better summarize his life than the publication of one of his books at a time he was "double-timing"—or should that be "quadruple-timing"—four different mistresses. He had the publisher secretly print a copy for each woman with her own name printed as the one to whom the book was dedicated.

Possibly one of the most devastating effects of Jean-Paul Sartre's legacy was the impact he had on the intellectuals, whose deadly crimes made Cambodia flow with the blood of its own people by the tens of thousands.

In order to understand Sartre, one must understand the philosophy of existentialism. Its investigations address that which is most personal within the human experience, recognizing the universality of the structures and conditions in which that personal existence is lived out. The first concern of existentialism is to give an account of how an *individual consciousness* apprehends existence. From this apprehension flows freedom, personal choice, personal authenticity, relationships, etc.

Sartre's most famous philosophical work is *Being and Nothingness,* published in 1943, in which the primary question he addresses is, "What is it like to be a human being?" He concluded that there is no explanation for the brute existence of things; it just so happens that things are there, and that is all there is to it. Life is absurd in that its very existence is unexplainable. But since man is in this "hurled" or "dumped" state he must choose for himself and author his own values. In a sense, man has never arrived but is always the product of what he does and chooses, which works into the scheme of his character, making possible the next choice. And against all this choosing and becoming, there ever looms the prospect of death. Man, in short, is in a bind—determined, yet free; free, yet enslaved.

For the want of a better analogy, Sartrean existentialism is the secular version of New Age philosophies, seeking to escape the technopoly of modern consciousness and finding one's own mantra to authenticate oneself by pulling oneself up by his or her own existential bootstraps. Against the absurdity of life's origin and the fear of life's extinction, a person chooses and feeds into his personal history ingredients that will then be inseparable from the product, which in turn prepares him for the next choice. It is understandable why he titled one of his books *Nausea.*

The criticism of Sartre's atheistic philosophy is really the criticism of atheism itself. In one of Sartre's major disproofs of God's existence, he argues for the unsuccessfulness of man finding God by himself. All he may at best prove by that statement is that he did not "find" God. By no rational means can he establish that, therefore, there is no God. Left in a desert, a man may die without food, but that does not establish that no food exists.

As for Sartre's ethical theory, it is one of antinomianism—a lawlessness. It is a philosophy that is unlivable—in fact, so unlivable that there is a strong indication that Sartre gave a tacit nod to theism, if not a clear avowal of it, in his last days.[9]

Notes

Introduction
1. Paul Scherer, *The Word God Sent* (New York: Harper & Row, 1965), 11.

Chapter 1   Anguish in Affluence
1. Andrew Fletcher, quoted in Harold A. Bosley, *Sermons on the Psalms* (New York: Harper & Brothers, 1956), 40.
2. L. E. Aute, Sheila Aute, "Who Will Answer?" © 1967 Ediciones Musicales BMG Ariola S.A. All rights in the U.S.A. administered by BMG Songs, Inc. (ASCAP). All rights reserved. Used by permission.
3. Robert Fripp, Michael Giles, Greg Lake, Ian McDonald, Peter Sinfield, "Twenty First Century Schizoid Man" © 1969 E.G. Music, Ltd. (PRS). All rights in the U.S.A. administered by Careers-BMG Music Publishing, Inc. (BMI). All rights reserved. Used by permission.
4. Robert Fripp, Peter Sinfield, Ian McDonald, Greg Lake, Michael Giles, "Epitaph" © 1969, 1971 E.G. Music, Ltd. (PRS). All rights in the U.S.A. administered by Careers-BMG Music Publishing, Inc. (BMI). All rights reserved. Used by permission.
5. Immanuel Kant, *Critique of Pure Reason*, trans. Norman Kemp Smith (New York: St. Martin, 1965), 857.
6. J. P. Moreland and Kai Nielsen, *Does God Exist?* (Nashville: Thomas Nelson, 1990).
7. Auguste Comte, quoted in the introduction to A. J. Hoover, *Don't You Believe It* (Chicago: Moody, 1982).
8. Arthur Schopenhauer, quoted in Hoover, *Don't You Believe It.*

Chapter 2   Straying through an Infinite Nothing
1. Etienne Borne, *Atheism* (New York: Hawthorn, 1961), 61.
2. Paul Edwards, ed., *Encyclopedia of Philosophy,* vol. 1 (New York: Macmillan, 1967), 175.
3. Madalyn Murray O'Hair, *What on Earth Is an Atheist?* (New York: Arno, 1972), 39–43.

4. See Peter Angeles, ed. *Critiques of God* (Buffalo: Prometheus, 1976) and Gordon Stein, ed. *An Anthology of Atheism and Rationalism* (Buffalo: Prometheus, 1984).
5. Frederick Nietzsche, "The Madman," a section of *Gay Science* in Walter Kaufmann, ed. *The Portable Nietzsche*, (New York: Viking, 1954), 125.
6. Quoted in *The Veritas Forum* (a public discussion of faith at the Ohio State University), fall 1993 special issue, 1.
7. Ibid.
8. Stephen Jay Gould, quoted by David Friend and the editors of *Life* magazine, *The Meaning of Life* (Boston: Little, Brown, 1991), 33. A fuller context of this quotation is found in chapter 6.

Chapter 3   The Madman Arrives

1. Viktor Frankl, *The Doctor and the Soul: Introduction to Logotherapy* (New York: Knopf, 1982), xxi.
2. Joyce Barnathan and Steven Strasser, "Exorcising a Soviet Ghost," *Newsweek*, 27 June 1988.
3. Thomas Common, translator, *The Philosophy of Nietzsche* (New York: Random House, n.d.), 28–29.
4. Ibid., 33–34.
5. Aldous Huxley, *Ends and Means* (London: Chatto & Windus, 1946), 273.
6. Ibid., 270.
7. David Friend and the editors of *Life* magazine, *The Meaning of Life*, 33.
8. Walter Kaufmann, *The Portable Nietzsche*, 103.

Chapter 4   The Homeless Mind

1. See Alisdair MacIntyre's *After Virtue* (Guildford and King's Lynn, England: Biddles, 1990).
2. Iris Murdoch, *The Sovereignty of Good* (London: Ark Publishers, 1989), 80.
3. Fripp et al., "Epitaph."
4. From a debate between Dennis Prager and Jonathan Glover at Oxford University, 3 March 1993, included in *Ultimate Issues*, vol. 9, no. 1. Glover's counterpunch was an equivocation on the illustration and philosophically contradictory.
5. Steve Turner, "Creed," *Up to Date* (London: Hodder & Stoughton). Used by permission.
6. Turner, "Chance." Used by permission.

Chapter 5 Where Is Antitheism When It Hurts?

1. Alfred, Lord Tennyson, "In Memoriam," VI, 2 in *Tennyson's Poetry*, ed. Robert W. Hale, Jr. (New York, London: Norton, 1971), 123.
2. Wilfred McClay, "Religion in Politics; Politics in Religion," *Commentary*, October 1988. Used by permission.
3. C. S. Lewis, *The Problem of Pain* (New York: Macmillan, 1966), 138.
4. King George VI, quoted by Leonard Griffith, *Reactions to God* (Toronto: Anglican Book Centre, 1979), 87.
5. Archibald McLeish, "When We Are Gods," *Saturday Review*, 14 October 1967.

Chapter 6 In Search of Lower Meaning

1. Stephen Jay Gould, quoted in David Friend and editors of *Life* magazine, *The Meaning of Life*, 33.
2. Philip Johnson has written a book, *Darwin on Trial* (Downers Grove, Ill.: InterVarsity, 1991) that startled the evolutionary world by exposing the fragile base on which it is built.
3. Alister McGrath, *Intellectuals Don't Need God* (Grand Rapids, Mich.: Zondervan, 1993), 15.
4. Ibid.
5. Quoted in Kenneth A. Myers, *All God's Children and Blue Suede Shoes* (Wheaton, Ill.: Crossway, 1989), 63.
6. Friend et al., *The Meaning of Life*, 194.
7. Ibid., 194.
8. Ibid.
9. L. E. Aute, Sheila Aute, "Who Will Answer?"

Chapter 7 The Science of Knowing and the Art of Living

1. Dietrich Bonhoeffer, "Who Am I?" *Letters and Papers from Prison*, Revised, Enlarged Edn. (New York: SCM Press Ltd., 1953, 1967, 1971), 221. Reprinted with permission of Simon and Schuster.
2. Stephen Hawking, *A Brief History of Time* (New York: Bantam, 1988), 175.
3. Norman Geisler, *Is Man the Measure?* (Grand Rapids, Mich.: Baker, 1983), 48.
4. Michael Polanyi, *Meaning* (Chicago: University of Chicago Press, 1975), 162.
5. D. H. Lawrence, source unknown.
6. Thomas Wolfe, "God's Lonely Man," in *The Hills Beyond* (New York: Plume/New American Library, 1982), 146, 148.
7. William Shakespeare, *As You Like It*, II. vii.

Chapter 8   The Romance of Enchantment

1. Kenneth R. Miller, "Life's Grand Design," *Technology Review*, February/ March 1994. Reprinted with permission.
2. The argument *to* design as distinct from the argument *from* design is a very important argument to understand. I have dealt with it more extensively in Appendix A.
3. Miller, "Life's Grand Design," 32.
4. John Polkinghorne, *One World* (London: SPCK, 1987), 57–58.
5. Christopher Morley, "No Coaching," quoted from Luccock and Brentano, eds., *The Questing Spirit* (New York: Coward-McCann, 1947), 418.
6. G. K. Chesterton, *Orthodoxy* (New York: Doubleday, 1959), 55.
7. Francis Thompson, *Complete Poetical Works of Francis Thompson* (New York: Boni & Liveright, 1913), 356–7.

Chapter 9   Truth–an Endangered Species

1. Malcolm Muggeridge, *The Green Stick: A Chronicle of Wasted Years* (Glasgow: William Collins & Sons, 1972), 16–17.
2. Ibid., 19–20.
3. I have dealt with the subject of truth-testing in greater detail in Appendix 2, "The Establishment of a World View" in my book *A Shattered Visage: The Real Face of Atheism* (Grand Rapids, Mich.: Baker, 1990), 189ff.
4. Marie Chapian, *Of Whom the World Was Not Worthy* (Minneapolis: Bethany House, 1978), 122–3.

Chapter 10   Love's Labor Won

1. Christoper Morley, quoted in a column by Ruth Walker in *Christian Science Monitor*, 20 November 1991.
2. G. K. Chesterton, *As I Was Saying*, ed. Robert Knille (Grand Rapids, Mich.: Eerdmans, 1985), 267.
3. Sandy and Harry Chapin, "Cat's in the Cradle." © 1974 Story Songs, Ltd. All rights reserved. Used by permission.
4. Albert Lister Peace, "O Love That Will Not Let Me Go," 1885.

Chapter 11   Crossing the Bar

1. Malcolm Muggeridge, *Jesus Rediscovered* (Garden City, N.Y.: Doubleday, 1969), 77.
2. Dietrich Bonhoeffer, "Who Am I?" *Letters and Papers from Prison*.

Chapter 12 Getting to the Truth

1. Richard Rorty, *Essays on Heidegger and Others,* Philosophical Papers, vol. 2 (Cambridge, England: 1991), 86, quoted by Gertrude Himmelfarb, *On Looking into the Abyss* (New York: Knopf, 1994), 14.

Chapter 13 Humanity's Dilemma

1. Blaise Pascal, *The Mind on Fire,* ed. James M. Houston (Portland, Oreg.: Multnomah, 1989), 115.
2. Ted Turner, quoted in David Friend and editors of *Life* magazine, *The Meaning of Life,* 73.
3. An autobiographical excerpt quoted by Ian Hunter in *Malcolm Muggeridge: A Life* (Toronto: Totem, 1981), 40.
4. Hobart Mowrer, "Sin, the Lesser of Two Evils," *American Psychologist,* 15 (1960): 301–304.
5. Anna Russell, "Psychiatric Folksong." Used by permission.
6. Peter Kreeft, *The Snakebite Letters* (San Francisco: Ignatius, 1991), 23.
7. John Z. DeLorean with Ted Schwarz, *DeLorean* (Grand Rapids, Mich.: Zondervan, 1985), 275.

Chapter 14 The Philosopher's Quest

1. C. S. Lewis, *Beyond Personality* (London: Geoffrey Bles, 1944), 14–16.
2. Archbishop William Temple, quoted by David Watson in *I Believe in Evangelism* (Grand Rapids, Mich.: Eerdmans, 1976), 157.

Chapter 15 The Historian's Centerpiece

1. Sigmund Freud's essay, "Timely Thoughts on War and Death," quoted by Walter Kauffmann, *The Faith of a Heretic* (Garden City, N. Y.: Doubleday-Anchor, 1963), 356–7.
2. Jon MacQuarrie, *An Existential Theology: A Comparison of Heidegger and Bultmann* (New York: Harper & Row, 1965), 185–6.
3. Ibid., 186.
4. Giza Vermes, *Jesus the Jew* (London: 1973), 19.
5. Robert Browning, "A Death in the Desert."
6. Walter Kaufmann, *The Faith of a Heretic,* 376.

Chapter 16 The Believer's Treasure

1. Malcolm Muggeridge, *A Twentieth Century Testimony* (Nashville: Thomas Nelson, 1978), 72.

2. Christoper Browning, *Ordinary Men* (New York: HarperCollins, 1991), jacket copy.
3. Anonymous, "A New Leaf," James G. Lawson, compiler, *The Best Loved Religious Poems* (Grand Rapids: Fleming H. Revell, 1961). Used by permission.
4. James Stewart, *The Strong Name* (Grand Rapids: Baker, 1972), 55.
5. Alfred, Lord Tennyson, "The Lotus-Eaters," *Tennyson's Poetry,* ed. Robert W. Hill Jr. (New York: Norton, 1971), 51.
6. Chesterton, *As I Was Saying,* 237.

Appendix A: Questions and Answers

1. Norman Geisler's books *Christian Apologetics* (Grand Rapids, Mich: Baker, 1976) and *Philosophy of Religion* (Grand Rapids, Mich.: Baker, 1988), present his arguments in detail.
2. This summary of Dallas Willard's theistic defense is excerpted from J. P. Moreland and Kai Nielsen, *Does God Exist?* (Nashville: Thomas Nelson, 1990), 197ff.
3. Ibid., 206.
4. Ibid., 210.
5. Ibid.

Appendix B: Mentors to the Skeptic

1. For further reading on this subject, I would recommend Norman Geisler's *Christian Apologetics.*
2. Ronda Chervin and Eugene Kevane, *Love of Wisdom* (San Francisco: Ignatius, 1988), 212.
3. David Hume, "My Own Life" from E. C. Mossner, *The Life of David Hume* (Oxford: Oxford University Press, 1980).
4. David Hume, *Enquiry Concerning Human Understanding* (London: 1748; New York: C. W. Hendel, 1955).
5. Geisler, *Christian Apologetics,* 14–15.
6. David Hume, *Treatise of Human Nature,* ed. E. C. Mossner (Harmondsworth, England: Penguin, 1969), VII, 8.
7. Colin Brown, *Philosophy and the Christian Faith* (Downers Grove, Ill.: InterVarsity, 1968), 95–96.
8. Sören Kierkegaard, *Diary of Sören Kierkegaard,* ed. Peter Rohde (New York: Citadel, 1971), 44.
9. Geisler, *Is Man the Measure?* 48.

DR. RAVI ZACHARIAS, president of Ravi Zacharias International Ministries, was born in India. His ancestors came from the highest caste of the Hindu priesthood. He immigrated to Canada in 1966 and graduated from Ontario Bible College and Trinity Evangelical Divinity School. He was honored with the Doctor of Divinity degree from Houghton College, the Doctor of Laws degree from Asbury College, and did special study in the English romantic poets at Cambridge University. Having spoken in more than fifty countries, Zacharias is also the author of *Cries of the Heart, Jesus Among Other Gods,* and *Deliver Us from Evil.*